WAR'S END

Other Works by the Author

Embodied Mind
Fully Alive, as Roy Laurens
The Second Gutenberg Revolution, editor

WAR'S END

The Revolution of Consciousness
in the European Community

1992

R. Patton Howell

Introduction by Rollo May

Saybrook Publishers

San Francisco   Dallas   New York

19740941

2-90

Library of Congress Cataloging-in-Publication Data

Howell, R. Patton, 1921
          Wars End, 1992, The Revolutionary New Thought in the European Community / R. Patton Howell.
        p. cm.
        Bibliography: p.
        Includes index.
        ISBN 0-933071-31-0 : $17.95
1. European Economic Community. 2. Europe—Economic integration.
I.   Title
  HC241.2.H64 1989
  337.1'42–dc20
                                    89-10159
                                    CIP

Cover design by Mike McIver
Book design and typography by The Special Projects Group
Interior art by Fred Huffman
Photography by Ellen Schuster
Title by Joan D. Howell

Saybrook Publishing Company
3518 Armstrong, Dallas, Texas 75205

Printed in the United States of America

Distributed by W.W. Norton & Company
500 Fifth Avenue, New York, New York 10110

For my dear wife, Joan,
and my children and grandchildren . . .

Elizabeth Mills, my editor, and Marcelline Watson, my associate of thirty-odd years, made this book possible. My deep and lasting appreciation to you both.

My friend, Dr. James Hall, and my son, Rev. Dr. Webster Kitchell Howell, suffered with me through the writing and contributed to it substantially. I owe to you a sincere debt of gratitude and also to the following people, who took time from their overloaded schedules to read the manuscript. The book reflects your valuable insights and suggestions, although you are in no way responsible for its text: Judith Applebaum and your Sensible Solutions, Dr. William H. Tedford, Bishop Paulos Mar Gregorios, Dr. Margaret Spencer, Dr. Larry Dossey, Professor Frederick Turner plus Ethan Ellenberg, Gayle Oler, Dr. Morris Berman and Erv Eatenson.

In addition there are the Europeans who so generously gave their time and interest to the project. I am deeply grateful for your kind help: Margaret Drabble, Michael Holroyd, Martyn Goff OBE, Josephine Pullein-Thompson, Francis King, Brian Aldiss, Prime Minister Garret FitzGerald, Proinsias de Rossa plus citizens of the world Dave and Iola Brubeck, Hensleigh and Barbara Wedgwood, Dr. Peter Koestenbaum and Dr. Donald E. Polkinghorne. Most of you are quoted in the book, and your contributions were so significant that I made notes of our conversations at the first available moment after they took place.

Quotes from Dr. Federico Mayor Zaragosa, Richard Hoggart and Ambassador Ian Christie Clark include speeches and press conferences; quotes from Altiero Spinelli also include a comment he made in the forward to *European Union*. The poem by Ernesto Cardenal is from a speech by Harold Pinter printed in *Index on Censorship*. This British magazine provided many of the quotes found in Chapter 10. It is one of the most valuable magazines I know, address: 39C Highbury Place, London N5 1 QP. The newspapers that have been resources for me: the *London*

Times, The New York Times, the *Berliner Morgenpost,* the Paris *Le Monde/Le Monde Dimanche.*

Other people quoted are private, not in the public eye. I have changed names and places and times and done whatever else I had felt was necessary to preserve your privacy, but to all you private people who have meant so much to me, let me publicly now express my heartfelt thanks for your help.

And I want to thank all of the people who read this book. It is about people, particular people, including you the reader.

CONTENTS

Introduction by Rollo May   *13*

PART ONE

ANTI-AMERICANISM

Chapter 1   There Will Never Be Another War in Europe   *21*

             The People of the European Community   *21*
             The People of the United States   *25*
             Dallas–Fort Worth Airport   *27*
             New York   *28*

Chapter 2   America as Anvil   *31*

             London   *31*
             Heathrow Airport   *35*
             Vienna   *40*
             The Channel Tunnel   *45*
             London: The Strand   *46*
             The London Press Club   *49*

9

Chapter 3   The Triangle of Power   *53*

         London: Belgravia   *53*
         Tea   *55*
         Visiting Europe   *61*
         The British Museum   *62*

PART TWO

IDEOLOGY, TERRORISM AND COMMUNITY   *68*

Chapter 4   The War for the Thoughts of the World   *69*

         Paris   *69*
         La Place Vendome   *70*
         The Marne Battlefield   *74*

Chapter 5   The Crocodile Club   *83*

         Strasbourg   *83*
         Brussels   *85*
         The Commission   *88*
            Business in Brussels   *95*
         Revelry by Night   *97*
         The Windsor Hotel   *101*

Chapter 6   The Rising of the Moon   *106*

         Brussels Airport   *106*
         Dublin   *108*
         The Dail Eireann   *113*
         St. Stephen's Park   *118*

PART THREE

THE THIRD DIMENSION OF THOUGHT IN EUROPE   *126*

Chapter 7   A Short History of European Thinking   *127*

         Milan   *127*
         The Monastery   *129*
         The Third Dimension of Thought   *145*

Chapter 8   Another Dimension   *151*

         Geneva   *151*
         The Old City of London   *158*

The Oxford-Cambridge Club *160*
Oxford *165*
The Oxford Hills *169*

Chapter 9   The Third-Dimensional Solution *171*

Frankfurt *171*
Bonn *176*
The Third-Dimension Solution *181*
Stuttgart *183*
Double Standards *184*
Fast Trains *187*

PART FOUR

THE MEANING OF THE EUROPEAN COMMUNITY *192*

Chapter 10   The Russian Hammer *193*

Stockholm *193*
Leipzig *196*
The Empire *198*
Russia *204*

Chapter 11   It Wouldn't Be Make-Believe *209*

London: Bloomsbury *209*
Hyde Park *213*

Chapter 12   Going All the Way *218*

Winchester Cathedral *218*
The English Channel *231*
Paris *233*

PART FIVE

AMERICA AND WAR'S END *236*

Chapter 13   The North American Community *237*

The United States of America *237*
The Only Game in Town *240*
The Business of the United States *246*

Chapter 14   Nurturing the North American Community   *249*

                  Education   *249*
                  Science   *251*
                  Journalism   *253*
                  Business   *255*
                  Community   *258*

Chapter 15   The Last Best Hope   *261*

                  Foreign Policy   *261*
                  A New World Order   *269*
                  The Chasm in the World   *271*
                  San Francisco   *273*

READING LIST   *279*

INDEX   *293*

Illustrations

The Twelve Members of the European Community (map)   *23*
The Administrative Structure of the European Community *90*
Percentage of Europeans Reading Novels   *150*
The North American Community (map)   *244*
Three Communities   *245*
World Order of Communities (map)   *268*
Five Possible Communities   *269*

INTRODUCTION

by Rollo May

Dr. May is internationally recognized for his out-standing contributions to psychology. He has received Phi Beta Kappa's Ralph Waldo Emerson Award for humane scholarship, the Christopher Award for affirming the highest values of the human spirit, the American Psychological Association's Award for Distinguished Contribution to the Science and Profession of Clinical Psychology and its Gold Medal Award for a Distinguished Career. Dr. May's latest book The Meaning of Myth *will be published in March 1990. Authorities who have read the manuscript regard it as a work of major importance for our time. He is the the author of more than twenty-five books, all still in print and translated into most foreign languages. His books* Love and Will *and* The Courage to Create *were international bestsellers. Perhaps more than any other scholar in his field, Dr. May is loved and revered throughout Europe. It is this special relationship with European culture that makes his introduction particularly appropriate for* War's End.

Once in a while I catch myself having a curious fantasy. It goes something like this.

A writer arrives at the heavenly gates at the end of his long and productive life. He is brought up before St. Peter for his customary accounting. Formidable, St. Peter sits calmly behind his table looking like the Moses of Michelangelo. An angel assistant in a white jacket drops a manila folder on the table which St. Peter opens and looks at, frowning. Despite the awesome visage of the judge, the writer clutches his briefcase and steps up with commendable courage.

But St. Peter's frown deepens. He drums with his fingers on the table and grunts a few nondirective "uhm-uhm's" as he fixes the candidate with his Mosaic eyes.

The silence is discomfiting. Finally the writer opens his briefcase and cries, "Here! The reprints of my hundred and thirty-two papers."

St. Peter slowly shakes his head.

Burrowing deeper into the briefcase the writer offers, "Let me submit the awards I received for my writing." St. Peter's frown is unabated as he silently continues to stare into the writer's face, and his tone is like Moses breaking the news of the Ten Commandments: "You are charged with *nimis simplicando*! Oversimplifying!

"You have spent your life making molehills out of mountains, that's what you're guilty of. When man was tragic, you made him trivial. When he was picaresque, you called him picayune. When he suffered passively, you described him as simpering; and when he drummed up enough courage to act, you made him a nonhero. Man had passion; you called it 'satisfaction,' and when you were relaxed and looking at your secretary you called it 'release of tension.' You made man over into the image of your childhood erector set."

The writer steps back. "Your honor, I only tried to let man speak for himself!"

St. Peter levels a long bony finger at the writer. "*You* thought everybody could be fooled. Everybody but you. You always assumed that you, the fooler, were never fooled! Not very consistent, is it?"

St. Peter sighs. The writer opens his mouth, but St. Peter raises his hand. "Please! Not your well-practiced chatter. Something new is required . . . something new." He sits back, meditating. . . .

And about that time I find myself meditating too.

What is this human dilemma that requires something new?

It has to do with inner reality and with what is outside. In other words, that which arises out of a man's capacity to experience himself and others at the same time in an inner reality.

Now to sharpen our definition: We are not simply describing two alternate ways of behaving. Nor is it quite accurate to speak of our being subject and object simultaneously. The important point is that our new human dimension is a process of oscillation which integrates the two. Writing in any genuine sense lies not in the capacity to live as "pure subject," but rather in the capacity to experience *both* modes.

I shall not go into the wide implications of this capacity here. I shall only add that we readers have the same human dimension as we authors.

We have assiduously avoided confronting this new dimension. Out of our seemingly omnipresent rationally reductive tendencies, we omit aspects of human functioning that are essential. And we end up without the "inner person to whom these things happen." We are left with only the "things of information" that happen, suspended in mid-air.

We need to confront, for example, the *historical dimension* of ourselves and the human beings we read about, as well as the history of the culture in which we live and move and have our being. It is a failure to see things in their historical inner dimension which has made us blind to the dangers in our phenomenal growth.

We need, furthermore, to confront *literature*. The classics are that because they have ministered to human beings when they were written and to different ages and cultures ever since. Literature is the self-interpretation of human beings.

Literature carries two other concerns that we need to confront; namely, the perdurable *symbols* and *myths*. These communicate, in ways that bridge different ages and cultures, the essence of what it has meant and means to be human. Symbols and myths are the nonmaterial structure that is the basis of our culture, and it is the symbols and myths that are ailing in a disruptive time like our own. They speak directly to the new human dimension. How can we minister to the ailments of human beings if we are strangers to their deepest language?

But if we confront the new human dimension, we shall at least be dealing with human beings rather than with some absurd and truncated creatures reduced to isolated parts of information with no center whatever, parts that we can read about since they fit our information machines. It will mean giving up some of our own power needs and clarifying our needs to control. We can then have some hope that we may endure.

Dr. Howell brings these existential reservoirs of the human spirit to bear upon the future of the United States in a new and dangerously changing international environment. He writes with a scholar's understanding of the deepest language of human beings and finds in the European Community the emergence of a revolution in consciousness that everyone concerned for this country should seek to understand. Whatever problem he may have with St. Peter, it will not be *nimis simplicando*. There are no absurd truncated creatures here, rather an important new human dimension. His work deserves our joining him on this pilgrimage.

Rollo May
Tiburon
San Francisco, California
June 1, 1989

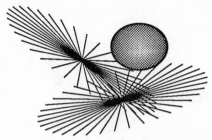

*L*isten! I must tell of the beginnings,
Of corpses buried in the walls of worlds,
Of how those men and women worth a story
Burn and consume the powers they're kindled by;
And how their acts, mortal and cast away,
Are crystalled in the melt of history.

— Frederick Turner,
Genesis

PART One

Anti-Americanism

THERE WILL NEVER BE
ANOTHER WAR
IN EUROPE

THE PEOPLE OF THE EUROPEAN COMMUNITY

War is the perennial subject of Europe's literature. *All Quiet on the Western Front* ends as Paul Baumer, thinking that now they can take nothing more from him, dies and lies upon the earth as though asleep. In *War and Peace* Andre watches mesmerized as a cannonball drops at his feet and explodes. Shakespeare's Henry V cries, "Once more unto the breach" at the storming of Harfleur, and Childe Harold winds his horn for the last time as he saves Christendom from bloody destruction.

The history we read of Europe is of war—continuous, incessant war. The soil of Europe is soaked with the blood of battle. But in the past forty-five years, since World War II, there has been no war in free Europe. This is a startling circumstance.

On the other hand, since 1945 the United States has engaged in armed conflict in Korea, Cuba, Vietnam, El Salvador, Santo Domingo, Nicaragua, Grenada, Libya and the Persian Gulf. There have been more wars during this period than at any other time in history. During 1987, two and a half million people were killed in war. And in 1988, some thirty wars were being waged throughout the world.

War's End is about the discovery of a revolution in consciousness. The revolution, which involves the transcendence of nationalism, is happening in the European Community, a community comprising most of the nations of free Europe. This radical change in the consciousness of Europeans has become a model for peace in the world.

Democracy has won. Now what? How can Russia and China restructure themselves without dissolving into chaos? The future of humankind hangs in the balance. The solution lies in the people of the European Community who are learning new ways of thinking about each other, ways that enable them to live together prosperously and peacefully despite their many differences, which they continue to cherish and protect. They have had no charismatic leaders to guide them, or government laws to force them to live in peace.

These ordinary people have gone beyond self-interest to find common human interests and goals—in trade, negotiation, literature, art, communication and travel, for example. To put it simply, members of the European Community have found room in their thoughts for each other. The result is that their consciousness has evolved to the point where they are no longer capable of warring with each other. There will never be another war in free Europe.

The developing European Community is not a government. Rather, it is a collection of agreements between independent nations that enables their citizens to bypass the laws and boundaries of their national governments

THE TWELVE MEMBERS OF THE EUROPEAN COMMUNITY

■ European Community

    Ireland   France   Denmark   Luxembourg
    England   Spain   Holland   Italy
    Belgium   Portugal   West Germany Greece

▨ Russian Europe

and get on with the human concerns of living. In 1985, members of the European Community decided to try to reach agreements on four major areas of relations by 1992:

- Removal of national barriers to the free movement of goods.
- Relaxation of the labor laws, allowing the free passage of workers from one member country to another.
- Establishment of uniform trade regulations for member nations in dealing with each other and with the rest of the world.
- Removal of national barriers to the free flow of capital.

These agreements are well on the way to being approved. Their acceptance—some before 1992, some after—will be the symbolic achievement of an international community rather than a supernation.

To get a feeling for what the transcendence of nationalism implied in these agreements means, consider the differences between the culture and standard of living in Greece and West Germany. Those differences are comparable to the differences between Mexico and the United States. Now try to imagine a North American Community that transcends nationalism as Europe is doing, that is, a North American Community that allows the free passage of workers and goods between Mexico and the United States. Are we, the people of the United States, ready for this? The West Germans are. If we are not, we may get a clue to the enlargement of consciousness that the people of the European Community are beginning to experience. It's worth looking into.

The new peace enjoyed by the European Community grows out of a radical change in consciousness. The old nationalisms put their trust in ideology; the new way of community puts its trust in people. The struggle between democracy and communism is no longer of central importance. Communism today is not viable. How can it be possible for Russia and Eastern Europe to restructure themselves without dissolving into chaos? We, the people of the United States, must enlarge our consciousness in order to make room for the very different peoples of Russia and Eastern Europe. We must be able to help them transcend their nationalism while we cherish their national and ideological differences—the way community is being practiced in free Europe today.

Change is accelerating in our world, and whether or not we are ready, it is giving birth to a new way of coexistence. Will we be helpless victims of change or will we choose our own destiny? If we learn the secrets of the emerging revolution in consciousness, we may lead the world into a new era of peace. In order to build a strong future for the United States, we would be wise to take the time to understand the people of the European Community. And in the process we would discover much of our own heritage, because the Marshall Plan helped to create the European Community.

THE PEOPLE OF THE UNITED STATES

After World War II, when Europe was in ruins, we, the people of the United States, enabled the nations of Western Europe to rebuild themselves through the Marshall Plan. We encouraged them to work together to make reconstruction possible. In fact, the Marshall Plan envisioned a kind of future European Community.

But where the United States lost this vision, the people of the European Community internalized and elaborated on America's initial impetus, creating a completely new kind of living. Europeans are still as cynical, greedy, unpleasant and glorious as ever—even more so. But, while enjoying their differences, they have made room in their hearts for each other. That is their secret.

As I write this introduction, I am preparing to leave for Europe. I'm a psychophysiologist specializing in language, and I've spent a lifetime consulting in countries all over the world, seeking the subconscious reasons that international projects work or don't work. My present commission is to uncover and explain European feelings about the United States and along the way to investigate this revolution in consciousness, which seems to be appearing for the first time in history.

As I think about the contrasts between Europe and my family and our home here in Texas, I am reminded of a small slice of American history. Looking over our land, I can see where the forest of evergreen live oak trees, coming up from the Rio Grande, crosses with a growth of deciduous post oak trees from the East. My grandfather named our place Cross Timbers as a symbol of the joining of East and West. He was the first human to claim this land for habitation. Before him the Comanches had come like the wind across the prairie grasses, leaving no trace of their passing.

In the 1880s, this spot represented the frontier of knowledge in the United States. The area west of here was as yet unmapped. When I was born, people here still had horses and buggies. When I leave this morning, I will ride a jet to New York and then to London.

The United States is only a tick on the clock that measures European history. We Americans are innocent of our land's past. We arrived late and created this nation entirely out of our own thoughts. In the context of world history, we are the innocents whose sacrifices will redeem the world. President Kennedy said, "Pay any price, bear any burden, meet any hardship, support any friend, oppose any foe, to assure the survival and success of liberty." We have a special role to play with regard to Europe in the next few years.

The world dominated by two superpowers is gone

forever. The United States is at a turning point; we can choose peace and prosperity, but only if we understand the psychological development of the new European Community.

There is a magic date associated with my pilgrimage—1992. By 1992, the European Community will have succeeded or it will have failed. Hidden forces threaten to abort the achievements of the revolution in consciousness. The thin tissue of community consent that now holds the European Community together can easily be torn apart. One current threat is West Germany's obsession for unification with East Germany, as expressed in its recent campaign to banish NATO's short-range missiles from Germany.

DALLAS–FORT WORTH AIRPORT

As the plane lifts off, revealing the stretch of Texas plain to the far western horizon, I get out my notes on the kind of methodology that would be appropriate for this investigation.

Information about the European Community is easy to find. Books are filled with information about trade and the numbers of dollars spent, but what do they tell us? Understanding how the European people have changed is not so simple. We have to understand the people themselves, their ways of thinking and feeling. We must be able to use our imagination to recreate their lives.

In order to understand the European revolution in consciousness, we must try to relate to Europeans whose lives incorporate this new kind of thinking. By plumbing the depths of these personal relationships, you may be able to create them for yourselves, in your own interior spaces. The process is the literary creation of inner reality. In this way, the people we encounter will become part of us, and we will know them.

Our method will be to look for essential people who pay attention to feelings and thoughts relevant to their lives. People concerned with literature are good examples. In attempting to engage a reader's attention, the writer is forced to deal in feelings. A writer who has also accepted some responsibility and leadership in the literary pursuit is even more useful to our understanding. We will also want to get in touch with businesspeople, government leaders, union members, shopkeepers and others who are guided in their work by their intuition and feelings.

But we must be careful. The opinions we hear will not necessarily enlarge our understanding. They might be information for a pollster, but we are not seeking information. We are seeking knowledge. Let us heed T. S. Eliot's lament in "The Rock."

Where is the wisdom we have lost in knowledge?
Where is the knowledge we have lost in information?

NEW YORK

How easy it is to confuse information with feelings. I am sitting at a bar in New York with Gunther Ball, a heavy-set German journalist who is visiting as a political expert. The bar is furnished very simply, with heavy, solid wood pieces. Its nineteenth-century ceilings seem to be two stories high.

Gunther and I are talking about how the Germans feel toward Americans after we criticized their sale of poison gas equipment to Libya. He tells me the German people feel less friendly toward us.

I say, "I don't doubt you, Gunther, but how did you get this information?"

"I got it from a public opinion poll by Emnid, you know, the German public opinion poll institute. I've worked with them."

"How do they select the people to question?"

He is getting uncomfortable. "Oh, demographics— you know, income, age, sex, occupation. They're representative."

I object. "Those classifications work only if the question is about the immediate self-interest of each group."

Gunther shifts in his chair. "Well, how about going back to our Who, What, When and Where days. Remember our good times then?"

I think, "Yes, Gunther, I remember, but we can't shrug this off." The question deals with feelings, but statistics don't express them very well. If a pollster asks how you feel about the United States, you're not likely to question your feelings seriously, first because the question requires a "yes" or "no" answer and second, because feeling are difficult to express. For example, what do you say when someone asks how you feel? Don't you reply "fine" without thinking about it? Even if you actually thought about what was relevant in your life and found a way of putting it into words, a pollster could only stuff you into one of these boxes used to classify people. Any parts of you hanging out would be chopped off, and your tender feeling would lie there bleeding and dismembered, unable to find appropriate expression. Feelings require a receptive environment in an atmosphere of mutual trust in order to reach expression. Unfortunately, we seldom make the critical distinction between feelings and information, and between information and knowledge; and few of us make the distinction between knowledge and wisdom.

Dynamic and forward-looking human scientists such as Nobel laureates Roger Sperry and Sir John Eccles go beyond the question of information to the reality of feeling and the kind of thinking that goes with it. They believe that such thought is subject to discovery, precise description and validation. They also claim that the predictive abilities of such knowledge far outweigh the predictive abilities of information. We will use their insights in order to understand the people of the European Community and what the European revolution in consciousness means for the future of the United States.

AMERICA AS ANVIL

LONDON

England is the door to Europe for Americans, the most accessible of the European countries because we share a common past, a common language and a common culture. We are going to find London especially useful in our investigation of the European Community because England is the most reluctant and critical member. England also affords opportunities for interacting with the literary people who are most sensitive to European feelings.

A good place to find these literary people is the English headquarters for PEN, the international association of Poets, Playwrights, Essayists, Editors, Novelists, Historians, Critics, Journalists and Translators. PEN has centers in most countries of the world. Its members stand for the freedom to write, and their best work has been in helping to free writers who have been imprisoned for their beliefs.

More important for our purposes is to understand that "Here Be The Story Makers." PEN is their lair, and here is felt their power. Information can change *what* people think, but literature changes the *way* people think without their being aware of it.

The English PEN Center is down by the Thames in Chelsea, Bohemian Chelsea where in past generations long-legged girls lay on the lawn listening to wind-up phonographs. "James Joyce? Darling! How delicious . . ."

I ask directions of a man in the lane. He pushes his cap to the back of his head. "You're already there, mate, and don't know it. You see the truck unloading the booze? That's it. Will they ask me in for a drop? Not likely, but I see they've asked you rich Americans. Why would I think you're rich? It's a word, mate—Richamerican." He strolls off chuckling.

Upstairs on the second floor, the oak-paneled PEN bar is packed chest to breast. A voice from the crowd: "After the writers' awards, you remember? Jean doesn't believe this, but 'struth, I was going just for a moment with this Irish poet to a pub where a poetry reading was going on, only never got there, but did get to a pub, but left—"

A female interjects, "You were thrown out, I expect."

"—and I got on the tube to go home, only I never got home."

"You got on the ring tube, you fool, and went around and around all night."

"—And I called Jean, and I said that I was somewhere near Covent Gardens. . . ."

A large man with a strident voice: "America . . . destroying the world in the interest of money, just money . . . financiers who never see the consequences of what they do."

His voice runs through the crowded room, seeming to touch fire as it passes.

A literary critic: "I remember touring California.

The architecture was such a sham. What are Americans doing there? Why are they doing whatever it is they are doing? American authors haven't told the American story. Are they meddling in the world? Yes, I suppose so, when one doesn't know who one is, has lost one's continuity of purpose."

"When the United States gets involved in the world," a man says, "it needs to learn to leave bad enough alone."

The strident voice again: "America . . . It doesn't matter whether it's peace or war . . . it's on a collision course. . . ."

The literary critic: "Who was it who said the Americans refer to their soldiers as boys? I suppose that means rambunctious and naive at the same time. I believe English people refer to their soldiers as men."

A man pounds on the bar. "The Yanks used to be overpaid, oversexed and over here; now they're over everywhere."

A woman says, "My agent tells me the only books the Yanks will buy are fucking books and fighting books. Fucking and fighting."

Antonia Fraser, the historical novelist, is greeting people at the door. This year's president of the English PEN Center, she is tall, blond and pleasant.

Two white-haired ladies are talking. "Antonia is distantly related to royalty, dear."

"Very distantly, dear."

The strident voice again: "The United States thinks it's so superior it can put the world right, and space as well, and it has poisoned itself with chemicals—all this for money. . . ."

Antonia's husband, Harold Pinter, the great English playwright who has influenced the theater perhaps more than anyone else in our time, is wedged into a corner by the bar, looking impatient with the strident voice. He says, "Being beastly to America is irritating and pointless. . . ."

Pinter's face tightens. "I gave a speech in Holland last week on U.S. imperialism in Nicaragua." I can feel his body vibrate with rage.

I turn to him. "Harold, imperialism is a cheap shot. It's too easy to put down the United States about Nicaragua. Some Contras were good guys, fighting the Sandinistas because they wanted freedom and democracy for their country. Unfortunately, the CIA only backed the Contras who could be controlled. The great majority of Americans are opposed to Contra aid. Most of us agree with you that the Sandinistas aren't as bad as our government portrays them—not that bad."

Harold gives me a long look compounded of anger and pity. "The speech is going to be published in the *Index on Censorship*. Read it."

A woman struggling to leave the bar with her drink intact bats her eyes toward Harold. "Isn't he too handsome and elegant to be so serious?"

With all the festivities and libations, it is fortunate that I am close enough to walk home. Suddenly Pinter's look of anger and pity flashes back and hits me like a blow to the chest. I grab the nearest lamppost for support. Pity! What did he see? Me running for shelter, hiding behind the "most Americans don't agree with our Nicaraguan policy" excuse? Was he thinking of other intellectually glib old men in Nazi Germany, pretending they couldn't hear the cattle cars in the night? Of course, I'm not a German living under Hitler, but I do accept the benefits of citizenship in the United States of America. Doesn't this also imply taking responsibility for my country's actions in Nicaragua? It isn't enough to say I don't agree with them.

The PEN Center vibrates with rage against the United States, and Harold Pinter expresses its essence. His rage resounds throughout Europe. His magnificent house in Campden Hill Square has become the epicenter of his self-righteous wrath against the United States. He has

used its energy to form his band of "twenty just men,"
using an archetypal anti-Americanism as the anvil of his
forge. His words have tapped a primordial, blood-
pounding rage that runs deep in the common European
psyche.

Before going to bed I sit down with my notebook to
record the evening's conversations. Once more I am
struck by the rage I encountered at the PEN Center. It
awoke in me an old sense of guilt and shame, the
counterpart of rage. Could I find a secret deep in my own
psyche that would help explain these feelings? I had
participated in the betrayal of Europe after World War II,
which culminated in America's failure to support the
Hungarian revolution in 1956. The Russian forces had
only left Austria in 1955. Vienna was the scene of the
intrigue that led to American assurances of help to the
Hungarian freedom fighters, whom we later betrayed.

This morning I am convinced that I have to return to
Vienna to reexamine my own buried feelings from that
time. Perhaps I can get a clue to the unconscious origins of
the rage I saw and heard expressed at the PEN Center. A
friend is providing a ride to Vienna.

HEATHROW AIRPORT

I am standing at the end gate watching the landing
of a three-engined corporate jet with a golden cockerel
painted on its side.

In my pocket is a box containing a small medieval
crucifix. Thirty-odd years ago it had hung around the
neck of Janos. I had known him before World War II as
a graduate student from Hungary at Princeton University.
He was a brilliant student and a brilliant writer, with a
small, slim, supple body barely able to contain a prodi-
gious energy. I had expected him to become one of the

important thinkers and writers of our time. During the war he worked in Washington as an intelligence liaison with a small Hungarian resistance group; afterward he returned to Hungary as a university professor and married Rena, the Magyar beauty of the season. His dark intensity offset her red hair and vivacious manners.

In 1956, Janos took his young wife across the border into Austria at a temporarily unguarded place where he was to pick up U.S. guns and ammunition. The goods weren't there. The United States had mountains of such weapons stashed near the Austrian-Hungarian border and had given the Hungarian freedom fighters reason to believe that those weapons would be available when they revolted against the Russian occupation. But we betrayed them. We betrayed ourselves. And all of free Europe connived at the betrayal. Janos left Rena and crossed back into Hungary to fight the Russian tanks with his bare hands.

The sound of the jet pulling up jerks me back to the present. The door opens and the steps are lowered. A big, blond man shoulders his way through the door and bounds down the steps, shouting, "Come on, we have to get out of here."

I'm 6'1", and still he looms over me. His hand is outstretched. I put my hand behind me. "I told you I would never shake hands with you again, Paul."

His round face breaks into a grin as he puts his arm around my shoulders and lifts me off the ground. "That was thirty years ago. It's time you forgave me."

"Never! You crushed my hand, you bastard. I couldn't use it for months."

He bustles me up the steps, and before the door is dogged shut, the jet is moving.

His young wife is leaning against the door to the main cabin.

"Hello, Jocelyn. Good to see you. How are you still putting up with this monster?"

She winks. "He's a pussycat with me." Jocelyn is as petite as Paul is big. Paul didn't marry until late in life.

He had been too busy building his business. But when he did tie the knot he had managed to find a beautiful woman who was also stable and intelligent.

In the middle of the cabin is a conference table with swivel chairs around it and couches at each end.

"Buckle up!" Paul says. "We'll talk after we're airborne."

I lean my head against the high back of the chair and relax for a minute. My hand is tingling in remembrance of that time thirty years ago.

The Hungarian revolution had been suppressed by Soviet tanks and troops sent in from Siberia. I was sitting in a jumble of rocks near a fringe of trees that marked the border. I saw some movement in the trees and shifted position, trying to watch the exact spot. Before I knew it there was a tousled blond head below me. I reached down to help him up. But he took my hand and was over the rock and on top of me, his grip crushing my hand and his Russian rifle embedded in my stomach. I had to grit my teeth to keep from screaming. When he was sure I couldn't use that hand, he let go and rifled through my pockets for identification. Satisfied, he put the gun aside and sat down facing me.

"Janos, where's Janos?" I asked.

Eyes like blue ice glinted at me. "He won't be here."

"But—"

"No one will be here."

"But—you mean—"

"Dead. Burned meat." His upper lip curled and his nose crinkled as he smelled death again. His face came apart for a moment. With an effort he regained control and became impassive.

I could see he was very young, maybe only eighteen years old. "Who are you?"

"I'm Paulus; I was his student. He said you could get guns, but you didn't come through."

Janos, my friend, was dead, and I and my country had failed him.

He picked up the gun.

"Put it down. You can't take it."

He wouldn't put it down.

I pushed my face into his. "If they find it on you, they'll put you in jail, maybe send you back. You killed the Russian who had it—and others?"

He nodded.

"They would send you back. Leave it. Leave it! I can get you to the United States. Do what I say."

When Paul arrived in the United States after leaving the burned and broken bodies of his betrayed countrymen in Hungary, he found *The King and I* and *My Fair Lady* playing in the local movie houses and Elvis Presley singing "Hound Dog" on the radio. Paul arrived with only a couple of hundred donated dollars and never asked for anything else. Now he owns an international heavy construction company headquartered in Los Angeles.

An older and wiser Paul claps me on the shoulder. "Come on, let's talk. You know I've been flying to Stuttgart every few days to see Heinz about the pipe-laying machinery he's building for me. I have to see it and feel it. This cross-channel tunnel from England to France can mean a big job for us. I'll pick you up tomorrow on my way back to London, but I won't talk to Rena."

Paul had never forgiven Rena, Janos's wife, for precipitously marrying a rich Viennese after Janos was killed.

Hungary and Vienna are symbolic of our failure to respond to Stalin when the world was divided up at Yalta. The true story of Yalta has never been made public. Averell Harriman was President Roosevelt's advisor there, and Harriman's assistant was a friend of mine. We spent a stormy Atlantic crossing talking about Yalta. Harriman was capable of great interior thought and saw Stalin for what he was. But the tragedy of the Yalta Conference was that while hundreds of thousands of hours were devoted to military and political strategy, few were spent exploring the reasons that we were fighting, and few were spent thinking about *how* Stalin thought as he fought. Harriman knew that Stalin had killed perhaps twenty million of his own people—middle-class farming Kulaks—for nothing more than the ideological purposes of Communism. The Russian people had acquiesced in those killings, and some had even written poems to justify the slaughter. Harriman had read them. He also recalled from his knowledge of Russian history a remark made by Stalin's predecessor Ivan the Great, who said that he scythed his people down occasionally because it made them grow back better.

Harriman also knew a little about Stalin's devastation of the free people of the Baltic states. He had heard of desolate villages, their inhabitants having been rounded up like animals in the woods and slaughtered. He knew how Stalin thought.

Though Harriman knew better, the staffs had managed to arrange the agenda so that a sick Roosevelt and an exhausted Churchill would talk to Stalin as though, beneath his strategy and ideology, he was capable of caring about others. And they turned over to him the lives of people who had looked to us as saviors.

Hitler made the infamous bargain to give Stalin half of Poland. We, the United States, gave Stalin all of Poland plus East Germany, Czechoslovakia, Hungary, Bulgaria, Romania, Latvia, Lithuania and Estonia. Hitler's motives were evil and ours were good. But who made the worse bargain? If we hold the people of Germany responsible for Hitler's holocaust, we must be willing to take responsibility for the holocaust Stalin visited upon the new slave

states of his empire. Today we are helping the Mujadeen
of Afghanistan fight for their freedom. We are helping
Savimba in Angola. We are even, for god's sake, helping
the Contras. We lost our nerve at Yalta and later in
Hungary when we didn't let any of the surplus rifles and
ammunition stored conveniently nearby reach the freedom fighters. We let a political agenda and strategic interests come before our deepest spiritual integrity.

VIENNA

They've banned automobiles from the central section
of Vienna, the original medieval walled city. In the early
morning mist it might still be that ancient city built on
the flat marshy land at a bend in the Danube. The dark,
towering mass of St. Stephen's Cathedral reaches up out of
the clutter of low buildings surrounding it. Past the cathedral, and after some turns, a lane winds between two old
buildings. Farther down, the lane widens onto a parapet
of the old city wall that runs out to form a defensive point.

This piece of wall dates back to the Islamic invasions
of Europe. In 1683, a vast Turkish army of 300 thousand
soldiers had moved up through Greece, Romania, Bulgaria and Hungary to strike through Vienna into the
heart of Europe.

Imagine the Islamic forces spread out below, their
fine-limbed Arabian horses and brightly colored silks
draped over polished steel armor, their wooden towers
and ladders moving ever closer. Vienna has been under
seige for a long time. There is no food left in the city. The
defenders, only twenty thousand, are propping themselves
against the parapet for strength.

The Islamic commanders know the city is about to
fall. Today's attack will overwhelm Vienna and pave the

way for the conquest of Europe. The fate of Western culture is awaiting the commands to attack these walls. A silence falls over the scene.

But look up to the high ground, the Kahlenberg rising above the city's plains, and see a solitary rider on a huge horse, standing black and immobile where the trees begin. It is the king of Poland. He finishes surveying the battleground and settles his helmet on his gray head, framing a grim, lined face. His calvary filter out of the trees to form behind him. He checks his line of warriors and without a word moves out. The ground shakes as the dark mass crashes through the flank of Islam, carrying all before it.

Thus began the long withdrawal of the Turkish Empire. Everyone who is heir to Western culture should mark that day. The female figure of the Winged Victory of Samothrace should be moved from the Louvre and mounted on the parapet of this wall, which points like the prow of a ship into the future of the West.

There are no more warriors here now. There were none in 1956, when the United States betrayed Europe. When the Hungarian people died fighting the Russian invaders for their freedom, we were the only viable force in Europe, the bright warriors from the magic land across the sea, but we dared not offer the least help. It was another victory for the Russian Empire and another defeat for the freedom of Western thought.

The Polish king, whose country we gave away to Stalin, had been true to his commitment, but we, as a nation, lost our nerve. We betrayed Hungary and we betrayed ourselves.

Today we pretend that outrage to our spirit never happened. But we will not be able to know ourselves or understand our relations with Europe until we face our part in the Hungarian revolution.

As individuals we all wonder who we really are; we dream of being able to discover our true nature through some test: Are we cowards or are we capable of heroism? As a nation we were tested in Hungary in 1956. We had assured the freedom movement that we would support them, and when the Hungarian people committed themselves to revolt, we discovered we were not the people we had hoped we could be. We had lost our spirit.

After the Russians brutally suppressed the revolution, they executed fifty thousand Hungarians and made hundreds of thousands more disappear into the maw of the Russian Gulag. We had valued our strategy over freedom and hope.

What comes to mind is a dark street in New York not so many years ago. A young woman was attacked on the street with apartment windows open all around her. She screamed and her attackers paused, but no one came to her aid. They continued attacking her and she screamed and still no one came. No one even called the police. People closed their windows and drew their curtains as she screamed, sobbed, cried for help and then died. How can the people who turned away live with themselves?

People in Vienna have gone back to the old Beidermeyer style of living that developed under Metternich's secret police. Social interaction—real living—takes place behind drawn curtains; if a friend is taken in the night, no one knows it. Austria hasn't drawn a deep breath since World War II. Just look at the map. Austria is a spear sticking into the Russian Empire, but it's a blunt spear, determined to pose no threat. Hear nothing. See nothing. Say nothing.

Here on Vienna's walls overlooking the Russian Empire to the east, let's acknowledge old shame and bitterness. Let's not pull the curtains on our past mistakes, but learn from them instead.

In this regard Frederick Turner is a good teacher. We're having dinner with him tonight in the quiet, brick-vaulted room of an old Viennese restaurant. Frederick has just returned from Budapest, where he has been collaborating on the translation of Hungary's great poet Miklos Radnoti. Frederick is himself one of the world's great poets. His latest book-length epic poem, *Genesis*, has won praise from critics around the world.

Frederick is talking about the Hungarian revolution: "You remember the priceless old buildings around the square in Budapest, where the most publicized slaughter took place. When the tanks had finished chewing up the people, they started in on the buildings and leveled some of Hungary's most important architectural heritage for blocks around. The repression after the revolution was absolute.

"Well, the Russian general strode across the broken and burned bodies and the smoking ruins, nodding at a job well done. That night at a raucous dinner party, he doubled over with terrible pains and was rushed to a hospital.

"My friend Mari was a nurse in the hospital where this Russian general lay wasting away, dying. The Russian medics were so incompetent and poorly supplied that even a general could die for lack of a drug that was available in any civilized hospital. Mari hates Russians the way a Pole, rather a Hungarian, would, but she couldn't just let him die. She obtained the drug and gave it to him, and he recovered.

"Some months later he showed up at her house with a military chauffeur and a great air of ceremony. He had a gift for her, he said. With a flourish he presented her with a box of cheap candy.

"In 1956, I was a Marxist working for the Campaign for Nuclear Disarmament in England. The word came down from the Communist party bosses, who were mostly middle-echelon British trade union officials, to see that no aid reached Hungary. It was Hungary that broke my connection with the Communist party. John Paul Sartre gave a speech denouncing the party and canceling his membership. Nothing could ever be the same after that betrayal of freedom.

"America wouldn't save Hungary in part because France and Britain chose that moment to go into Suez. America was also betrayed by Europe. The Europeans thus hate the Americans for the same reason Iago hates Othello and Claggart hates Billy Budd. To one who has forever degraded himself morally—as Europe did with the Terror, the Holocaust and the Gulag—the innocence of the noble U.S. spirit was wormwood, insufferable. Actually, there's a difference in the way England perceives America as compared with the Continent. England is jealous of America, jealous of its fullness of being. England didn't betray itself by crime or cowardice as Germany and France did, but by small-mindedness, . . . by modesty felt as an innate superiority.

"I grew up in England. Remember I was a student at Oxford when you were there in 1965, and I wanted to write epic poetry. I knew that if I tried to do it in England they would peck me to death, so I came to America. Here it's only the academics who try to peck you to death, and academics don't count for much in the United States. But around the American academy, like beautiful organisms living in the dead stone of a coral reef, I find remarkable human beings, some of the finest I have known. Epic doesn't faze them at all."

Regardless of Frederick's valid insight that the United States was betrayed by England and France, we did betray Hungary and, in so doing, ourselves. That betrayal acquired a mythological dimension of guilt within American leadership that became a central influence in the escalation of the Vietnam war under Lyndon Johnson. Our leaders were driven by the unconscious agenda that *this* time we would be true to our spirit, and communist aggression would be stopped. For Europeans, however, Vietnam became the symbol of the American betrayal of Europe and its hope for peace, a symbol that allowed them to use us as a scapegoat and draw the curtains around their own betrayals.

THE CHANNEL TUNNEL

On the flight back to London, Paul pretends to be busy, and I wander about the plane.

The cabin forward of the conference room is an electronic center, with computers and transmitters and an electronic drafting table. Jocelyn runs communications. No one is around Paul for long, not even his wife, without being put to work, his work.

Further forward is the cabin for sleeping, with three bunks on each side and racks for hard hats, boots and all-weather gear. Paul's office is a little cubbyhole next to the cockpit. When I come in, he rings the pilot. "Buzz the tunnel for us."

The construction of a tunnel under the English Channel is one of the most awesome projects of the European Community. The paperwork involved in negotiating to subcontract its construction is supposedly keeping Paul at his desk now. I gather there are political as well as construction forces at work.

Shortly, the plane banks and there on the coast of England is a huge hole in the ground. As we pass overhead, I can see the movement of construction equipment within a ring of derricks. The tunnel has been a contentious issue between England and the Continent. England is having a hard time giving up its autonomy and security as an island, which Shakespeare described so well in *King Richard II*.

> . . . this sceptred isle, . . .
> This fortress built by Nature for herself
> Against infection and the hand of war,
> This happy breed of men, this little world,
> This precious stone set in the silver sea,

The tunnel is a threat to the English. However, the Thatcher government has reluctantly gone along with the project in the spirit of the European Community. At the moment the English are objecting to the use of the fast French trains in the tunnel. But the tunnel will be much more than fast, cheap transportation to the rest of the European Community; it will be a physical joining in the common earth below the continent, a symbol of the thousands of years of intermingling of the thought and blood that make up Europe.

"Very impressive, Paul. It's obvious that this tunnel will be important for the people of the European Community."

Watching him closely, I say, "You're avoiding something, Paul."

Paul settles back in his chair for a moment, averting his eyes. "What happened with Rena?"

I take Janos's crucifix out of the box and hold it out to him. "Remember, you gave this to Rena after you crossed the border. She gave it to me after she remarried. I've kept it all these years as a reminder, so I would never forget what we Americans did at Yalta and during the Hungarian revolution. But I've finally resolved that for myself. You take it now."

Paul's upper lip curls and his nostrils crinkle. He rubs his massive hand across his face. He's smelling the burning flesh of his mentor, Janos, again. He pushes his hands at me. "You're crazy. That would be like putting my hand on a hot stove."

I notice a brownish smudge in the silver work of the cross. It looks like old blood. I try to get it out with my nail and sit rubbing Janos's cross, rubbing and rubbing.

LONDON: THE STRAND

Back in London I feel better able to deal with the rage I saw expressed at the PEN Center. I look up Pinter's speech. He defines U.S. foreign policy as "a classic case of depraved moral position" that quite simply means "Kiss my ass or I'll kick your head in." He further accuses the United States of "systematic, calculated, cynical, blatant, vicious lies," and of instigating or abetting "murderous acts." "Every effort" he says, "must be made to persuade the Western European governments to act independently of American influence!"

It occurs to me that Jungianism might provide some insight on this. Jung postulated a collective unconscious in which archetypes become landmarks of thought upon which the mind can orient itself. Has the United States become a useful archetype in the context of developing European thought?

At one time the Statue of Liberty provided a good visual image of the United States archetype. The statue and its accompanying inscription, "Give me your tired, your poor . . . ," announced to the world that here was a country with room in its heart for everyone, where the best dreams of Europe could be realized. Here were youth, innocence, energy and creativity—the opposite of Europe with its world-weary discontent, cynicism, hypocrisy and self-interest. The United States represented the possibility of peace.

As Europe was fighting to rebuild and find itself after World War II, it depended on the bright, caring United States. But we betrayed our promise. The United States archetype failed. In Jung's scheme, each archetype has a dark side that is loosed if the archetype fails its social purpose. Could it be that Europe's anti-Americanism actually describes the dark side of the archetype?

On the dark side of the archetype would be images of guns and soldiers used to achieve national interests, the gangster with the machine gun and the mushroom cloud of Hiroshima. It would be bloated businesspeople with greedy eyes clutching bags of money.

Using the Jungian archetype as a model, how can Pinter's anti-American words describe the new European

Community? His tone of voice and body posture suggested his outrage and revulsion toward the United States, and he defines the topic of his speech as "U.S. imperalism." Our friends in Europe use this word more than any other in referring to the United States. Everyone knows the United States has no empire, so why do intelligent, articulate wordsmiths like Harold Pinter use the word? Because the people of Europe have developed no language as yet to express their new way of living without war. In their rage at our betrayal, the word imperialism symbolizes any warlike force used to achieve national goals. We were certainly guilty of war in Vietnam, Nicaragua and elsewhere in the world. At present, anti-American language is the only means available to describe the European Community, by defining it in terms of what it is not.

Without knowing how or why, Europeans have become people who no longer need warlike force to attain national goals. It isn't that they are able to do things Americans are incapable of. The fact is that their thinking has evolved to the point where they are no longer able to carry on warlike activities among themselves.

Pinter's "depraved moral position" is a description of the United States that actually implies its opposite—the way Europeans are preserving and cherishing their local and national morals while moving at the same time to bypass boundaries and transcend rigid nationalism. His description of U.S. foreign policy as "Kiss my ass or I'll kick your head in" is extreme, but it further illuminates the radical change in European thinking, which consigns violence to interior experience rather than exterior action. When Pinter accuses the United States of "systematic, calculated, cynical, blatant, vicious lies," he is simply describing our normal government policies that protect national self-interest.

The anti-Americanism of my British friends thus defines the new thought taking shape in the European

Community. For them the United States represents the antithesis of the European Community.

THE LONDON PRESS CLUB

My literary preoccupation with anti-American feelings at PEN has been pushed to its limit. Let's try to find some perspective at the Press Club. It is a place full of old stories and memories. Perhaps we can go back to a time when feelings for the United States were reasonably simple, to see how today's more tangled feelings developed. It's the little things, the currents of thought barely noticed, that build the future.

The Club has recently left the International Press Center tower and burrowed underground into the embankment at the bottom of Fleet Street. The newspaper companies are leaving hallowed Fleet Street behind as they move to their new fairy city of glass towers down by the old Thames dock area—Americanization taking over.

The new quarters are snug and comfortable, insulated from the outside world and full of smoke, as in the old days. A grizzled reporter turns from the unending club Snooker game: "Do I remember? Of course I do. . . . Was it twenty-five years ago? Well, that's a generation—not so long ago, is it then? Thursday, November the 22nd. No, I didn't remember that, but I do remember the time of day. It was seven o'clock. I was working for the *London Times* then. We had torn up and redone the front page maybe four times and finally put the paper to bed. And then, at seven o'clock, every wire service teletype in the city room went crazy—AP, UP, Reuters . . . PRESIDENT KENNEDY ASSASSINATED. I was up all night. At some point I went to the Press Club, where I hoped to find the reporters who would laugh at anything; they weren't laughing that night."

From the bar: "I was there. You could see out the Club then, over the Thames. I remember like it was yesterday, see; this feeling down my back that it had all gone wrong. Listen, you ask anyone in the Western world what they were doing when they heard that news, and they'll know—as clear as if it were today. If there's any one single thing we all have in common everywhere, it's the memory of that day."

"Great Caesar fell," a boozy voice murmurs. "Oh what a fall was there. . . . Then I and you and all of us fell down, as the Great Bard said."

Someone whistles a bar from the musical *Camelot.* "Camelot! That's it. How did it go? It never rained and everything was perfect."

An excited voice breaks in: "No, no, it was 'right makes might' instead of 'might makes right'—a socko story."

The grizzled reporter: "Well, that night was the end of Camelot. 'One brief shining hour,' that's about what he had. Remember in the movie version the king, that sod Richard Harris, sends a lad back to tell the story of Camelot. . . . Who told the story of the Yank Camelot? Not the Yanks!"

A thin-faced young man with wild red hair speaks up. "Well, I don't remember because I was a baby, but I do know that if you went into any Irish cottage, and there were many without running water, there would be a picture of the damned Pope and a picture of damned Jack Kennedy and damned little else." He broods over his drink.

A white-haired man, barbered and elegantly dress-ed, is standing up. "I was there. To the world young Jack Kennedy was the symbol of hope. We young people were going to put things right." He winces, as if from a bad taste, and walks out.

Trust reporters to nose out the stories that clutch the heart. Have I stumbled upon a key image here, a symbol that marks the change in English minds from respect and affection to . . . what? A backlash of rejection resulted from an unrealistic dependence on the United States as a magic Camelot, a promise of hope for the world.

In 1963, President John F. Kennedy was the living American archetype. He personified youth, innocence, energy and creativity—and the hope for an end to war. He was King Arthur, the once and future king of Camelot, returned to redeem all peoples.

He had visited Ireland the year of his assassination. The people had greeted him almost as though he were a living saint, making tentative gestures to touch him with reverence as he passed among the crowds. He represented the child of Europe, the United States, returned to rescue the parents, a fairy-tale motif as old as culture itself. The Marshall Plan made the fairy tale seem true—here was a selfless help from the United States to Europe.

But there is a resentment of the child who saves the family. As Europe began to recover its own identity, it no longer needed the savior-child archetype projected on the United States. The turning point was the death of Kennedy.

The assassination of John Kennedy was itself an archetypal image—the killing of the king, something that may have actually been done in old Nilotic tribes. Then an enantiodromia, a changing of opposites, took place: The United States no longer carried the bright shadow of Europe, lost in World War II, but took on the dark shadow that Europe was growing beyond.

What was this dark shadow? The old negative image of Europe itself—colonialism, the use of military force and a certain cultural inflation and presumption of superiority. Perhaps anti-Americanism allowed Europe to deny its own dark past that had culminated in the world wars. America carried the shadow just as it had carried the savior image.

By seeing the United States as the dark, disowned side of Europe itself, the Europeans began to unconsciously define themselves in a new mold. If the United States was nationalistic, they were open to transnational and cultural values; if the United States was materialistic and greedy, they unconsciously identified with a major thesis of this book—*the importance of persons over property*. If the United States was militaristic, Europe could identify with disarmament.

By carrying the changing patterns of Europe's archetypal projections, the United States unwittingly participated in the growth of the new consciousness in Europe. Jung would be fascinated to see the individuation of Europe riding on the dark side of the American archetype. This image became charged, moreover, with the as yet unexpressed emotions of betrayal surrounding Yalta and the failed Hungarian revolution. We took out our guilt by waging war in Vietnam, they took out theirs by blaming us for betraying peace in Vietnam. Kennedy's assassination was the turning point in European thinking, and it was from this point in history that the policies of the European Community were forged between the anvil of anti-Americanism and the hammer of Soviet threat.

THE TRIANGLE OF POWER

LONDON: BELGRAVIA

An intimate dinner party is being held for Michael Holroyd and his wife, Margaret Drabble. It is in a small house in the mews in back of the Duke of Hamilton's townhouse. These mews—named for the sound made by the falcons there—were originally designed for falcons and horses and now make attractive cul-de-sacs for private residences. The lane is still cobbled, and one can imagine the carriages clattering out into Belgrave Place and around to the front of the grand houses, where lords and ladies would be waiting.

Michael is an eminence in English letters. He is the biographer of Lytton Strachey and Augustus John, and he recently received an unprecedented advance of over a million dollars for his *Bernard Shaw: The Search for Love.*

Michael is also the spokesman to the world for literary London. Quiet and unassuming, he is a powerful man even though he doesn't feel like one.

As a writer, Michael is in touch with his inner feelings, and he has a finger on the pulse of European society. It is therefore important for us to understand the feelings of Michael Holroyd, and people like him, in order to understand the European Community.

Michael is telling the story of a fellow writer who, on the eve of going to Brussels for a few weeks, stops off at his publisher's to pick up the galleys of his latest book. The publisher holds up a set of galleys and says, "This is our best book of the year." The author is glowing with pleasure when the publisher hands him another set and says, "And here are your galleys for correction." Michael, who is dark-haired and pleasant, is saying, "Now, was that kind? That's not the way to send someone off."

Pouncing on the opportunity, someone says, "But Michael, it demonstrates that publishers are turning authors into galley slaves."

Laughter.

Michael's story touches off a discussion of the European Community, because its administrative center is in Brussels. I ask Michael what he thinks about the community and its relation to anti-Americanism. He gives my question his full, serious attention as is his way. "The European Community goes back a ways. In the sixties and seventies England was divesting herself of empire, remember. We were consciously seeking to be less, to diminish ourselves. Perhaps that was the kind of atmosphere the European Community needed. But on the other hand, it was easy to be envious of an enchanted land like the United States that was prosperous and growing."

From across the table: "The United States was hope during a time when Europe couldn't handle hope. Perhaps we English could only handle despair. In 1967, for example, England devalued the pound just as the English had been devaluing themselves. Even worse, by leaking the information the Bank of England more or less asked the world to speculate it out of some five billion dollars. But I think this was part of our effort to separate ourselves from a failed American dream that assigned spiritual worth to money."

Margaret Drabble, a direct, powerful person, is talking about one of her sons becoming a fellow of Balliol College at Oxford. "He's making very little money, of course, but what he wants from life is value and respect."

Margaret has a unique place in English letters. Not only is she a prominent novelist, but she is also the editor of the *Oxford Companion to English Literature*. She writes in Hampstead, where she lives with her children from a previous marriage, and Michael lives and writes in West London, fifteen minutes away. They get together on weekends. It's an unusual but very successful marriage.

Margaret and Michael reinforce each other's conversation in a natural, loving way. They are talking about Paul Johnson, the English historian: Margaret has read his book *Modern Times*. "You know what a conservative he is," she says, "and I disagree with him. but his point about the Marshall Plan being meddling is interesting. I don't think that was meddling, but 'meddling' is a key word for the United States: meddling in Vietnam, meddling in Grenada, meddling in Nicaragua, meddling in Libya."

It is interesting that every time the conversation turns to the European Community or to its global interest, someone refers to the United States. Even Margaret, in her fairness about the Marshall Plan, seems to find it necessary to describe the current situation in anti-American, rather than European, terms.

TEA

After dinner we retire to this lovely old living room, French doors opening onto a fragrant garden. There are

tea and cookies, and we are discussing Margaret's book
The Radiant Way. The book is about the England of the seventies, "the brave new world of Welfare State and County
Scholarships." Someone suggests that this also describes
almost any other European country at the time, but the
conversation drifts back to the minor character George.
George escapes from this "brave new world" to the United
States, where he finds himself serving on committees instead of performing as an artistic producer. He stays for
money and is destroyed in the end by New York's greed
and lack of intellectual values. Margaret's major characters remain in England to serve English society. They are
"the elite, the chosen, the garlanded of the great social
dream."

John Andrews, a book editor, is with us. Rosy-faced,
sitting upright in his chair, teacup in hand, he says, "Ha!
Those are great quotes from Maggie's book, but the elite
were those who, by graduating from Cambridge or
Oxford, became the arbiters of England's despair and de-
cline, who presided over the more and more equal distribution of less and less. Cambridge produced its Marxists
and its traitors, but it also produced the class of social servants that Margaret describes so well. Class is bred in the
English bone. Class still rules England, you know, only it
is the class of intellect.

"This class worked out our remarkable adaptation to
socialist despair in the seventies. Complete freedom from
censorship of thought for the intellectual class. And to
balance that, censorship of action for the lower classes
through socialist cradle-to-grave care. Intellect and literature could be free of censorship only by censoring the
actions that might result from them. I should say that our
actions are self-censored. Self-censorship of behavior is
like breathing for us. We are born doing it. It's quite cozy.
And it worked for Europe. Our urban wasteland became
cozy. Quite an achievement."

Intellectual coziness! This is not an idea, but a way of
thinking. Is something as subtle as this, a different

quality of thinking and feeling about each other, likely to be the key to the success of the European Community in the future?

Martyn Goff says, "Let me tell you a story about the United States." Martyn has just retired after many years as chief executive of the Queen's Book Trust, which Michael Holroyd chaired. He is now chairman of Henry Sotheran Limited, an antiquarian book company. The Book Trust has been successful in fostering literacy through contests and fun and games. Martyn is saturnine, handsome and vital.

"In the seventies I was asked by the U.S. State Department to tour the major universities and libraries across the country, talking up the Book Trust approach to reading books. That trip was the germination of the Center for the Book at the Library of Congress. It required the cooperation and help of American publishers and editors, which I understand was freely forthcoming."

John mutters, "Editors don't read manuscripts any more and publishers can't read, except for the figures on balance sheets. That's Americanization."

"Well, John," Martyn says, "it's much more than that. I remember one afternoon coming into a midwestern town whose university had one of the great libraries. The librarian and his wife met me and took me out to dinner, at 5:30."

The civilized English people present, who eat at 8:00 P.M., recoil in shock.

"And they had nothing to drink. I mean no alcohol."

More shock.

"Then after dinner they took me to see a new shopping mall. I explained that I didn't want to see a shopping mall, I wanted to see the great library. It took a visit to a second shopping mall before we finally got to the library. Later I suggested I would walk back to my hotel. 'Oh, but you can't walk,' they said. 'We'll drive you back. We can't let you walk.'

"This was my biggest problem all through the trip. Everyone was so friendly, they wouldn't let me walk. Do you know that you can't walk out of Chicago's O'Hare airport? I tried to and was stopped by two police in a police car.

"I heard a typical American story in Chicago. There's a well-known bookstore near the University of Chicago, and the proprietor is a famous character. I went in to meet him. He said that it was nice to meet another Englishman, because an English salesman for Penguin had been in just the other day and had asked him for an order. Then he stopped and looked at me until I foolishly fed him his line and asked if he had placed an order.

"'No,' the proprietor said. A robber came in just then and, in the excitement, shot the English salesman dead—right where I was standing apparently. He said the salesman had missed a good order."

Martyn lounges back in his chair. "He never changed voice or expression while telling me that story. He got me, indeed, he did. You think it was just a story? No, he showed me a piece about it in the newspaper.

"When I got to Washington, I encountered the Peace Corps—their new imperialism. Their students used to come here, to Europe, to learn about their literary and intellectual roots. Now, they are only concerned about 'fixing things,' but they don't have any cultural perspective about what to fix or why. And then these young people leave the countries they're meddling in before they have to face the consequences."

Going to the French doors opening onto the cozy, perfect, English garden, I say, "Martyn, it seems to me your story and your anti-American tone are about a feeling that the United States betrayed Europe. I know you respect the United States, but I think you felt betrayed when the dream that the United States under President Kennedy would bring unending peace and prosperity could not be fulfilled.

"For the last twenty years you have all been using anti-American symbols to orient your new, amorphous ways of living together. You can't seem to put those qualities of living into words. They slip away from you like a dream on awakening. Instead of using the good old United States of America to define European thought by what it is not, it's time you defined it by what it is. What's the message? Where is the European Community going, and how is it changing?"

John then looks around the room with a sharp glance. "Very well, let me try, using points from Martyn's speech to the International Publishers Association the other day. The information revolution, for example, started in the United States. Europe is very much into it, but information is only a very surface kind of thought. It has no meaning in itself. A different kind of thought—a deeper thought—is needed to give it meaning. When we use words, we feel them. It is an interior knowledge. And it seems to me that the United States loses knowledge to information. On the other hand, we in the European Community have the depth to—"

John puts a hand to his cheek. "Ah yes, I see I am still using the United States as a referent. I admit it is useful, but perhaps, as you imply, it is a habit one might put aside. Let me start again. We in Europe are developing an inner speech that leads to growth, an enlargement of thought. It has something to do with the accumulation of six hundred years of reading mixed into the European soil. If nothing else, it is the reading itself, bringing conscious and unconscious, civilized and primitive feelings together. We've talked about Jung's racial memories. They accumulate, you know. They live in fantasy. One can't help but feel that fantasy is atrophied somewhat in the United States. . . . Sorry. . . .

"I'll try another angle. The ability to communicate and hold depths of thinking and feeling within ourselves. For us the food of this kind of thought is our feel-

ings expressed in well-used words, the literary use of
words. Our feelings hold the secrets of our hearts. They
are our community. But we wordsmiths haven't yet found
the words to express our European Community."

Returning to my chair I say, "What do you think,
Martyn? Has John put his finger on it? I remember that
the Canadian scholar Marshall McLuhan was your
friend. You said he was having some second thoughts
about his slogan 'the medium is the message' before he
died. Would McLuhan have been willing to say that reading literature, the process of author and reader creating
inner realities, is the message? The message of European
thought is expressed through the medium of internalized
words; that is, your reality is interior rather than exterior. You Europeans have trouble expressing the message
because the medium you are using is internal."

John breaks in, "I'm going to pretend I didn't hear
that convoluted nonsense. Let's have some fun 'banging off
the good old United States of America,' as you say. Did you
read about the Americans giving a remote African village
a state-of-the-art, solar-powered water pump to replace
their old bucket system? As a result, the villager who had
been controlling the water lost his authority. The village
boys he had paid to haul the water were out of work, and
so spent their days terrorizing the village. Social life
broke down and everyone starved. Meddling. Not fore-
seeing the consequences."

"The cultural milieu of Americans is a fascination
with facts," Martyn breaks in. "They are astoundingly
well-informed but have no depth. They have no opinions
of their own; they constantly seek opinions in a
competitive rush to gather the most information."

Neither John nor Martyn is angry with the United
States, nor are they anti-American. It's worse than that.
They are using the United States as an archetypal symbol
for their inexpressible thoughts and feelings. Anti-
Americanism is a way of indicating where European

thought departed from American thought, leaving us behind.

VISITING EUROPE

Any American businessperson or tourist in Europe will experience this anti-Americanism. It may never be expressed aloud, but it is there, behind the smiles and hospitality. When Europeans are unconscious of it, it is especially difficult to deal with. The "bottom line" does not determine business deals between Europeans and Americans. In the end, an unconscious agenda of dislike and distrust is the determining factor.

This unconscious agenda may be used to our advantage, however. First, we have to understand how anti-American phrases have become ways of talking about a community consciousness in Europe for which there is as yet no language. We need to understand that there is no personal hostility and recognize that, although we can't change anti-American feelings, we can go around them to reach our European hosts as fellow human beings. The best way is to read a few European novels. Margaret Drabble's *The Radiant Way* is an example. The characters are essential English people. You will be overwhelmed by their differences from Americans, but you will also laugh and cry with them, despise them and love them. The literary experience will imperceptibly change you.

Another example is *Ruins* by the bestselling English author and dramatist Brian Aldiss. The leading English character goes to the United States to work as a song writer, but eventually comes home to England and finds himself. The literary experience of coming back with him from New York and sharing with him the differentness of English people will change you. Europeans will intuitively recognize the change in you and respond.

The response is not because you have become more like a European, but because you have shared a human experience. Brian, who has a very English accent, tells the story of dining with an American lady from Georgia. They were each so enchanted with the other's exotic accent that they achieved a friendly rapport.

There is no reason to apologize for the United States. Remember, American business supplied the tools that made winning World War II possible and that helped rebuild Europe after the war, making the European Community possible.

THE BRITISH MUSEUM

It's night. The cab stops in front of the British Museum. No lights are showing behind the expanse of marble columns. The driver says, "Take it from me, it's closed, but if you want to get out here . . ."

A policeman at the door lets me in. Another policeman in the dim vestibule points to the left down a long hall. Footsteps clicking on the marble floor make a lonely reverberation.

Faint sounds of voices and music near the end of the hall, a right turn, and suddenly there is a gush of noise and light. A tall man in red livery approaches and then announces me to the three-storied room swirling with color.

I seem to have been transported into the midst of a Bacchanalia. Before me is an antique fountain; by its side a young man is playing the pipes. Beyond looms a Greek temple. I snag drinks from a passing nymph and wander on, finding delicious tidbits of sausage and pastry.

What an idea, a party in the British Museum. We seem to have collapsed time, wandering through coruscations of other ages.

I run my fingers idly over a small boulder maybe a

foot across. It has been split down the middle and the face polished. There are faint marks . . . the hairs on my neck stand up. This is the Rosetta Stone! I can see hieroglyphics crowded in the irregular, top part of the face, then Hebrew characters, then Greek at the bottom. Here is the key, the irreplaceable key to the writings of humanity's past. What Prometheus of thought conceived such a dream, half of an ordinary boulder waiting centuries to open the door to the beginnings of human thought?

I wander into the galley housing the Elgin marbles, surrounded by Athenian temples, the gabled friezes of the Parthenon. . . . There, at another fountain, surrounded by wine, women, song and food is our friend John, his white hair springing up from around his flushed face. "By the way," he says, "I have to warn you of something."

"Warn *me?* I must warn *you* not to send these treasures back to Greece. They would have been destroyed if Elgin hadn't brought them here. I hear Mellina Mercouri has talked England into returning them."

"Ah, well, old fellow, can't refuse a beautiful woman, you know. But that's what I want to warn you about. As you see, we're still devaluing ourselves. Mustn't do as I do, but as I say. Our last conversation has stuck in my mind. I realize you were puzzled by your English literary friends displaying so much unconscious animosity toward the United States. It is not that they wish the United States ill. Remember, thirty years ago—that's only a generation— the sun never set on the English empire. Indeed, we ruled the world. Think of the power and splendor that implied.

"We gave all that up. The United States didn't take it from us. We gave it up voluntarily in response to the kind of thinking embodied in your Marshall Plan. Your caring about us touched us, and the balance shifted. The way we thought had changed. There were enough people who could face the reality of colonialism, what it meant to hold other people captive against their will—and reject it."

"John, you've put your finger on my conviction that feelings and thought change the world. Your politicians could not have divested England of its empire if the sensitivities of enough people had not expanded so that they decided to give it up willingly. That's inspiring!"

"Ah, but there's more to it, don't you know," John says. "As we divested ourselves of empire, we must have devalued the very thought that had made it possible. We became in thought as well as in geography an insignificant island nation. But fortunately for us our intellectual class continued to develop. In the new world of thought we find importance not in empire but in being able to work peacefully with our fellow members in the European Community.

"I'm becoming more conscious now of how we use anti-American archetypes to express our deepest ways of thinking. It's as though Europe and the United States were two antithetical sides necessary to make a whole. We need our anti-Americanism for the moment. But remember, you in the United States haven't lost the spirit that made the European Community possible. You may have mislaid it for a few decades, but you haven't lost it altogether.

"I merely want to warn you not to keep on following our example. Don't devalue your true spirit to the world. Stick it to them, old boy."

I leave my dear friend among the detritus of his empire. But if his story is about the recession of old, imperial power, what is the source of this new, burgeoning power in Europe? If the storytellers are truly powerful people in the world, then the publishers here tonight are their masters. They have gathered from all over the world in this haunt of ancient temples.

The glaring lights and mysterious shadows, the high, piping music and the champagne combine for a moment, and I see a wizard wearing a cloak of cabalistic design stirring a steaming brew in a cauldron.

I realize I am seeing the figure of J. A. Koutchoumow, the secretary general of the International Publishers Association (IPA). His sharp features are pointing downward, not into a steaming cauldron, but into a Greek fountain, and I shake the magic out of my mind. What could I have thought? This is a man who has nothing but goodwill for the world.

I remember a high official of the IPA taking me aside at lunch and saying, "You were pushing Dr. Mayor hard at the conference."

Dr. Federico Mayor Zaragosa, the director general of UNESCO (the United Nations Educational, Scientific, and Cultural Organization), was chairing the panel of speakers at the IPA. At first I thought the official was joking. My relations with Dr. Mayor were friendly and, I thought, sincere on both sides. Then I realized he was seriously concerned for Dr. Mayor.

His eyes were probing me as if to ask, "Are you the enemy?" Why should I be? But . . . of course! UNESCO would think of the United States as the enemy. The United States had withdrawn its support because of UNESCO's anti-American campaigns in the world. UNESCO's first leaders were English, and they made it a center of ferment for European thought. The IPA is also controlled by Europeans, *and* it is allied with UNESCO.

Suddenly it breaks over me: this alliance is the source of the magic. I remember Koutchoumow saying, "We here are what a world government might be in our global village, with the Minister of Education, Science, and Culture already designated in the person of the director general of UNESCO, and it is ours, the publisher's ministry. Today's publisher can no longer wait for the reader to seek the books he needs. The publisher must steer the reader toward the book," he said, "using reading campaigns . . . as UNESCO does."

The invisible control of the flow of thought: a new kind of wizardry has been let loose upon the world, and I can see the pattern of a triangle of power.

PEN is one point of the triangle. Its centers in nearly every country in the world are sponsored and supported by UNESCO. They represent the creative point, interacting with people's inner thoughts.

The second point is UNESCO. It sponsors and provides support and money not only to PEN but also to teacher-training centers, libraries, museums and research centers, and for art, race relations and gender studies, publishing and information facilities. It is also a major publisher itself. In other words, UNESCO's tentacles reach into every cultural activity in every part of the world. It is the top point of the triangle, the governance of thought.

The third point of the triangle is the International Publishers Association. It has been active in forming and being formed by UNESCO. It is the point of power.

At this moment I resolve to check out the UNESCO connection. I figure I can wangle an appointment at its world headquarters in Paris for tomorrow morning and fly over. It's hard to get used to the idea that most places in Europe are only about an hour away.

The psychological dimensions of European anti-Americanism are taking shape. It has played its part in shaping the thought that has led to war's end in the European Community. Now we need a better handle on institutions like UNESCO that may be using anti-Americanism for other purposes. There is a feeling in the air that arrangements that are now being made will change the world profoundly, in ways no one could have predicted even a year ago.

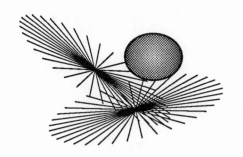

PART TWO

*Ideology, Terrorism
and
Community*

THE WAR FOR THE
THOUGHTS
OF THE WORLD

PARIS

Ah, Paris! Paris is so . . . anti-American. When Americans speak perfectly good French, the French pretend they don't know what we're saying. Instead, they have the rudeness to answer in English. How can they tell we're American?

It is an incomparable Paris morning. Old tree-lined streets lead up to the UNESCO plaza by the Seine. The low, enduring French buildings on the opposite bank reflect serenely in the river. The UNESCO building is better designed than the United Nations in New York. It seems to belong here. The eight-story Secretariat building must house more than a thousand people and, although massive, its Y-shaped design and futuristic entrance curve as though to embrace you.

A slight, Levantine man is waiting for me in the reception area. For a moment I'm puzzled, then realize we have met before. "Do you remember me? I'm—"

"I know who you are." He remains impassive as he cuts me off, then turns away brusquely to lead me upstairs.

A woman who is trying not to frown takes over. Is it a coincidence that I know her also, from New York? I remember her as being a little dumpy and sloppily dressed but with a sharp analytical mind. She is slim now, with a European haircut and expensive Gucci clothes. "Mary, it's been a long time. How do you like working here?"

"It's been a little difficult since your country abandoned us." She's giving me that it's-all-your-fault look. "I don't know why they are seeing you," she says, and with an appraising glance, "but perhaps it is your publishing connections . . ."

The rest of the day is spent with the kind of frustration that only a well-organized bureaucracy can create— polite evasions, misunderstood questions, unavailable documents. However, I do get the break I am hoping for. During an interlude I am surreptitiously passed an invitation to dine with a man named Lazlo Kanosz tomorrow night. I hope he wants to talk privately. I am eager to know who he is.

LA PLACE VENDOME

It is evening and I am sitting at a sidewalk cafe near the Place Vendome, reviewing my notes of the day's bitter scenes of rejection and evasion by the bureaucracy. It was not Dr. Mayor, director general of UNESCO. Movie-star handsome with a dark Spanish intensity, Dr. Mayor does not like the United States at all, but he is sincere in his desire to be fair. It is scary that he doesn't seem to realize that his administrators are determined to put the United States down.

The first director general of UNESCO was biologist Julian Huxley, the brother of British author Aldous Huxley. During Huxley's tenure, literary London created the socialist images that UNESCO supplied to the world. While anti-Americanism existed when UNESCO was under European control, it wasn't until the directorship of Amadou M'Bow, the Soviet-aligned African, that UNESCO became a *virulent* and *effective* anti-American organization, effective because it structured the way people felt about the United States without their ever realizing it.

I remember suggesting to Dr. Mayor when we first met in London that the United States was justifiably concerned with a UNESCO dominated by anti-American ideology.

"First, I am no M'Bow," he had said. "I am sorry, but I cannot do anything about the past. I have accepted the task of reforming and revitalizing UNESCO because to me, as a scientist, its goals reflect my most central professional concerns.

"I would like to soothe the people of the United States, and I hope the United States will rejoin UNESCO. But America is and has been arrogant in its approach to us. All I can do is the best job of running the organization I can, and pledge that I will personally stand for the absolutely unimpeded flow of information, without any kind of inhibition."

Dr. Mayor's words brought to mind the English writer Richard Hoggart, a previous director general of UNESCO, and a story he had told about its bureaucracy. "At a conference of ministers from scores of countries," he had said, "a resolution was made calling on writers not to flout the prevailing philosophies of their states. One delegate bobbed up and asked, 'What about the writer's freedom of expression?' At that point I was called away from the platform. When I got back I found that a wily aide had conflated the two calls amazingly into one acceptable resolution: Whilst respecting the freedom of writers, states will nevertheless ensure that they do not flout the prevailing philosophies of their states.'"

Hoggart had also said that "the authentic voice of the bureaucratic organization is blithely confident that it enunciates reasonable democratic sentiments; the defense of the status quo (however bad that status quo may be) soon, and virtually always, becomes a primary moral principle, not a second-order rule."

He had two epigrams for bureaucracies: "The business of government is to govern, a bureaucratic code for our business is to stay in power," and "You can't make an omelette without breaking eggs, another codified bureaucratic justification for staying in power, if necessary by dubious means."

Another astounding resolution was "We reserve the freedom to interpret ourselves to ourselves," where "we" refers to the government; "freedom," the right of the government to do whatever it chooses; and "interpret," the government censorship of thought.

With bureaucrats like that around him, Dr. Mayor is going to find it impossible to fulfill his pledge of an "absolutely unimpeded flow of information." He had also said, "I am proud of our well-known Collection of Representative Works, for example, which now contains over nine hundred titles translated from sixty different languages." How will he be able to monitor the anti-American bureaucrat responsible for the selection of the Collection of Representative Works?

Dr. Mayor hasn't yet had Hoggart's experience with how a bureaucracy can use language to reverse your meaning right before your eyes.

Twilight fades into darkness, leaving only a feeble light from the lamp on the corner. Where is the power in the world? Is it in thoughts? Or is it that plane coming in for a landing at Orly? It could be carrying a nuclear bomb that would vaporize my thoughts in a nanosecond. Probably UNESCO, with its power to control thought, is a more real threat than the bomb.

My notes on Ian Christie Clark, former delegate and ambassador from Canada to UNESCO, are very revealing about the organization and the source of its power in the world. "UNESCO's founders—the United States, France and Great Britain—deliberately set up a political organization," Clark said, and the United States "ended World War II as the champion of decolonialization and world organization. UNESCO is the result of things long sought and obtained by the United States; in repudiating UNESCO, the United States not only repudiated the sanctity of nation states as the sole source of power in world government, it also risked repudiating something that for fifty years has been at the core of its conception of its world role."

Fortunately, the United Nations is a sham world government. If it were not, the world would be ruled by a majority of small warlike nations obsessed with their own self-interest. Ambassador Clark is locked into an outmoded ideology of world government based on the "sanctity of nation states as the sole source of power." And he knows very well what kinds of nations these are. He describes them as having "every reason to want to believe that their poverty and backwardness are caused by past exploitation by the colonial powers." And he says that "they find it appealing to believe that this was merely some trick of technology, some unfair advantage the Europeans deliberately engineered to suppress and exploit the rest." He admits that "this may seem preposterous, grotesque, unfair [but notes that] it is a fact of contemporary international politics. World opinion," he concludes, "has proven to express not the lofty idealism of liberated mankind as imagined by the Americans—I should say North Americans—but the tawdry reality of international life—issues of primary concern to the Third World."

Clark is mesmerized by our original dream of world government ruled by one-nation, one-vote democracy. He knows exactly how that original dream has been tarnished by the "tawdry reality of international life." He is a man living in a dangerous illusion. He implies there is no alternative for peace except through material aid and democracy. If we bring the Third World nations up to our level of material consumption and education and impose a democratic structure upon their societies, then we will surely have peace, Clark supposes. How blind and arrogant a view this is. It is particularly painful because he is a talented and intelligent man of goodwill. He believes there is no alternative to the United Nations and UNESCO, but all he has to do is raise his eyes and look upon the European Community. Peace only comes from peaceful people, not from ideological plans and structures imposed from without.

U.S. policymakers think that a nation state with democratic names for its governing institutions will become benevolent and large-minded and that it will care for others. They think that supporting and promoting poor nations is a way to world peace. Words and systems are not people, however. And only the minds and spirits of people can lead to peace and prosperity. The first realistic opportunity for peace between nations is happening in the European Community. The forces conspiring to defeat the European Community may succeed, and so it is the European Community that needs all our help at the moment.

THE MARNE BATTLEFIELD

The next evening, I am in a taxi driving past the Paris suburbs that surround the World War I Marne battlefield. The bodies of American soldiers had been piled up in windrows here as they were killed in a selfless, wholehearted effort to "save the world for democracy." Our soldiers saved Europe for something even better than democracy, the transcendence of the European Community and the end of war in Europe altogether.

During the day I had called a friend in New York who is connected to the United Nations. "Charles, do you know anything about a man named Lazlo Kanosz?"

There was a long silence. Then, "I'm sorry but that is an area I can't get into. Kanosz was a powerful member of the U.N. Secretariat. He has been retired for many years but is still a high-powered individual. However, I can relate some almost common knowledge about him. During World War II his family managed to send him to school in the United States. He was just beginning his graduate studies at Harvard when the United Nations was created; with the help of Harvard and his family's connections he obtained a good position at the U.N. Secretariat, and so he left graduate school behind. Those were heady days, I expect. He spent his life governing the developing world."

There was another long silence. "But it all came to an end for him in the Congo. Dag Hammarskjold ended it when he ended himself. Dag was his mentor, and Kanosz apparently worshipped him. He experienced first-hand what being God can do to a person, even a great human being like Dag. He drifted out of the political mainstream of the United Nations and finally shifted some years ago to the intellectuals at UNESCO. He has become very wealthy from his own efforts. That's the best I can do for you. Does that help?"

"Hell, yes, that's plenty. This is just personal curiosity. Let's have lunch when I get back. Thanks Charley. Ciao."

My friend was letting me come to the conclusion that if this man had become very rich by his own efforts, he was not likely to be connected with Moscow, which was what I had wanted to know.

The taxi pulls onto the grounds of a small, Grecian-style villa set in the midst of an extensive property. Lazlo greets me in his library. He is sleek and handsome, with graying hair and clever, sparkling eyes. His skin has a slightly oily Mediterranean sheen. We move across the expanse of marble floor, and my feet sink into a huge white and blue Kermani rug. It is one of those rooms with plaster cupids on the ceiling. Marble columns frame windows overlooking the grounds on one wall and bookshelves on all the others. The old leather bindings give life to the cold stone, and a long narrow table stacked with books announces this as a working library. There are books in several languages, including Russian. At the end of the room is a huge fireplace circled by a couch and big easy chairs.

After dinner we sit overlooking his estate. "I'm impressed. You live like a king here. I was surprised and honored to receive your invitation. Are you connected by any chance with UNESCO?"

"Not exactly, but you must be wondering why I asked you here. Nothing hostile, I assure you. A piece to a puzzle of mine, you might say. You were teaching the psycho-physiology of form and language at the graduate school of the Portsmouth Polytechnic during the Falklands unpleasantness. Since Portsmouth is the base for the English fleet, that was an interesting coincidence. Then there was the quixotic and futile arrangement you tried to set up after the Hungarian revolution."

I can feel myself flushing. "Now wait just a minute."

Lazlo is examining me. "Surely you don't feel guilty after thirty years? Actually, your efforts weren't quite as futile as you thought, as it turned out. You didn't know, but I had an interest in that affair. You were trying to move money overnight from Panama to Viennese banks—unsuccessfully.

"But you inadvertently opened an avenue for me to get my favorite cousin and her husband out of Budapest. I prevailed upon Eleanor Roosevelt to transfer a large sum of money to the communists through your conduit, and the dear lady thought she was rescuing two freedom fighters when the facts were actually au contraire. They were communists who had backed the wrong party faction. That is one reason I asked you to meet me here, to give you a tardy thank you."

My shoulders are tingling. "Just a minute! Have you had any contact recently with a man named Paul Schorr? I can find out if you have."

His eyes shift. "I see that I have been gauche, and it has been a long time since that has happened. Let me assure you that your friend Paul is almost as cunning and devious as I. I would never seek information from such as he, and he has told me nothing, absolutely nothing, about you or your affairs. My source was elsewhere. It is simply standard procedure for me when I wish to . . . ah . . . establish relations with someone, no?"

"I think you were about to say, make use of someone."

"No, not in the sense you mean. Please, let me explain.

"The United States will have some hard choices to make in the near future. The question is whether your society is still flexible enough to regain the spirit of the Roosevelt–Kennedy era. The United States has made more than its share of mistakes recently, but the first mistake was putting the United Nations headquarters in New York."

"Let me tell you, Lazlo, about a redwood grove I know near San Francisco that was pivotal in the founding of the United Nations. It's in a valley that winds away three or four miles to the sea, where the redwoods rise up straight to over a hundred feet in the air. They have been growing a thousand years or more. It's always quiet. The founders of the United Nations came there to meditate when they were drafting its charter."

"I didn't know that."

"Hah! So there is something you don't know."

"San Francisco might have been suitable. But you must admit that Paris is the obvious place for the United Nations."

I let myself sink deeper into the soft, stuffed leather chair. "What difference does the location of the United Nations make when its organ, UNESCO, has been sitting here in Paris like a Machiavellian spider, in the center of a worldwide web designed expressly to control world thinking."

Lazlo gets comfortable in his chair. "Too true. But what are you going to do about it?"

"Well, we won't give them any money until they are ready to cooperate, and then we'll ream them out." A feeling of the sun about to rise comes over me. "I am being foolish and arrogant. It's not in our power to change UNESCO, nor is it in yours. But you seem to be bypassing UNESCO as though it were irrelevant to what's happening in the European Community. In fact, I think you've given up on UNESCO, even though you're still connected with it."

Lazlo beams. "Well, perhaps we can actually speak meaningfully, now. What a pleasure. You are, I take it, prepared to accept several contradictory realities about UNESCO? Good.

"One reality is that for the first thirty years of its existence, it served as the center for the intellectual ferment of what is now the European Community. Anti-Americanism was useful to this European ferment and has left its stamp upon UNESCO. In any case, it has been taken over by the erstwhile colonial states. Not only is Europe not in control, but it has relinquished control. UNESCO has served its purpose for Europe, and its legacy of anti-Americanism is being used for very different purposes by the colonial states who are now in control."

"Ian Christie Clark said that it is turning against Europe now—a taste of your own medicine."

"Very well, if that pleases you. But notice that the European nations do not strike back. They accept things as they are and work peacefully, going around the unpleasant realities. The United States is only capable of striking back, a sign to the Europeans that your country is undependable. But to continue, it is true that the states who hold the balance of power in UNESCO are violently nationalistic and especially opposed to the countries of the European Community, where nationalism is losing its political power."

Pulling out my notebook and flipping through it: "There was something Clark said about that. . . . Here it is. I remember thinking how tragic his point of view was. He said that in the evolution of our international system the nation-state continues to be the principal repository of power and focus."

Lazlo stands up in irritation. "Your friend Ian is indeed a tragic innocent. He has not the slightest surmise of the implications of his statement. Do you? No! You are also an innocent."

"Well, yes, as a matter of fact I think I do. In its original dream of achieving peace through world government, the United States thought by imposing democracy on a country, it would create a people capable of sustaining democracy. We are beginning to find out, however, that people come first, that they are more important than government. When we created the United Nations, we Americans never considered the possibility that a world government might not be democratic and benevolent. At the United Nations, as well as at UNESCO, the warlike nations have taken over for their own self-interest the American-inspired ideology of peace through world government. The important struggle in the future will be between two forces: the warlike nations seeking their own ends through world government and those peoples able to live in a community of nations where local differences are cherished and protected while national boundaries are transcended and bypassed. The European Community is the model for these new peoples."

Lazlo, still standing, looks as though he is going to give me a pat on the head. "That is moderately perceptive of you. Being an innocent, I wonder if you can accept the implications of what you have said. All of the contradictory realities of UNESCO exist at the same time. Federico Mayor, for example, as director, represents a European past that is still an important influence. But like Ian Clark, he is committed to an ideology of world government based on nationalism. Both of those honorable men are enemies of a new kind of world order based on communities of nations such as the European Community. The worldwide UNESCO and United Nations network failed in the development of peace and prosperity. But it might succeed, with the acquiescence of these honorable men, in the violent acquisition of power in a future world government. All the realities of UNESCO are contradictory except for their violent and total commitment to a world government. When contradictory realities converge, the possibilities for power are quite astonishing."

"Okay, Lazlo. I get it. Here at the center of the European Community is the single greatest threat to its existence, UNESCO. It has managed to take over a dangerous ideology of peace through world government that men of goodwill cannot deny. Yet all the time under their very noses, the people of the European Community are developing a true end to war through the resolution of personal conflicts."

"You are still missing something. It only took a few Nazis, with the charismatic Hitler as their leader, to create and control the nationalistic aspirations of the German people for leibenstraum for their super-race. In Russia only a few communists were needed to control their ideology of national security against the evil designs of outsiders. Even nation-states that are democracies require only a few leaders to move people to violent excesses of national self-interest. . . ."

"I see what you mean. Whatever it is that is bringing about the end of war in Europe has had to come from the European people directly. In a world order using the European Community as a model, a few leaders alone could not put the people on the roller coaster to war or warlike adventures."

Lazlo raises an elegant finger. "What an amusing American colloquialism. But you still do not have it all, my innocent. These few leaders you mention, who are they? They are real people who depend on the use of power—the bureaucrats of the United Nations and UNESCO, businesspeople, politicians. Most of them believed in a European supernation as the ultimate example of and model for a world state, but they are coming to realize belatedly that the European Community is not and cannot be a supernation. They are beginning to see that they will inevitably lose power in a world order based on regional communities rather than a world order based on the imposition of power. These people are only identifiable by someone such as myself. They cross borders and occupations and political affiliations. They leave no wake as they move."

"Okay, I agree I'm out of my depth."

Lazlo is patting my arm. "My poor innocent, these people are capable of sophisticated mischief. May I bring something to your attention that I am sure you have not conceived of? Most of the nations that hold the balance of power at UNESCO and the United Nations are nations that also either export terrorism or exercise some form of it internally. I am by no means suggesting a sinister conspiracy, but rather a vague, tacit understanding among world government supporters that extends from terrorist organizations to the most pristine bastions of democratic idealism. I merely suggest that if you follow your investigations further, pay attention. Do not be concerned; merely pay attention to what transpires."

The taxi is honking outside, and Lazlo walks me to the door. "My friend, you leave me with a slight modicum of optimism. We old bureaucrats learn to live on slight modicums."

As the taxi pulls away, he is still standing in the light of the open door. His figure dwindles in the distance and is gone.

After writing down our conversation that night, I go to bed and dream that I'm struggling with Lazlo. At breakfast I think, "That man Lazlo is out of my league. He certainly stirred up my psyche. He could be a formidable opponent if I am headed in a direction he doesn't want investigated."

The extent to which I'm willing to commit myself further to the investigation depends on the answer to an important question. I am sitting on the porch of the old homestead in Texas surrounded by my children, grandchildren and great-grandchildren to come. How much does my family's future depend on what is happening in Europe? Right now my hunch is that it depends a lot.

If that's true, the next question is, what is important? I think most American families would agree that without a deep and relevant understanding of the explosive changes of thought taking place in Europe right now, American foreign policy and economics are worse than useless. They could do our families harm.

We've got to get out in the world and vibrate with the feelings of joy, anger and despair felt by the European people. We surely can't depend on the bureaucrats and their statistics for our understanding of European thinking.

What kind of thought is important, and where can we best find it? Vienna turned out to be a good place to start for deep emotions. People in London helped formulate an expression of those feelings, and they brought us to Paris. Here we have encountered subtle forces maneuvering to control the future of the European Community and perhaps the world. Now to investigate the administrative centers for the European Community. I'll drive to Strasbourg tomorrow.

THE CROCODILE CLUB

STRASBOURG

Strasbourg is a dreary, old factory town. It has bred anarchists, Marxists, communists, and now, finally, socialists. My friend Elizabeth Mills, a sometime resident, has told me about having had to periodically leave the depressing apartment of a friend so that the friend's Marxist cell group could convene in private. It was winter, and to kill a few hours, she would walk the gray streets, the same color as the thick, sooty sky and the drab dress of its citizens. The pungent smells of beer and onion tart pour from the many winstube lining the city's streets. And amid the ugliness, conspiracy flourishes.

Strasbourg is the site of the European Parliament, which meets in a modern auditorium designed like a theater in the round with an attractive vaulted ceiling.

With all this, the atmosphere is still miasmic. Altiero Spinelli, who is the leading member of Parliament and now in his eighties, has worked untiringly for the European Community in this theater. Altiero is a true European hero. In his early years he was a communist, then during World War II he worked in the underground resistance. The dream of most resistance groups at the time was anti-nationalistic. They wanted to get rid of the nation-states that were causing the war so that they could "live happily ever after" in a European supernation that would impose peace and security upon them.

The irony was that they were giving their lives heroically to defeat a Germany that was trying earnestly to accomplish their dream.

In their dream, of course, the European supernation would be governed by benign Marxists who would take from each according to ability and give to each according to need.

There was a double irony. If the dream had come true, their benign ruler would have been Stalin, a worse monster than Hitler. Stalin would have wreaked upon all of Europe the unspeakable repression and slaughter to which he subjected the eastern part.

Altiero Spinelli was able to understand the consequences of Stalinist rule and so became a socialist. He proposed to "transplant into Europe the great American political experience." Altiero and his friend and ally in the European Parliament, Ortensio Zecchino, have had the wisdom to assure Europeans that in their program "member states will retain their sovereignty." For them, this is a vital concession. They have been fighting as politicians ever since World War II for a United States of Europe. But the European Community was never intended. It happened while no one was looking, and it is difficult now for the veteran politicians who fought for one dream to realize that what is happening in Europe is not their outmoded dream of a supernation, but the emergence of a new kind of relationship, a true community of nations.

BRUSSELS

The train is rolling slowly across the flat, rich farm lands of Belgium as we approach Brussels. Coming into view, the city is an island of green with the tops of a few buildings rising cautiously above the trees.

The administrative center of the European Community resides in Brussels, a small city of some two hundred thousand inhabitants. Belgium would be lost if dropped into Texas. Strangely enough, Belgium and Texas are about the same age. The Catholic people of Belgium, French- and Flemish-speaking, revolted from Protestant Netherlands in 1830, and Texas revolted from Mexico to become a separate nation in 1836.

Belgians identify with Americans in other ways. On the night of the 1988 U.S. presidential elections, for example, twenty-five hundred guests, eighty percent of them Belgian, swamped an election-night party. Dan Quayle was more highly regarded there than he was in the United States because Europeans had heard his free-trade positions.

To Brussels, 1992 signifies the years of work that have gone into drafting the new trade agreements for the European Community. In a recent speech in the neighboring city of Bruges, Prime Minister Thatcher praised the agreements, which would create a Europe open for enterprise with free markets, widened choices and reduced government intervention.

I'm meeting an old and dear friend, Peter Koestenbaum, for dinner. Peter is a round ball of electric intellectual energy. After a long career as an eminent professor of philosophy, he has been called to a ministry of consulting and lecturing to governments and businesses. His activities carry him all over the world. His current best-selling books are *Socrate et le Business* (Socrates and Business) and *The Heart of Business: Ethics, Power and Philosophy*. Peter has learned how to find the human spirit and thought that lie behind and give relevancy to life. He has just finished a whirlwind tour, speaking to the World Economic Forum in Davos, Switzerland, meeting with the Volvo Company in Sweden and with Renault in Paris.

At dinner he is saying enthusiastically, "You're in the right place. Over the centuries these Benelux countries on the North Sea have developed the art of negotiating. The individual cities were always as important as the government, and historically it was a question of getting everyone to agree, even the farmers outside the cities. In their form of democracy, negotiating was more important than voting. That's why the bureaucracy here is the best in the world. They nitpick and obstruct, but they do it from an age-old tradition of including everyone in the negotiations."

"That's perceptive of you, Peter. But let's hope that the European Community can avoid the lure of becoming a supernation. Any bureaucracy, even this one, can succumb to power. We don't want Europe to drown in a sea of red tape, even as the community is being born."

Peter smiles. "Don't worry. The traditions here are strong. The early Pan-European movement after World War I started here. They were pacifists and the idea of Esperanto as a world language grew out of that."

Ah, it's good to be with Peter. I lean back and say, "But that was one-world thinking, making peace by making everyone the same. Esperanto didn't work. What we have is better. The different peoples of the European Community speak each other's languages. Especially the young ones."

We're eating in a large and very good restaurant overlooking the lights of the city. Peter says, "European restaurants have waiters from every country in the Community. Young people are scattering all over Europe to work. They're deepening their sense of the languages of each country. They're making room in their minds for the personal intimate differences in the ways various ethnic groups live. Whether or not they're reading as much literature as their parents, they're developing the kind of thinking that leads to war's end.

"Ethnic is the key here. With national controls dissolving, the differences become ethnic. Ethnicity is people. People, especially people with room for others in their minds, can negotiate differences without war. Nations aren't people, but rather systems for controlling them. There's never been a time in history before the European Community when a nation wouldn't plunge its people into war rather than give up control.

"It's the same with the European companies I am helping. They are beginning to understand that leadership is not control, but rather it is spiritual and philosophical ways of thinking."

Peter calls this new way of thinking the deep structures of the psyche, where one faces the inner creations of the experience of death, the anxiety of difference, and the alienation from Gaia, or Nature. No wonder his message is so hot in Europe. Most people here are ready for it. Some people are ready for it in the United States.

"Ethnic differences are fine, Peter, but what about the minority of Europeans who can't handle them? I tried to put in a transatlantic call today, for instance, and got a Flemish-speaking operator. I spoke perfectly good French, and in French she said she didn't speak French. I said that I was an American whose countrymen had died in Flanders fields so she could be playing political games with the telephone service. How could she expect me to speak Flemish? She finally put the call through, in perfect English."

Peter laughs. "So what do you expect? The key word is negotiation. Following the European Community model, Belgium has acted to defuse the ethnic conflict between the French- and Flemish-speaking Belgians by giving each group control over its parts of the country, thus insuring the people's freedom to be different. Of course, the people involved have to have enough room in their heads to celebrate each other's ethnic differences. If enough of them do, it will work out—the metaphysical unity of differences is a state of mind."

Peter is off the next morning for a speech in Mexico and then back to the United States. Over breakfast I think about how the United States actually started the European Community in the first place, but no one here seems to have heard of that. In 1947, George Marshall gave a talk at Harvard University in which he outlined his thinking about what was to become the Marshall Plan. "There must be some agreement among the countries of Europe," he said, "as to the requirements of the situation." Marshall Plan aid was then made "conditional upon the continuing effort of participating countries to set up a permanent organization."

President Eisenhower later welcomed "the efforts of a number of our European friends to achieve an integrated community." In 1962, President Kennedy said, "The nations of Western Europe are joining together to find freedom in diversity. . . . We do not regard a strong and united Europe as a rival but as a partner. To aid its progress has been the basic objective of our foreign policy for seventeen years."

A quote I still remember from his inaugural address: "The world is changing. An old era is ending. The old ways will not do."

THE COMMISSION

The next morning I'm to meet an old friend I had known in the Middle East. Claude Deplessy is a well-known economist and banker who works closely with the bureaucracy, the permanent civil servants of the European Community Commission. Brussels, as a city, seems made up of generations of impeccable, proper bureaucrats. It is the perfect city to host the Commission.

I've walked through the Grande Place, the old medieval marketplace surrounded by cozy, tightly packed, rococo guild houses, and have arrived in the newer section, with tree-lined streets and more open spaces. Twenty-five hundred trade, industry and nonprofit organizations have offices here. The European Community Commission building rises out of their midst. The building is reminiscent of UNESCO headquarters in Paris, only without the French flair. UNESCO is in the shape of a Y; the European Community Commission has four wings thirteen stories high, radiating from a circular, central structure.

Claude hasn't changed. He is still slim and impeccably dressed, with dark hair and luminous eyes. He is also absolutely dependable. I spend the day at the Commission going over charts and agreements with him, and he invites me to attend a diplomatic party at his house tonight.

Here are highlights of what I learned during the day (see the chart on pages 90–91).

The Commission is not a governing body. It is an administrative body of seventeen members, headed by Jacques Delors, a French socialist. It initiates proposals to release and bypass national restrictions in order to meet the 1992 goals. The Commission requires over ten thousand bureaucrats, all permanent. The proposals of the Commission go to the European Parliament in Strasbourg.

Through the leadership of Altiero Spinelli, the Single European Act was agreed on in 1985. This act gives the European Parliament the function of approving and amending all proposals of the Commission before they go to the Council of Ministers. The Parliament represents people rather than states. Its members are elected by direct vote of all the people in the European Community.

THE ADMINISTRATIVE STRUCTURE OF THE EUROPEAN COMMUNITY

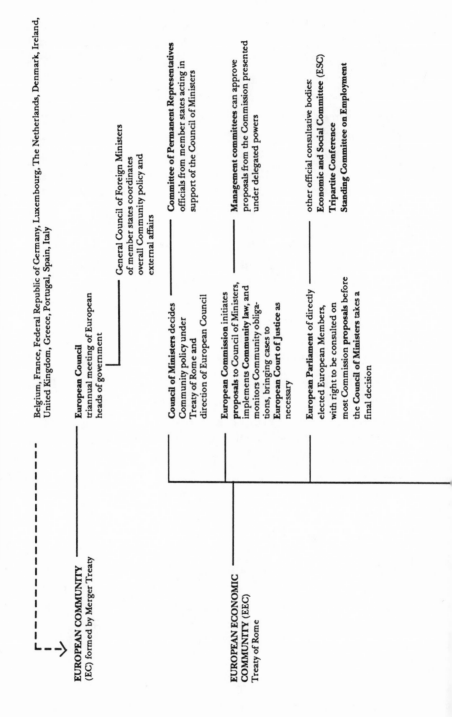

EUROPEAN COMMUNITY (EC) formed by Merger Treaty

Belgium, France, Federal Republic of Germany, Luxembourg, The Netherlands, Denmark, Ireland, United Kingdom, Greece, Portugal, Spain, Italy

European Council triannual meeting of European heads of government

General Council of Foreign Ministers of member states coordinates overall Community policy and external affairs

Council of Ministers decides Community policy under Treaty of Rome and direction of European Council

Committee of Permanent Representatives officials from member states acting in support of the Council of Ministers

European Commission initiates proposals to Council of Ministers, implements Community law, and monitors Community obligations, bringing cases to **European Court of Justice** as necessary

Management committees can approve proposals from the Commission presented under delegated powers

EUROPEAN ECONOMIC COMMUNITY (EEC) Treaty of Rome

European Parliament of directly elected European Members, with right to be consulted on most Commission proposals before the **Council of Ministers** takes a final decision

other official consultative bodies: **Economic and Social Committee (ESC) Tripartite Conference Standing Committee on Employment** multinational representative organizations established independently to monitor and influence Community policy

European Court of Justice interprets and applies **Community** agreements, arbitrates disputes between member states and judges complaints from individuals or corporations about the effects of Community legislation

European Investment Bank — an independent body to encourage development of the common market through investment loans for certain types of of projects

now administered by EEC institutions, with ECSC **Consultative Committee** representing producers, consumers, workers and dealers, with whom the **European Commission** must consult

EUROPEAN COAL AND STEEL COMMUNITY (ECSC) established by **Treaty of Paris** to plan development of coal and steel industry

EUROPEAN ATOMIC ENERGY COMMUNITY (Euratom) established under **Treaty of Rome** to encourage civil nuclear industry

COUNCIL OF EUROPE —— Committee of Foreign Ministers —— European Commission of Human Rights
Consultative Assembly   European Court of Human Rights

ORGANIZATION FOR ECONOMIC CO-OPERATION AND DEVELOPMENT (OECD) —— Council

The Council of Ministers, which has the executive function in the European Community, has sixteen members, one from each state, except France, Great Britain, Germany and Italy, which have two representatives each. Their tenure is tied to the government in power in each of their states, and the Council has the ultimate power. Proposals passed on to the Council by Parliament normally go into effect only by unanimous consent. However, under the 1985 agreement, certain proposals "which have as their object the establishment and functioning of the internal market" no longer require unanimous consent. They can be approved by a "qualified majority."

There are seventy-six votes possible in the council, so a qualified majority is fifty-four votes. Great Britain, West Germany, France and Italy can each cast ten votes. The other eight member states divide the remaining thirty-six votes among themselves. Thus, it takes twenty-three votes—or, say, France, Italy and Greece—to veto a special proposal. All other proposals may be vetoed by only one vote.

Keep in mind that these organizations do not make up a government. They are a forum for community in the highest and best sense of the word. In theory, serious issues must have unanimous agreement. In practice, the Council, Commission and Parliament work out policies by negotiation. There is a continual dialogue between the Council, representing each member state, and the Commission, representing the Community, as each decision is gradually reached. The Parliament is the consultative body for these decisions. It can influence decisions, but it cannot make them. Proposals for agreements between European Community members originate in the Commission, go to the Parliament for debate and perhaps changes, and are approved or disapproved by the Council.

The Court of Justice plays an active part in the Community. It has upheld Community agreements above national laws. It has also upheld the Parliament's right to block budget decisions by the Council and the Commission and to veto any draft directive of the Council. The Court, which meets in an ugly building on a barren rise of ground in Luxembourg, is composed of one jurist from each member country.

The Council of Europe, which consists of the European Commission of Human Rights and a European Court of Human Rights, is not formally connected to the European Community. The Council of Europe is a name given to the meetings of European heads of state, which are held three times a year.

Many Europeans of the supernational persuasion are beginning to refer to actions of the European Community as "laws." They are not. They are administrative expressions of agreements between members of the community.

The European Community does not have a unified structure of administration. There are actually three European Communities that were set up at different times by different treaties. In 1951, U.S. leaders masterminded the creation of the European Coal and Steel Community. The treaty, signed in Paris, joined the coal and steel industries in a single "common market." In 1957, the Treaty of Rome set up the European Atomic Energy Community and the European Economic Community. In 1965, the three communities were merged, in name only, as the European Community; however, they still operate under their original separate treaties.

The 1992 goals of the European Community, as noted earlier, are:

- Free movement of goods.
- Free movement of labor.
- Free movement of capital.
- Coordinated trade with the world.

The Commission has drafted most of the three hundred pieces of administrative agreements that need to be ratified in order to achieve these goals.

In 1992, the European Community will consist of about 330 million people who are able to bypass national borders, as compared to 244 million people in the United States and 122 million in Japan. It will thus be the largest trading bloc in the world, encompassing more than forty percent of all trade. In 1983, its trade balance with the United States turned from a deficit to a surplus; in 1984, the surplus reached $13 billion, in 1986, it reached $27 billion, and it is still growing.

Will things get better for the United States after 1992? No, they will get worse. After 1992, the European Community will become Fortress Europe. The discovery by Europeans that they can prosper in peace has given them a sense of enormous self-confidence. They will still be our friends, but tough, competitive and confident friends. We'll be doing things their way, which will extend to our dealings in NATO, the United Nations and UNESCO. They will be in a position to take over the leadership of the world. The United States has been the natural leader of the world, but if we want to retain that leadership, we must learn from the European Community.

The development of the European Community is frequently referred to as a move toward unity. Those are politicians talking. The essence of the European Community is diversity—the freedom of people to agree on particular relationships and ways of living that transcend national controls.

This freedom for diversity was created by individuals thinking in new ways. Since ways of thinking are hard to express, economic terms are often used to describe them. Economics is a discipline that attempts to quantify ways of living. Thus, information about the European Community is commonly communicated in numbers, such as how many tons of wheat were stored in a warehouse on a certain date. This information is valuable, even necessary, in our ever more complex world, but it is not relevant to understanding the meaning and value of the European Community.

Claude gets nervous when he doesn't have facts. He can't stand ambiguity in his life. He predicts trends and occurrences from an economic standpoint, by the rigorous statistical analysis of factual information. Over the years I've kept a private score card on his predictions, and so far he would have done better flipping a coin. Leaving predictability out, however, his information is an impeccable language. It must after all be people who give information meaning. Economics as a language is useful, but economics as a reduction of people to numbers is in trouble. As we were leaving the Commission building, I told Claude a joke: An economist is someone who sees something work in practice and then makes a theory about it.

Claude didn't think it was funny.

Business in Brussels

Imagine some middle-sized, midwestern city like Des Moines, Iowa, as the site of the entire U. S. bureaucracy that controls commerce. Now you have a good picture of Brussels, Belgium.

These low-land cities by the North Sea have survived for a thousand years on business negotiation. By tradition, business has been synonymous with government. Such successful European Community projects as ESPRIT and BRITE were developed and promoted by industry and bureaucracy working as one.

The rules of business have been care, caution and confidence. Today, European Community bureaucrats are generally reserved in their dealing until they have sufficient confidence in their associates. There is no Freedom of Information Act in Brussels as there is in Washington. The Belgian bureaucrat in not likely to cooperate with an American businessperson unless trust has been established first.

In the European Community, governments and businesses negotiate all the time, unlike in the United

States, where government and business are separated into contentious interests. The European Community bureaucracy wants to know what businesspeople are thinking and what they are seeking. Brussels exists to help people bypass barriers, but only if companies have satisfied the requirements of integrity and credibility.

So how does an American go about establishing a relationship with the Brussels bureaucracy? Many consultants and lobbyists are available to help, and they charge very little—say seven hundred fifty dollars per day, as compared with Washington's many thousands of dollars per day. But trying to buy influence does not play as well here as it does in Washington. And when it is an American spending the money, modest though it is, it is probably wasted because European Community bureaucrats perceive it as using money to try to buy their confidence. They would much prefer that people approach the proper official of the lower rank first and work their way up gradually. They expect the initial and all succeeding inquiries to be in writing, and they expect them to be carefully presented. They need to understand the issues and know the people involved before negotiating.

If you want them to understand you, you must first understand them. The remaining chapters of this book lay the basis for a psychological understanding of Europeans. On an operational level: a simple lunch in a good restaurant is more appropriate and more impressive than an overly lavish production. You must take your time and don't push; be truly open to the kind of understanding that changes you; they can tell. A sincere American can do as well here as anyone else.

Strasbourg is more like Washington. Members of Parliament generally come from the ranks of the political organizations of their respective countries. Money and power help oil this political machinery a little better than in Brussels. The European Parliament has become more important recently, and it now has the power to amend all 1992 Commission proposals in two readings before sending them to the Council.

The Court of Justice in Luxembourg is not to be overlooked. Some creative justices there are breaking new legal ground.

The trade federations and union organizations in Brussels are also worth looking into. They have a lot of influence with the Commission. Proposals discussed first with them tend to succeed better.

REVELRY BY NIGHT

Claude lives in his family's ancestral home, far enough from the center of Brussels to have some land around it. I'm greeted at the door by his wife, who is just as I remember, pretty, petite and proper. I enter to the discrete hum of conversation. A harpist is playing in a corner, trying not to interfere with the talk. Claude is with a group that seems to be dominated by a large, physically powerful man with blunt features and long hair falling over his collar.

Claude sees me and steps over to greet me. "Let me introduce you to an honored guest, a member of the European Parliament who is here to consult with us on the European Unity Treaty. I might add he is a member of the famous Crocodile Club."

The man glances up, irritated at having his conversation interrupted, and nods.

"Yes," I say, "I have heard of the Crocodile Club. It is named after the Crocodile Restaurant in Strasbourg where some of you meet to put teeth into Parliament's bite."

This doesn't seem to go over too well, so I try, "I am fond of Strasbourg beer, especially La Belle Strasbourgeoise."

Claude tries his hand: "Dr. Howell, a citizen of the United States, has recently been at UNESCO."

The crocodile man finally decides to engage in conversation. "UNESCO was created by the United States and reflects the shortcomings of the United States. The United States declared it wanted peace through world government, but it would not give up its sovereignty to the United Nations so that peace could be brought to the world.

"We Europeans have been held impotent for the last forty years by the lack of a European will to become a United States of Europe. Now that we have an elected parliament we are making progress. We boldly drafted the European Union Treaty."

"Didn't that draft go beyond the powers that the Treaty of Rome allocated to the Assembly in 1957?" I venture. "The 1985 Single European Act has since changed it, but you did fall under the Treaty of Rome at that time."

He doesn't bother to turn around, replying over his shoulder, "We grasped the power we needed. No national government has dared ignore our draft of the European Unity Treaty."

Turning slightly to me, he continues, "The European Community has been called an economic giant but a political dwarf—but no more! All nation-states will be superceded by the supernation."

I move into the group. "You say the European Community has been impotent politically for forty years. Yet during that time it has become an economic giant. Perhaps it is necessary for the European Community to be a political pigmy in order to be an economic giant. But far more important than its economic growth has been its success in ending war in a Europe that previously had always bred war."

Flipping through my Strasbourg notebook, I read a quote from Altiero Spinelli: "A major transformation has occurred in the consciousness of Europeans, something that is completely new in their history. European people have removed obstacles to free trade and have bypassed nationalist controls while preserving their national traditions. This is a kind of integration that has never occurred before, a new meaning to community." It is possible that this major transformation in the consciousness of Europeans could have occurred only in a period of political impotence.

The Crocodile Club man turns red in the face. "Don't quote Spinelli to me. That is out of context. You know he is the founder of the Crocodile Party and the architect of the European Unity Treaty. Altiero's remark about the integration achieved—which is nothing but negative integration—focused on process. We need positive integration focused on the establishment of institutions. We must exist as a supernation or not at all."

A serious-looking young man, nervous but determined, breaks in. He is tall, angular, blond and blue-eyed. "Sir, the young people of Europe have developed the ability to hold multiple loyalties simultaneously. We can be loyal to our countries, to the European Community and to the world. We find no problem in observing a multitude of different systems such as patriotism, Europeanism and international ecological concerns. This gentleman from the United States did quote Spinelli out of context, and I'm sure he knew that very well. I agree that we do not need mischief-makers here. Spinelli also said that the main obstacle to creating your supernation was the lack of a central authority—no king. He wants to make the European Commission king, so that the Parliament can exercise true political power. Let me say that the European youth do not need to be coerced by a central political power."

The big man turns on him. "Young man, if you were a member of the European Parliament you would understand better . . ."

The young man draws himself up. "Sir, I am a member of Parliament, a delegate from Germany since the last election."

There is an embarrassed silence and the group begins to disperse. After a moment the large man gives a stiff bow to the young man, glares at me and stalks off. In a low voice I say, "I apologize for being provocative, but if Altiero were here, he would agree with both our statements. After all, he is a poet and a writer. He can feel the major transformation in European consciousness of which you are an example. But he has also spent much of his life as a politician, being tested by his party in the fire of controversy. He knows how to amass power and use it toward a humane end. He is left behind, however, when humanitarianism occurs spontaneously without the use of political power. This is outside his experience. He can only go on seeking more centralized political power, even though such power is the antithesis of his attempt to go beyond nationalism. It is one of the human tragedies of our time."

The young man holds my eyes for a moment, nods in agreement and fades into the crowd.

The party is winding down. Claude comes over looking concerned and says, "Come sit down and have a drink before you go. My friend from the Crocodile Club left immediately after talking to you. He looked furious. You know how closely the Parliament works with the Commission. You must realize how important he is to me."

"Claude, I'm sorry. Don't ask me to any more diplomatic parties. Really, I didn't get a chance to say very much. Let me explain and you decide the kind of damage I've done. You've heard me talk about Altiero's theories before, that a major transformation of consciousness has led to a widespread diffusion of new thinking among more and more people, until in the United States and Europe it has broken out in such new ways of living as the New Deal, the Marshall Plan, and especially the European Community. Okay?

"Well, your crocodile friend—and a crocodile is a dinosaur, you know—while having done a lot of good for the European Community, is poised to begin drafting the constitution of the United States of Europe. Now that the people of the European Community are getting rid of the evils of nationalism, he is about to force a regression by forming a supernation of Europe. He justifies this by assuming that the European Community is the result of planning, rather than people, and that more planning will be even better. I'm afraid I baited him—and he exposed his views on world government.

"He's a good man, a typical socialist politician with communist connections, and he was doing his normal political thing when he encountered a young man whose quality of thinking has actually made the European Community work. Your crocodile friend tried to discount the young man, but he turned out to be a fellow member of Parliament, probably from the Greenpeace movement."

Claude's wife, coming up to us says, "How could you . . ."

Claude says, "It could have been worse. It was only about reality rather than policy."

He pauses. "I was going to go over to the Commission to work on some external agreements with you tomorrow. I think at the moment I'd better just bring my notes to your hotel."

"I'm sorry, Claude. . . ."

THE WINDSOR HOTEL

Hotels are not my favorite places, but the Windsor is one of Europe's best. The next morning I awake refreshed, thinking about the young Parliament member from Germany. It was a treat to be in the presence of a person who is able to think in seemingly antithetical ways at the same time. I'm reminded of something once said by Richard Hoggart. While I'm rummaging through my briefcase for the London notebook, there is a knock at the door and Claude arrives. I read the passage to him: "There are signs of a growing wish for a renewed sense of the reality of the human scale. Across Western Europe, to take only the continent we are now in, you can detect, especially among young people, a disenchantment with old-style, nationality-bound political parties, in favour of causes that flow across national and party boundaries and are rooted in a concern for mankind as a whole, its universe and its history, as in the Greenpeace movement and the rise in the claims of ethnic minorities. Contrary to popular opinion, those minorities are less enclosed than are old-style nationalists; their interests move naturally from their local groups, direct to at least the continental, bypassing the nation-states."

"Do you realize you might have been entertaining angels last night and never have known it if I hadn't inadvertently caused you a small embarrassment? But let me beg your pardon again."

Claude smiles as he sits down. "You are forgiven. Even my wife more or less forgives you. And the young man is certainly an interesting phenomenon. It helps clarify some of my thoughts about the developing European mentality."

Claude is feeling a little guilty, apparently, about banishing me from the Commission. He reveals some surprising thoughts about UNESCO, and I have never heard him speak this freely before.

"Let's compare what's happened with UNESCO and with the European Community," he says. "They were both inspired by the United States. They inhabit similar buildings in European towns not far from each other— UNESCO in Paris, the European Community in Strasbourg, Luxembourg and Brussels. UNESCO was created in 1946 by the United States, Great Britain and France at a meeting in London with forty-four other states. At that time there were twenty member states. The European Community was started by six member states in 1957.

"The goals of both were similar: peace, prosperity, freedom through cooperative activities between nations. Neither has the power of a supernation to impose peace.

Let us consider which has succeeded and which has failed. Since 1981, more than one hundred thousand people have died from war in Uganda. In Ethiopia, more than five hundred thousand have died since 1974; and in Mozambique, more than four hundred thousand have died since 1981. That's over a million people dead in just three countries. Counting war as a conflict with at least a thousand deaths a year, the twenty-two wars underway in 1987, almost all of them involving UNESCO member states, resulted in well over two million deaths. The situation has worsened since then. On the other hand, since World War II not one single person has died in the European Community from war. There has been no war.

"Not only did the United States badger and, yes, inspire Europe to form the European Community, it also cajoled and coerced us to give up our colonial systems. When UNESCO was formed in 1946 with twenty members, it was an organization of Western culture. But as each of our colonies became independent countries, it joined UNESCO until by 1978 there were one hundred forty-four member states.

"The result has been the exact opposite of the development of the European Community. UNESCO has made the nation-state the focus of power, thereby encouraging war. On the other hand, the European Community, by dismantling encrustations of nationalistic regulations, has done away with war in Europe. While our erstwhile mentor, the United States, has been a warmonger, we have found peace and prosperity. In only the past year I have witnessed a refreshing self-confidence among the people of Europe. They are just beginning to discover what they have done."

"Claude, could we take that one step further and say it isn't so much what the people of Europe have done as it is what they have become? Aren't they discovering a common change in their natures, in the ways they think and feel, a common spiritual quickening? And in emphasizing how UNESCO has been taken over by peoples outside European culture, aren't you implying the un-thinkable—that UNESCO has failed and the European Community has succeeded because of the natures of their respective peoples and their ways of thinking? Their administrative structures are not basically different. The only difference is the people."

Later I realize what a damning indictment Claude has presented. UNESCO is an enemy of my country. It *is* the key point in the triangle of power that includes PEN and the International Publishers Association. And yet, and yet . . .

I remember Federico Mayor speaking on the founding of UNESCO, which was inspired by the spirit of the American people. "It was no longer seen as just the absence of war, but as a collective and continuing effort to integrate the growing interdependence of national and individual destinies." He saw it as "a great victory for the human mind and spirit to contribute to a future in which everyone will take other people's needs more and more into account." He said, "From manpower, we have begun to turn to mindpower."

Poor Dr. Mayor. When he tries to reconcile his dreams for UNESCO with its people, his actions become grotesque. The bureaucracy and member states are already sabotaging his dreams.

The parallels between UNESCO and the European Community extend even to their both having chosen 1992 as a symbol of progress toward specific goals.

In 1992, UNESCO will have an international conference on saving the environment. Its goal is to persuade the United States and England to rejoin. How-ever, Mr. Eggar, Undersecretary of State at the British Foreign Office, has already said, "At the last UNESCO Executive Board meeting in Paris there had been con-siderable evidence of the member states opposing even the fairly minor changes that Señor Mayor had introduced recently. . . . I made it clear that we needed to see that the necessary fundamental reforms had been achieved."

Regardless of the reasons, UNESCO has utterly failed in its goals of achieving peace, freedom, prosperity and understanding between nations. The European Community, however, in spite of formidable obstacles, has accomplished every one of those goals. This despite the fact that only forty years ago Europe was in ruins, with no food or shelter and packs of uneducated and undernourished children roaming wild. Even still, Europe is subject to constant threat from the encroaching Russian Empire.

Europe has its roots in many different cultures and embraces many different races. Neither race nor material resources nor education nor technology can account for the differences in results between UNESCO and the European Community. Only Altiero's theory of a major transformation in the consciousness of Europeans seems to account for it.

But it's time to go. We have a date in Dublin tomorrow.

THE RISING OF THE MOON

BRUSSELS AIRPORT

It's a rainy night and the runways shimmer with a confusion of lights. The stewardess drags the door shut and starts her countdown. A car's headlights swerve up suddenly beside us. There are hurried consultations, the door is opened, and a package is handed in. A furious but awed stewardess marches down the aisle and stops at my seat. Her voice comes from a glacial height: "Dr. Howell."

"Uh, yes."

"This package is for you."

I turn the attached card over. In his calligraphic style—Lazlo. Damn him, How did he know?. . .

The wrapping paper has the quality of watered silk. Inside is an antique inlaid box that might have been a jewel box, and inside that a slim used book, *Unequal*

Partners by Garret FitzGerald. I had spent an unsuccessful day in London trying to find a copy of this book. Here was my own copy. How could Lazlo possibly have known that I was looking for it? He must have heard that Garret had invited me to visit him in Ireland.

Dr. Garret FitzGerald, an economist with the heart of a poet, must have been president of the Council of Ministers of the European Economic Community when he was writing this book. That was before he became prime minister of Ireland.

It's an hour until Dublin. Let's see, Lazlo has marked some passages.

> In recent decades there has emerged for the first time in world history a sense of the obligations in justice that rich people owe to poor people.
> Until well into this century this concept had no real meaning in any kind of political commitment; indeed the reverse was true.
> This development is irreversible. Mankind has passed an important turning point in the development of its corporate moral sense. It may seem unnecessary to lay such stress on this point, but like most important revolutions in the thought of mankind, it has happened gradually enough to have escaped notice and rapidly enough to be quite astonishing.

Garret is a true prophet. Long before anyone else, he recognized that "for the first time in world history" people are thinking in a new way. Not only is the thinking original, it is exactly opposite our thinking during the millions of years of evolution. What are these uniquely new thoughts? Garret says they're about justice and morality . . . and here Lazlo has marked a passage about a new "level of sensitivity and commitment." I believe "sensitivity" is Garret's key word for this mysterious and mind-boggling revolution, which is not about ideas or ideologies or systems of government, not about *what* people think, but about *how* they think.

Garret perceives it as having appeared for the first time in world history "in recent decades," about sixty years ago.

The people of the United States were the first, in all their contentious differences, to demonstrate sensitivity and commitment in Roosevelt's New Deal of the thirties. After World War II our Marshall Plan demonstrated the same enlarged sensitivity to Europe and the entire world. It was in the United States that the desire to help weaker countries emerged for the first time in history. Before, the reverse was true. Strong countries took from weak countries.

We won the thoughts of the world, then. But today it is the European Community that is setting the example.

DUBLIN

During a phone conversation with Paul the subject of Lazlo comes up. "He knows about the Hungarian business, Paul, and other things that couldn't be just coincidence."

Paul's voice shakes the phone. "You better believe I didn't tell him anything. However, he's involved in a consortium I'll probably be working with. I can tell they are people who have purposes beyond just making money. They see the cross-channel tunnel as promoting a way of living rather than just strictly business—very subtle people. Lazlo sounded me out about it. I told him I'd take the money and leave everything else to them. You can bet they have contacts wherever they are needed. On the other hand, there's a group competing directly with them connected to old-fashioned political interests. Those people are treacherous. I wouldn't touch them with a ten-foot pole. Take care of yourself. Don't get in the middle."

Next morning there is a meeting at Trinity University, that ancient, walled, intellectual community in the center of Dublin. Trinity's medieval library is the repository of the most famous Celtic work of art, *The Book of Kells*.

I find a close-knit group of students in the gate house room above the arched entrance to the university. We start with the subject of the European Community.

A thin-faced boy speaks up. "It means I have a home beyond Ireland, in a community of nations. I can go anywhere in that community to study or work and I know I will be accepted. You don't know what it's like to have been a colony. We belonged to England, and they treated us as though we were animals. Now we're going to Europe as members of an international community. It's the United States now that excludes us and treats us like second-class people."

A red-haired girl: "I was working as a waitress in Manhattan and putting a good bit aside until they caught me. It was so degrading. My aunt took care of it all, but she acted superior like all Americans do. I felt so exploited!"

"The United States decides what is right and wrong and imposes it on others as though they should agree with them," another student says.

The girl speaks up again: "And my aunt has become a born-again Protestant. The fundamentalist revival in the United States—you wouldn't believe it. It's so bad, and growing. It shouldn't be allowed. It should be stamped out!"

It is clear that the United States is no longer regarded as the land of opportunity. "You Europeans have been boosting yourselves by using anti-American symbols in your thinking. In the process you've created a new world of peace and prosperity here in Europe. You're about to inherit it, but do you know anything about it? What do you know about the European Community?"

Silence.

"You will be citizens of this Community when you graduate. Have you studied it here at Trinity?"

Finally, the thin-faced boy offers, "I haven't heard of any course on that subject. I must admit that it does seem as though we are able to speak more easily about what is wrong with the United States than about what is right with the European Community. Of course, we have a general idea, but . . ."

"Let me suggest this to you: Essentially it is the result of a radical change in the consciousness of Europeans, and it is new in the history of the world. Don't feel badly that you don't know much about it. Not many Europeans have been able to express what is going on, and I'm struggling with it myself. Give me an example of a European Community activity you're involved in."

"The Coffee Run," an intense, dark-haired boy offers, followed by laughter tinged with malice from the entire group.

"We all collect money during the year, and then in the summer we send as many of us as we have money for to Nicaragua to help harvest their coffee crop. When we come back, we're asked to speak all over because we've been witnesses to the U.S. oppression of the Nicaraguan people."

I'm a little angry. "Let me tell you, I'm just about fed up with European talk about this U.S. oppression of the Nicaraguan people. Who has been on the 'Run' to help the oppressed people of Czechoslovakia or Romania lately?"

A tall strawberry-blond girl stands up. "Dr. Howell, you're being cynical. You're taking unfair advantage of us. You know, Norway is giving, I think, twenty-three million dollars and Sweden, thirty million dollars to Nicaragua for relief against U.S. oppression. The United States stands accused by the entire world. Don't you think the German people were responsible for the Jewish Holocaust? And don't you think you are acting like a German who doesn't want to admit responsibility for his country's atrocities?"

I am hit by a flash of myself at dawn hanging onto that lamppost in Chelsea, after Harold Pinter devastated me. The strawberry blond sits down with a smug little smile.

"I'm ashamed for myself and for my country about a great many things. Who would be interested in hearing my heart's thoughts about Nicaragua?"

"Yes."

"Yes, if you mean it."

"Go ahead."

The intense, dark-haired boy stands up. "I would very much like to hear what you have to say."

"Thank you. First, let me say that I have recently become convinced that we are all involved in a truly international war for the thoughts of the world. In this war it is how we think that is important, not what we think. We can't afford to live just on the surface immediacy of information. We need to live in our inner spaces.

"That is what this ancient university is about. And literature is the battleground of this war. I think we all know the difference between thinking deeply in our interior spaces and thoughtlessly repeating slogans.

"Very well, in Nicaragua the United States lost the thoughts of the world. We failed there because we inanely repeated our slogans about the communist menace, without making room in our interior thoughts for the living Nicaraguan people. It is not up to you or me to decide whether the Contras or the Sandinistas should prevail there. The U.S.'s tragic, fatal blunder was to provide arms so the Contras could kill people, *before* the Contras had developed a literature and a common ferment of deep interactive thought about what they were doing. The CIA didn't want thought. They wanted people who would sell themselves for money. Contra—to be against—is only a slogan and a very poor one.

"By contrast, the Russians supplied the Sandinistas with arms *after* the Sandinistas had created a literature, a vision and a dream for the Nicaraguan people.

"Harold Pinter quoted from the poem "Lights" by the great Sandinista poet Ernesto Cardenal, who is now Nicaragua's Minister of Culture. I have it here in my notebook, and I'd like to read it to you.

> We've landed. Comrades clad in olive-green
> > come out of the dark to embrace us.
> We feel their warm bodies, which also come
> > from the sun,
> which are also light.
> > It's against the darkness, this revolution.
> It was the dawn of July 18. And the
> > beginning
> > of everything that was to come.

"Where is the Contra literature? We in the United States thought we could use the communists' own tricks of violent revolution against them. We had our 'guerillas in the mountains' looking down on the Sandinista towns. We didn't realize that 'guerillas in the mountains' are first thoughts that later become a few people, then regiments, then armies. We left out the thoughts, the literature. How could we have made this mistake, when our own revolution was the first, the quintessential revolution of thought?

"The Sandinistas are busy making their own tragic mistakes now. They have repressed the free thought of the Nicaraguan people to the extent that now all they can hear are their own slogans. I'm content to leave them to it.

"You know in your hearts that the people of the United States want to help others, not to hurt them. The Sandinistas have succeeded in this war for the thoughts of the world simply because they have been, in thought, successfully anti-American. That's why Europe focuses on Nicaragua.

"Please remember that the United States is the oldest and most successful pluralistic society of people who live together in personal freedom and equality. In our kind of society confusion is inevitable, and we move slowly to change our ways of thinking. We need your goodwill. We need you to believe in us.

"Read Garret FitzGerald's *Unequal Partners*. He points out that an enlarged sensitivity to others is evolving right now. For the first time in the history of the world, there are people who can care for people they have never seen. The mutuality of this caring makes your European Community possible, and it can mean the salvation of the world. Don't turn away. We all need each other as we change over to this new kind of living."

The meeting ended well. The long bonds of kinship between Ireland and the United States are palpable, even in these students, when their feelings are aroused.

Walking toward St. Stephen's Park, I think of the Irish revolutionary folk song "The Rising of the Moon":

> At the rising of the moon,
> At the rising of the moon.
> and so on
> And the world is turning over,
> At the rising of the moon . . . .

The world is turning over, and a new age is coming for these young people. The development of the European Community brings a promise of peace and prosperity. Europeans have gone beyond the boundaries of nationalism to community. They have found a way to embrace each other's national differences.

THE DAIL EIREANN

Garret FitzGerald's office is a light airy room with modern furnishings. His hair is graying, but he is still the most handsome statesman in Europe and the most imposing. We are discussing my arrival in Dublin. "Here I am on the walkway into the Dublin terminal and the end of it is filled with a poster of healthy, good-looking Irish college graduates who are portrayed as the bright future of Ireland. But I'm told that all except one have left Ireland to find work elsewhere."

Garret frowns at me. "Who told you that?"

"Janet McCally. She and her father worked their hearts out in your campaign to reform the divorce and abortion laws. When you lost, she left for a job in London.

"I know that as an economist and leader of your country you have to be concerned with goods and services, but Ireland's greatest treasure and its best exports have always been its thoughts. The problem is to keep the thinkers here and export only their thoughts. Think of George Bernard Shaw, Yeats, and Sean O'Casey, who all wound up living in England."

Garret stirs impatiently, his face darkens. "They leave because we can't generate the jobs to keep them."

"But maybe it's thoughts that generate the economics that generate the jobs to prevent them having to go to the United States. Which comes first?"

Garret rises to his feet. He's not tall, but broad and powerfully built. His dark eyes aim at me like the barrels of a gun. "I know where the Irish don't come first—the United States. If Janet McCally had gone to New York, she would have been denied a work permit. She would have wound up, as so many of our talented young people have, as a wage slave, working illegally as an au pair or worse, and for starvation wages.

"In the European Community, at least Janet has the right to go to London or any other city to compete freely for a legal job in which she can use her full talents and qualifications. She's not a subperson in Europe as she would be in the United States. As part of the European

Community, moreover, we have possibilities for economic growth."

I'm suffering the discomfort of not knowing what to say when the bell rings. It's time for us to go to the Dail, Ireland's parliament. Garret gets me through security and we enter the most attractive government hall I know. The room is small enough to be intimate; it is almost a circle, the seats converging on the speaker's dais. The Dail is preparing a resolution to commemorate Nelson Mandela's seventieth birthday, his twenty-fourth in a South African prison. All of the political parties want to get into the act. The passion to wish Mandela a happy birthday becomes more intense as each speaker tries to outdo the last.

An old man in the front row rises to speak. He has the dignity of an elder statesman and the obvious respect of the other members. He tells the story of the oppression of the African National Congress and its leader by the South African government. Then he compares that situation with the oppression of Nicaragua by the United States.

He was honored, he says, to be chosen to represent Ireland and the European Community as an official observer of the Nicaraguan elections. He says he can guarantee that the Sandinistan government represents the will of the Nicaraguan people just as the African National Congress represents the will of the South African people. It is clear that in this assembly Nelson Mandela is a symbol for censure of the United States.

Running through the speeches is a theme that only the little countries of Europe have the right to stand with Mandela. His crusade against oppression is identified with their crusade for the European Community, implicitly excluding the United States of America.

The good feelings of political unanimity overflow through a side door down into what is the most civilized and wonderful part of this building's architecture. Underneath the Dail is a good Irish bar. I have lost track of Garret, but an acquaintance buys me a Guiness Stout.

I find myself standing next to Proinsias deRossa, leader of the Workers' Party. Actually, Proinsias is pronounced Frank. His black Spanish hair and eyes are electric with vitality. He has a knack for getting his name in the papers nearly every day.

"No, you are wasting your time," he is saying. "England was Ireland's enemy in the distant past, but not today. England is obligated to defend the partition of Northern Ireland. We want union with Northern Ireland, but not through terror or bloodshed. We need England's cooperation to achieve union and in time we will get it, even if it is sub-rosa. We don't need union now. When it happens is not vital. And when union does happen, we'll have the same problem with the Prots that the English are now having with the Catholics. Plus we'll have the same problem integrating the IRA into our democratic society that we had after Irish independence.

"The solution for both the North and the South is to cooperate, to negotiate our problems. We can only find that solution in the European Community. The greatest obstacle to solving our problem is the Irish Americans meddling with the IRA. Americans must not support the IRA with words or money. It's the worst kind of meddling. Don't do it!"

One of the organizers of the Mandela birthday greeting moves up on my other side. "Did you know the American CIA is responsible for Nelson Mandela being in jail? Twenty-four years ago they discovered where he was hiding and turned him over to the South African police."

A burly member of the Dail says, "Yes, that's true, and did you know that the CIA engineered the election of the prime minister in Australia's recent elections?"

After that, what with the constant flow of stout and the Mandela occasion, the United States continues downhill all the way to the bottom.

It's late when I turn in my security badge and leave the Dail. Walking across the deserted bridge over the river Liffy, I become aware that someone is following me. I look behind: a slight gray man, gray hair, gray skin. He catches up with me as the bridge opens into Dublin's main drag, O'Connell Street. It's full of lights and people, mainly teenagers going into and out of pubs. From alongside he mutters something I don't catch.

Then, ". . . a rocket factory near the border . . ."

I had been enjoying a pleasant buzz, which suddenly disappears. "I'll talk to you at . . . at the fountain." A fountain to Anna Liffy, a popular meeting place, is just ahead.

He makes a secretive gesture. "I have a private place where—"

"I'll talk at the fountain or not at all."

He hesitates, then shrugs, and we walk on.

We sit on the edge of the fountain and I say, "For both our sakes I want you to understand; I don't want anything to do with people who will kill me if they think I've betrayed them. I don't keep secrets. If you tell me any secret information, I will instantly broadcast it to everyone on O'Connell Street. That's why we're sitting here. I won't be blackmailed by secret involvement, and I won't be set up by knowing about any rocket factory."

He looks at me, memorizing everything about me, his thin lips getting a little thinner. He is starting to move when I say, "Lighten up. How do you think I got to be as old as I am."

He smiles a bitter smile. "You don't leave me anything."

"I will leave you something. More than a rocket factory, or an operational plan. I'll leave you a thought. O.K.?"

His expression doesn't change, but he slacks down on the rim of the fountain.

"O.K. Think of the Irish revolution, its eight-hundred-year struggle to get free of Britain. It was a great revolution because it was a literary revolution. In song, poetry and prose, its every defeat was written into a victory of thought. The Irish soul was never defeated. The greatest revolutionary act was Yeats's poem *Easter Sunday*, and every bullet-pockmarked wall on O'Connell Street still testifies to that greatness.

"At independence, the IRA was heir to the greatness of Ireland's literary soul. Now look at the IRA in Northern Ireland today. Forget the terrible provocations and betrayals by the British and the Prots, and tell me if you yourself have a soul. No, wait. Leave that. Do you have a thought, a dream besides pulling everyone around you down to bloody destruction?

"The IRA gave up dreams in order to solve an organizational problem. You sold your soul for organizational secrecy—just for an organizational technique. Secrecy destroys thought. No one dares think. You censor yourselves, which is the ultimate censorship. The tragedy is not that you have killed *people* needlessly; you've killed *thought* needlessly.

"Find your literature again. Literature drives out secrecy and maximizes thought. . . ."

He is getting up. Without looking at me, he says softly, "That's not leaving much."

His slight figure moves quietly down O'Connell Street and disappears into the darkness of an alley.

You're leaving the only chance you'll ever have—your literature. . . . But in my secret Irish heart, I say, "God bless you."

ST. STEPHEN'S PARK

I'm sitting on a bench feeding some ducks. Irish trees surround me, with little folk undoubtedly nearby. The headlines of the Dublin newspaper jump out at me, ROCKET FACTORY RAIDED. Coincidence? Lazlo and Paul and Claude have all implied that I should be careful not to be caught in the middle. Lazlo maintains that all terrorist groups, including the IRA, are allied with the warlike ex-colonial nations that control UNESCO and the United Nations. They all support nationalism and the old ways, and if they have their way the European Community won't make it. They would rather see it become a supernation. Some businesses and political groups in Europe who fear the ambiguity of community are also unwitting allies of the terrorist nations.

It is the ambiguity of the European Community that makes it vulnerable. No one can say what the Community is. New forms, whether historical or literary, defy definition. They have a patchwork quality at first that makes them difficult to describe. It is easier to refer to them in economic quantitative terms, but that is only one kind of information, not meaningful in itself. Europe needs new language forms with which to talk about its new revolution—invisible because it is a revolution in consciousness.

In order to arrive at new language forms, we need to understand the essence of the European Community, how the Community is relevant. Relevance . . . that brings Maury Berman to mind. I dig into my briefcase for the notes on our last meeting.

Morris Berman had returned from speaking at an international conference in Hanover, Germany. He is a famous human scientist who has managed to capture the imaginations of the scientific community and intelligent, curious readers alike. Perfectly in tune with himself, he makes room for others to expand freely into his world. His book *The Reenchantment of the World* was a big seller, and his latest book, *Coming to Our Senses*, promises to do even better.

I had been telling him about my European Community investigation. "I'm looking for the feelings of the relevant person, not the average person as expressed in some statistical poll, but the mythical, sacramental person whose feelings are plugged into what is essential in life."

"Our deep interior experiences of mind and body constitute the real events of our lives. They are what is relevant," Maury said.

"Body, the body's mind, feeling tones, rhythms of thought spreading through time from primordial hearts. Maury, *you've done it*; by making me concentrate on my senses, you've broken a language barrier I've not been able to surmount. Do you remember what the great German theologian Karl Kohner said, 'The more I become my body, the more I become spirit; and the more I become spirit, the more I become my body.'?"

"Yes, I like that," Maury replied. "A more current example of the body's relevance is one I mentioned in my book. It's from the popular comic strip by Lynn Johnston, "For Better or For Worse."

Mother is sitting in front of the radio listening to the news report; young daughter, home from school, is babbling to her about what happened in school that day ("And then Johnny took a frog out of his pocket, and . . ."). Finally, mother turns to daughter and says, "Elizabeth, be quiet! Can't you see I'm trying to listen to the news?" Elizabeth goes to her room, thinking to herself: "I thought that's what I was telling you!"

"Right. News from the media is information. It is surface thinking."

Maury continues, "The rationally processed media fail to resonate with what is most familiar to us, our inner lives. What is relevant in our lives reflects the things that matter most to us, that are experienced in the body. The human drama is storytelling first and foremost."

"What I've been doing in the European Community, basically, is immerging myself in storytelling."

"I wrote about this in *Coming to Our Senses,*" Maury said. "Storytellers assume that human beings are not rational, that their deepest and most significant experiences are lived on a level that is largely invisible, a shadowy region where mind and body move in and out of each other in an infinite number of elusive combinations that can only be evoked through feeling tone and resonance. Storytelling also assumes that this shadow world is what life is really about, that it is the crucible in which life, in the final analysis, is really made. Truth has always been a mode of storytelling. In this mode, the facts were above all what happened on a psychic level. Indeed, if this got left out, it would be fair to say that nothing happened, that there was no story to tell. The essential truth is an interior one; to omit this is to give the reader nothing significant.

"The collective mental baggage of a civilization reaches, like a geological formation, far below the visible level. This isn't the surface thinking of ideas, but the deep interior thoughts of how life is lived."

I lean over and say, "Our immediate surface perceptions are truly irrelevant. Television, newspapers, information books, especially schoolbooks, don't reveal what is going on."

"Especially schoolbooks," says Maury. "It all starts in school."

"You're right. Think of your school years. What should have been relevant was numbingly irrelevant to your life. Think of all the boring books. They were not about your relevance to the world around you or to your roots in the past. Completely unlike the books that could whirl you away to other worlds, secret worlds that belonged to you, which you created with the art of the author.

"We don't think about it while we're in school because we're dancing as fast as we can to someone else's tune. But test it now. Children have a sense of what rings true and what is irrelevant. How sterile and irrelevant is surface information like Dick and Jane. The children who have to read *Dick and Jane* books are capable of the most elaborate kinds of make-believe, yet their reading is not rich in make-believe, which is surely their most important mental exercise. The *Dick and Jane* kind of information is irrelevant. In fact, the kids who learn to read with books like *Dick and Jane* may well wind up hating reading.

"We've been cheated as children and we're cheating ourselves now. As adults we've become addicted to the boring, irrelevant information we stuff down ourselves every day from TV, newspapers and books. We've become infoholics. Try a vacation without TV or newspapers. . . ."

"Infoholics, I like that." Maury snorts.

"Do you remember *A Delicate Balance* by Albee? It didn't do as well as *Who's Afraid of Virginia Woolf,* but I liked it better. I can't do justice to Albee, but let me tell you how the play has become an inner reality unique in my mind. It's about relevance.

"This woman's sister is an alcoholic. Friends are visiting. The alcoholic sister is oh, so charming, but the woman is tense and bitter. The family finally get her to one side, and she bursts out with something like, 'You see charming. You don't know what's going on. I see vomit on the floor. I know the smell and the cleaning up. She's giving you information. I'm giving you relevance—smell, feel, despair. By staying on the surface, being charming, she's walled herself off from that vomit on the floor. I can't forgive her for that.'"

Maury: "I see what you're getting at. Go on."

"Well, I guess relevance is this woman's feeling of being caught on the flypaper of information. The information says everything is all right, but her senses tell her she's being destroyed in a surface illusion. She knows that isn't all there is, but she can't get free of it. She is being cheated. Books of information, as well as television and newspapers, cheat us, feed our infoholism. Literature knows the vomit on the floor."

It is Maury's way, as a philosopher of history, to doubt the surface information and seek "deep interior relevance."

What can we find in the surface history of Europe since World War II to account for the existence of the European Community? What has changed that would correlate with the radical change to community?

The quality of European leadership has not changed. There have been no charismatic political figures. In fact, the crocodile man in Brussels complained of years of political impotence. There has been no radically new ideology. Neither education nor science has undergone any radical new changes. There seems to be little surface development to account for the European Community.

What have we learned about the European Community that seems particularly relevant to our lives and that has undergone a radical change? First, Claude in Brussels observed that war has ended in the European Community during a time when there have been more wars in the world than ever before in history. That is certainly a radical change. Joseph Brodsky, the Nobel laureate in literature, suggests a new kind of human thought that helps explain Claude's observation: "For someone who has read a lot of Dickens to shoot someone in the name of some idea is more problematic than for someone who has read no Dickens."

Then, we have Garret FitzGerald's discovery through economic analysis of an enlarged sensitivity to others, which has appeared for the first time in history. And, he says, it is not only new and unique, but also irreversible, a revolution in the thinking of humankind.

In addition, there is the purely political instinct of

Altiero Spinelli, who senses a radical change in the consciousness of Europeans that has never happened before—
another inner change.

And we cannot ignore the evidence of the Greenpeace movement, presented by the young member of the
European Parliament in Brussels. He said that his young
cohorts, the coming elite, had observed in themselves a
new way of thinking. That is, they could think in different paradigms simultaneously, and they could maintain
loyalties to their own countries, to the European Community, and to international ecological concerns, all at
the same time.

All of these changes demonstrate Maury's "deep interior thoughts of how life is lived," thoughts that reach
"like a geological formation far below the visible level."
And they correlate with the emergence of the European
Community.

We must follow Maury's way. As a philosopher of
history, he distrusts surface information while seeking
interior relevance. A study of the history of the European
psyche seems the only way to understand and give linguistic form to the European Community.

On returning from the park I find I have received a
letter from Lazlo. How could he have found me? Paul? No,
after our talk I believe Paul would be particularly careful.
Lazlo must have me under some kind of surveillance. It's a
note on handmade parchment illuminated around the
borders. Is it scented? By god, it is! He is inquiring after
his gift—his "bijou," he says—of Garret FitzGerald's book,
Unequal Partners. He delicately suggests that "perhaps, you
are not in the habit of writing letters." He suggests another meeting on matters that might be of mutual concern.

He's right. I'm terrible about writing letters. But I'm
going to write one this time.

Dear Lazlo,

The copy of *Unequal Partners* was exactly what I needed exactly when I needed it. To consider how you could possibly know this is so irritating that I refuse to think about it. I do thank you. I'm sure you can imagine that my thanks are given somewhat grudgingly. When I am with you, I can hear the whisper of strings being pulled. Does the puppet master consider the possible resentments of his puppets? He should.

However, by the time you receive this letter I will be gone. I have a pilgrimage to make through the history of European thought, a pilgrimage to find new language structures. The European Community needs to find a literature for its revolution in consciousness for all our sakes. You will not know where I am, so I suggest that we not consider a meeting at this time.

PART THREE

*The Third Dimension
of Thought
in Europe*

A SHORT HISTORY
OF
EUROPEAN THINKING

MILAN

It isn't that I don't agree with Lazlo's support of the European Community, it's that his support takes the form of secret intrigue and intricate maneuvers. The European Community is the expression of a revolution in consciousness that is the antithesis of the kind of manipulations of which Lazlo is a master. This new revolution is characterized by an enlarged sensitivity for others, empathy for others and interior room for them to live intimately in one's mind. Lazlo has a massive intelligence that enables him to understand the importance of the European Community to the world, but his being was honed in the bureaucratic intrigues of the United Nations and a one-world ideology. Like Altiero Spinelli, he can appreciate the European Community, but he can never be part of its spiritual life.

So Lazlo does what he can do best for the European Community. But when I catch him using me as a pawn in his maneuvers, I get nervous. For the sake of an advantage in his game, he would sacrifice me without a second thought. However, there is no way Lazlo's people—or anyone else—could have followed me here to Milan. One theory on eluding surveillance is to act on impulse and never look back: Think like the hunter, not the hunted. I passed through Geneva and, after emerging from the tunnel under the Alps, criss-crossed the central plain of the Po River on local buses.

Imagine a classical scene from the Roman Empire, the white columned compounds of Roman villas that once dotted this rich plain. I'm sure many of the farm buildings here today were built atop the foundations of those villas. A few of the original Roman families remain by virtue of their defensive location and their strength of purpose. These are people who managed to defend themselves against barbarian invasions and, later, bands of pillaging marauders.

Here in Milan is the little out-of-the-way church where Leonardo da Vinci painted *The Last Supper*, also the palace built by the Sforza family, which contains the drawings of da Vinci's mechanical inventions. Milan possesses physical ties to the Renaissance and spiritual ties to the lost classical age of thought.

Outside the Milan station, which resembles a palace, a communist parade is forming up. Anyone can join, raising a clenched first in the communist salute, shouting "Lutta" and other communist slogans, and waving at the pretty girls. It is innocent and fun these days. But when the United States invaded Grenada a few years ago things were a little ticklish for Americans. The Franciscan priest in a nearby church—known locally for the artistically arranged piles of human bones and skulls in its crypts—would loudly exhort the American imperialist predators who were raping unspoiled Grenada. With every "Grenada" a low rumble would rise from the congregation. Any available wall in the city was apt to have *Fuck America* spray-painted on it that year.

Now Italy is enjoying an unprecedented prosperity, due in part to its membership in the European Community. There is less anti-Americanism and more self-confidence, especially with representatives like Altiero Spinelli playing major roles in forming policy. For example, in the area around Trieste in northeast Italy at the head of the Adriatic Sea, the inhabitants were originally Austrian. By treaty they had to become Italian nationals, but they still speak German and live in an Austrian culture. The Italians who had moved in were regarded as interlopers and ostracized. What is interesting is that now both ethnic groups feel they have room to exist and keep their integrity because of the nature of the European Community.

I've made arrangements to go to a Cistercian monastery in the countryside outside Milan, located near an ancient road leading to Rome. The monastery has a good library; it'll be a great help to me in preparing my short history of thinking in Europe. I'm going to have to begin with classical times in order to follow the changes in thought that have led to the present.

THE MONASTERY

An outside stairway leads from the inner court up to the cells. Visitors live like the monks, with only a hard bed, small dresser, small table and chair, and a light. There is no heat and the cold walls suck out the body's warmth. But there is a wood fire in the library. The books with old calf bindings and parchment pages reflect the golden warmth through the room, with its low, vaulted ceiling. And the food here is marvelous, freshly grown or caught on the grounds and cooked to perfection. There are crisp, delicious apples off the trees, and the wine, fermented on-site from the monastery's own grapes, flows like water. One feels a sense of solitude and scholarly camaraderie here.

I am here to try to tease out the one significant thread from the tangle of thinking that makes up the European Community. Where does it begin? To facilitate the task I will use Maury Berman's method of paying attention to those ways of thinking that are relevant to people's daily lives.

I've found a shelf of *The Confessions of St. Augustine* in old calf bindings that have a deep amber glow from loving care. I'm looking for an account of his time in Milan, which was the capital of the Roman Empire in the West.

I imagine him in A.D. 385 as a thirty-year-old Roman yuppie called Augustinus. He is wearing a tunic, tight like a T-shirt, but reaching down to his knees and heavily embroidered at the hem. He has bright green stockings pulled up over his calves, and as he walks up the steps to the bishop's palace, his yellow silk cloak billows behind him. Ambrosius is one of the most powerful men of the Western empire. He is in a position to promote the newly appointed professor of rhetoric in the imperial bureaucracy. In fact, the bishop is the moderator between Theodosius, Emperor at Constantinople, and the Augustus of the West at Trier, in what is now Germany.

It is hard to see the bishop, Ambrosius, when he is not surrounded by throngs of people, but today is a quiet day. A secretary ushers Augustinus through the almost empty arcades with lofty ceilings and arches and a floor of inlaid marble mosaics. The hot air ducts under the floor keep the temperature even, and running water makes a constant murmur from the fountains. They come to a small room lined with heavy drapes. The bishop is sitting on a proconsul chair looking at a book. As Augustinus reclines quietly on a couch so as not to disturb him, he notices the bishop's eyes.

This is the way he described what he saw.

When he was reading, his eyes moved along over the pages and his heart searched out their meaning, but his voice and tongue remained silent.

I read it over and over. It is important enough for us to have a look at his original Latin.

Sed cum legebat (when he was reading) oculi ducebantur per paginas (his eyes moved along over the pages) et cor intellectum rimabatur (and his heart searched out their meaning) vox autem et lingua quiescebant (but his voice and tongue remained silent).

Then it hit me. Augustinus thought Ambrosius was reading in a strange manner because all the people he knew read aloud. They had to speak the words in order to understand them.

It was not the sword, he had been taught, but the power of spoken words that had created the Roman Empire. Through the word, mind was disciplined. The disciplined mind created law and justice. It also created military precision and soldiers who did not break. It was rhetoric, the speaking of words, that made this possible.

Augustinus wondered if the bishop had a sore throat or if he had been speaking so much that his mouth was tired. It couldn't have occurred to him that Ambrosius was simply, and of his own choice, reading with his eyes without declaiming the words.

Augustinus was a leading scholar of his day. North African by birth, he had attended the best schools in Carthage and was familiar with the great classical figures; even so, he had never seen anyone read silently. That was his discovery, that it was possible to read silently. His words testify to a change in the nature of reading which began to manifest itself in the twilight of the classical age.

But if reading silently, with the eyes instead of the tongue, was still relatively new in A.D. 385, what had reading been like before?

Have we endowed the revered figures of antiquity with abilities they did not have, abilities we take for granted today? It does seem probable that classical reading was used primarily as an aid to memory when making orations.

Readers must have already known the general message and read the words to check their memories. They would have read by sounding out the words and then . . . "Oh yes, that's the way it goes." The sequence would have been read, speak, then understand.

Today we read, understand, then speak. That is the difference.

The volume of written words that engulfs us today would have been inconceivable to Romans. They would have been able to read only a few books in a lifetime. Written words were rare—to be treasured, memorized and considered carefully by speaking and savoring them. They were often run together with little punctuation, as in a phrase often found on Roman public buildings: SENATUSPOPULUSQUEROMANUS (The Senate and the Roman People). Reading this with the eyes would have been laborious. Only when the phrase is said aloud— SENAT.US/PO.PUL.US.QUE/ROM.AN.US—does meaning take shape.

The human species developed language in order to carry thoughts and pass them on from one generation to the next. Linguistic thought developed with oral language. As words were spoken one at a time in a linear sequence, linguistic thought evolved to break experience down into separate pieces that could be strung together in the same way. Logic and reason were then born, but their birth tore open the human psyche. The source of the wound was self-consciousness, the alienation of linguistic thought from the body's feelings. While this linguistic thought consisted of the broken pieces alienated from the natural body, the body's thought was whole—perceptions, feelings, emotions.

Both animals and people have body thoughts, which represent the first dimension of thinking. Darwin said, "When my terrier bites my hand in play, often snarling at the same time, if he bites and I say *gently, gently,* he goes on biting, but answers me by a few wags of the tail, which seems to say, 'Never mind, it is all fun. . . .' [D]ogs do thus express, and may wish to express, to other dogs and to man, that they are in a friendly state of mind."

Rational thinking, along with oral language, was the second dimension of thinking, which only human beings have achieved. In this dimension humans are alienated from the natural world of animals, and from their wholistic, first-dimensional thinking.

Sophocles wrote *Oedipus Rex* about this alienation of rational thought from nature. Imagine you are a Greek nearly twenty-five hundred years ago seated in the crowded amphitheater in Athens. Even the air is Greek; everyone crowded around you smells the same, is dressed the same way. You are bound to your friends and relatives. You can't stand back from this event; it is you. Looking down the steep slope you see the actor in the blind mask of Oedipus, blood streaming from his torn-out eyes. He makes the ritual gesture . . . and you are him. You hear the actor's voice as though it were by your ear.

O light, may I behold thee nevermore!
I stand a wretch, in birth, in wedlock cursed,
A parricide, incestuous, triply cursed.

No other play expresses so well the unforgivable gulf between the linguistic, self-conscious man of second-dimensional thought and the feeling-bound man of first-dimensional thought.

For example, the great-great-grandfather of Sophocles might have been pretty much an animal. He probably couldn't read or write and hardly ever spoke. But he would have been a magnificent warrior, a man of strong feelings who never hesitated, never doubted, rarely thought. He created the estates that supported Sophocles as he immersed himself in the new second-dimensional thinking.

Sophocles was a man of logic and rational thought—immortal thought. In his play he shows how Oedipus in his "thyksos," his animal joy of life, kills his father and marries his mother. Then in his "hubris," his dark destiny, Oedipus uses his human, language-created thinking to logically track himself down as the criminal. This is the tragedy of man's dual nature from which, until recently, he could not escape.

This was the scene at the advent of reading, the human psyche torn by a new kind of thought—rational, linguistic, self-conscious and oral. But oral language was not enough to hold the increasingly rich harvest of thoughts to be passed on to succeeding generations. The only function of reading was to preserve oral language. It was an aid to memory. If archaic man had had a tape recorder, reading might never have developed. Archaic reading had no more thought content than a tape recorder.

To understand the quality of this ancient reading, we can look to the development of our own children. When learning to read, children act as though they are plugged into a tape recorder. They look at the word *president*, for example, and don't know what it means, so we suggest that they sound out each syllable: "pres - i - dent." They still don't know what it means, so we tell them to say it fast: "pres-i-dent." Then they hear it spoken and a light dawns: "Oh, *president*." They have to hear themselves say it before they can understand its meaning. For them it is read, speak, then understand, just as in classical second-dimensional thought. This phase of learning passes very quickly, sometimes unnoticed, but it is an example of an evolutionary recapitulation of two thousand years of archaic reading.

We notice similar tendencies in ourselves. Sometimes while reading silently we will sound out a new
word or move our lips as though we are speaking. We
may notice tiny muscle impulses in our tongue, which
with electrodes attached can be recorded as muscle nerve
firings. The old neurological patterns are still there. We
have evolved from them, but evolution keeps the past while
transcending it. We still hold within ourselves the
atavistic wound caused by the tearing of self-conscious
rational thought from the first dimension of bodily
feeling.

Silent interior reading occurs in late childhood.
Think back to when you were young. Say you are reading
the *Odyssey* laboriously, word by word, when suddenly the
words disappear and you are blown by the winds of that
wine-dark sea to a third dimension of thought, a secret
interior world. Such an experience could never happen
with *Dick and Jane.* You can't believe the afternoon has
passed when you hear your mother calling you to dinner.
Unbeknownst to you, you were the heir to Augustinus.

Augustinus learned to find in himself the ability to
internalize written language and create from it a proto-
third dimension of thought that was a proto-interior reality. He didn't have to go through the physical act of forming words and beating the air with their sound to understand what he was reading. He learned to create his own
inner landscape from a written text, without recourse to
anything beyond his imagination. It was as though his
mind had loosed itself from the ancient bondage of oral
language. Similarly, our minds recapitulate an evolutionary leap when, in learning to read, we find our own
secret world of inner spaces.

At the fulcrum of the development of silent reading,
then, Augustinus observed the beginnings of a new kind
of reading and thought. He obtained his preferment and
eventually became a bishop like Ambrosius. Notice in *The
Confessions of St. Augustine* how much the quality of his
mind differed from most of his classical precursors':

> I was not yet in love, but I was in love with love,
> and, from the depths of my need, I hated myself
> for not more keenly feeling the need. . . . What
> I needed most was to love and to be loved; but
> most of all when I obtained the enjoyment of
> the body of a person who loved me . . . I rushed
> headlong into love, eager to be caught. . . .
> Happily I wrapt those painful bonds around me;
> and, sure enough, I would be lashed with the
> red-hot iron rods of jealousy, by suspicions and
> fear, by bursts of anger and quarrels.

This is surprisingly modern. It is a journey inward, an intensely personal scrutiny of the depths and heights of inner thought, the kind of thought that developed with silent reading.

As a contrast, consider the classical thinker Cato, who was bound to the second-dimensional immediacy of oral culture. His thoughts were more powerful, more disciplined and more focused than those of Augustinus, but he was incapable of inner thought. "Delenda est Carthago" (Carthage must be destroyed) was his constant refrain, hammered home within the marble columns of the Roman Senate. By his words he meant killing or enslaving all the inhabitants—men, women and children—sowing the fields with salt, removing the culture of Carthage from the face of the earth forever. He could arrive at a brilliantly logical policy, but he could not empathize with the Carthaginians. His thoughts could never encompass the feelings of the Carthaginians. He had no space in his mind for negotiation.

Augustinus, on the other hand, developed a rich interior world that, while distancing him from Cato's logical immediacy of thought, gave him a perspective from which to embrace the experience of others. He was on the threshold of a new evolutionary leap to the third dimension of thought.

As bishop, however, he apparently suffered a relapse:

he began burning heretics. And in the sixth century, a hundred years after Augustinus and the brief burst of interior reading, there were no signs of people reading silently. As an example, we can look in on Benedictus, who established the Benedictine order in a community north of Rome and south of this Cistercian monastery. Imagine the hills of Tuscany with their steep folds of rich brown earth, where the community of Benedictus occupies the top of a ridge. Vineyards and crops are planted in terraces that drop away from the ridge. The buildings enclose a square, at the south side of which is the church and at the west, the dormitory for the brothers. The scriptorium and library form the east side, and the refectory and gate the north. There are no windows. Benedictus and a few brothers are sitting around a table in the library, a long, low, barrel-vaulted room whose walls are covered with religious scenes. The brothers are writing the *Rule of St. Benedict*, which prescribes the monks' daily activities. They write by first speaking the words, next honing them to get just the oral words they want, and then memorizing them. Finally, the scribe writes them laboriously on the precious, scarce parchment. One of the rules governing reading after the day's end is:

> From the fourth hour until the time of Sext, they will devote themselves to reading. But after Sext and their meal, they may rest on their beds in complete silence; should a brother wish to read privately, let him do so, but without disturbing the others.

From the way this is written, it seems that reading would ordinarily have disturbed others. Why? The monks must not have been able to read without declaiming. They could not read with their eyes, only with their mouths. They were only capable of second-dimensional thinking. The animal appetites and feelings of first-dimensional thinking were repressed by the severe monastic disciplines.

After the death of Benedictus the monastery was destroyed and the monks fled. The empire that had seemed so secure was dissolving in chaos. In the eighth century a manuscript of the *Rule of St. Benedict* turned up in the monastery of Montecasino, where during World War II so many American soldiers were killed as they stormed its heights. Of all the perils from which they thought they were saving the world, one of the more important may have been the salvation of reading from Nazi fires.

Both before and after Augustinus's time, there were others—Tertullian, for example—who practiced interior reading, but even in this last late blooming of classicism, when more books were published than ever before, the culture remained oral. There is little evidence of physical evolution, even less evidence of the evolution of thought. We must be content with fragments.

It is puzzling that in the hundreds of years after Benedictus, there were not even fragments to mark the interior development of reading. Sin was considered behavior—something one did, not thought—and its forgiveness, "satisfactio," was also considered an action. Penance was behavior, and even dreams were thought to be external events acting on the person. Only God was inner.

But beginning in A.D. 1000 there were evident signs of interior thought. Medieval law and monastic rules began to emphasize intentionality as well as behavior in ethical considerations, and by A.D. 1200 "contritio," interior repentance, was receiving more attention in the literature. One reads with increasing frequency of the recognition that sinners had thoughts. Even so, evidence of the development of interior reading is rare. Even Saint Thomas Aquinas in the thirteenth century declaimed his words in order to write them, speaking aloud until the words were polished. Only then would an assistant copy them down. How can we account for the evolution of interior reading and thought that had to have been going on in those years leading up to the Renaissance? My fantasy is that contemplation, that most inward of medieval mental journeys, provided an outlet for those who were able to internalize words and read silently.

In any case, without war or political transformation, trade or technological breakthrough, without a new system of ideas or ideology, without overwhelming exterior influences, the oral people were left behind by successively more and more of a new breed—interior people evolving invisibly toward a third dimension of thought.

Within two hundred years after Aquinas, the Renaissance was upon us. We call it the rebirth, and it must have seemed so. Cosimo de Medici was smuggling into Florence copies of classical texts bought from Arab traders. The Golden Age of Greece and Rome would be reborn.

But was it a rebirth or a birth? Wasn't this a new kind of human being, capable of interior third-dimensional thought and reading? During those birthing years they transformed two-dimensional, flat-surfaced painting into three-dimensional perspective, they internalized logic and created science, they internalized the story and created the novel. For example, Hero invented a steam toy that Watt used as the basis for creating the steam engine, and Fernando de Rojas and others internalized narrative. In classical times, stories had an immediacy bound to culture. But Renaissance readers found an internal theater of mental experience in which they could step beyond the closed circle of oral culture.

Fernando de Rojas was a Jew living in Spain toward the close of the fifteenth century. At least, he had been a Jew before he prudently converted to the Catholic faith during the Spanish Inquisition. He wrote a play entitled *La Celestina*, which did surprisingly well. Even more surprising, more people bought the book than saw the play. By reading the book, they were discovering an interior life that was not available from the immediacy of the play.

The play was about a boy and girl whom circumstances were holding apart. They had hired a procuress named La Celestina to help them. But in the writing, La Celestina had gotten away from Fernando; she was sly and crafty, and she had written herself into the lead. The boy and girl were familiar, cut-out abstractions. La Celestina, however, had become a real person to Fernando. He had never before experienced a real person living in his mind. To him it was like being possessed by a demon.

I can imagine Fernando walking home one night. Rather than the broad, ordered streets of Milan, these are narrow with jumbled buildings crowding overhead in a blackness darker than the street. The figure of La Celestina appears at the corner of his house beckoning him on. He goes to his room and opens the window. Without lighting a candle he gets into bed. Sometime in the night he becomes aware that La Celestina is in the room with him.

He awakens with a start and jumps out of bed. "Did you come in through the window?"

"If you like." It is the first time she has spoken to him.

He backs away from her until he comes up against the window. A chaos of black roof lines is growing against the morning sky.

In wonderment he says, "A new world is coming."

La Celestina has moved against him. She reaches her arms up. The hairs stir on the back of his neck.

"A new world has come for you," she murmurs. "Let your thoughts have eyes, so your readers can see. Let your thoughts have ears, so your readers can hear. Let your thoughts have weight, so your readers can know the deep earth. Let your thoughts have blood and feel the beat of the heart's feelings. Do this, for the new world is coming."

De Rojas had managed all these things, and *La Celestina* became the first proto-novel. It was the harbinger of a new type of literature, a literature in which the reader was able to internalize the words. This kind of reading was an outward and visible sign of the evolution of third-dimensional thinking.

After de Rojas, Cervantes wrote *Don Quixote.* Our imaginations are still intrigued nearly five hundred years later by this crazy old don attacking windmills that he imagines to be giants. Why are we intrigued? Because we also can imagine windmills as giants. Moreover, we can imagine him imagining. When you read *Don Quixote*, do you feel pity for someone hopelessly insane, or do you sympathize with the first person to become intoxicated with imagination? He is on an imagination binge; yet his fantasies serve a rational, self-conscious purpose.

As he and Sancho huddle exposed, waiting through the night, they imagine the ground moving deep beneath them, and truly it is. New kinds of people are being born, people who can read silently, who can read words expressing rational thought and transform those lifeless words into the living world of their body's perceptions, sensations and feelings. Readers are beginning the slow healing of the predicament of the human species, that of being caught in a tragic struggle between two warring worlds— the second dimension of rational language versus the first dimension of the body's feelings.

Throughout history there have been individuals, perhaps even groups, capable of reading with imaginative inner thought. Queen Berenice in classical times may have inspired such a group. But it was not until the Renaissance that their numbers reached a critical mass, which, along with authors of genius, has made modern third-dimensional reading possible. The author is the explorer of inner mental spaces. The reader creates from the author's map a third dimension of thought. They were both equally the midwives of the Renaissance.

In the short five hundred years since the Renaissance, the novel has exploded throughout the world, and all kinds of people have been reading novels, imaginative histories, biographies and essays. Such reading depends on the reader's ability to follow imaginative triggers in the prose that cause the two antithetical dimensions of thinking to "fire" together and create worlds of a third-dimensional reality. Authors and readers of creative writing co-invent inner reality. The author cannot claim to empower our creativity, for that can come only from our own mental spaces, furnished and peopled by the author's clues.

It may be no coincidence that movements to abolish slavery in the Western world coincided with the proliferation of novels. People were developing new mental room. Their perspective could embrace the personal reality of the horrors of slavery. During the American Civil War, Eliza crossing the ice in Harriet Beecher Stowe's *Uncle Tom's Cabin* became reality. Eliza and Uncle Tom became three-dimensional characters created by an interaction of readers and author. They could exist only within the interior spaces of the reader's mind, but still they were a greater reality in the North than the exterior reality of slavery. Northern readers did not merely observe slavery, they came to know it as an experience in which they were participants. It wasn't that they had become more compassionate; it was that their beings had expanded to include Uncle Tom and Eliza. Anything that hurt Uncle Tom hurt them.

Compare that mental quality to the classical mind. How many people in classical times even saw slavery as repugnant, much less tried to stop it? St. Paul, for instance, preached love but did not inveigh against slavery. The classical mind was incapable of making the connection.

Evolution didn't go the way Nietzsche thought it would. He imagined his superman as superrational. It is true that the material aspects of our lives are vastly superior, but this is only because of our greater ability to accumulate information. Our reasoning ability has not evolved since the time of Plato or Pythagoras.

Rather it is interior, third-dimensional, imaginative thought that has evolved to form people with super inner spaces in their minds. A new evolutionary step has imploded to enlarge our interior worlds dramatically. It isn't that we are more rational, but that we have more space in our minds to encompass and care for others.

Compare reason to inner space. When a second-dimensional, rational sequence of thought has been completed, it ceases to exist, does it not? Like a computer, it is either on or off. On the other hand, when you read a passage that results in a vivid inner experience, a sense of the experience remains within you, connecting to other experiences, deepening and enriching you as the years go by.

Consider how you tested your environment as a child. When your parents called you home for dinner and you delayed coming, you were testing the consequences of your actions. As an adult, the consequences of your actions become more serious. Don't you find that the ability to create vivid alternative worlds in your interior spaces helps you to assess the consequences of your actions before you take them?

Even though the novel has proliferated in Western culture and is irrevocably associated with changes in our ways of reading and thinking, the old rational use of language is still with us. Evolution brings along what it builds on. The rational use of language is taking over, in fact, in our new electronic information society. This information society is good for us only so long as we keep in mind the differences between second-dimensional information thinking and the third dimension of imaginative inner thinking.

Let us review the distinctions between the second dimension of classical, or informative, thought, and the third dimension of Renaissance, or imaginative, thought.

Electrodes hooked up to your head can show brain-wave changes when you switch from reading three-dimensional books to second-dimensional books of information. These changes indicate significant differences in mental functioning, which means that we may be able to quantitatively define this newly evolved third dimension of thought.

Hunger for power through information is more immediately satisfied than hunger for power though interior mental growth.

A book communicating primarily information fills us up. But when we read a book in which our imagination interacts with the art of the author, we fill the book up.

Information is transmitted *actively* but received *passively*. Computers, rather than books, are its most effective tools. The measure of information is not in meaning but in the accuracy of the transmission. The third dimension of imagination, on the other hand, involves the interaction of active transmission and active reception. The author gives artistic birth to a written possibility that the reader's imagination takes away, to create his own inner mental reality.

Information is immediate to the mind. Imaginative third-dimensional reading has the depths and heights of inner spaces. Let us be aware of these different realities of thought: third-dimension imagination and second-dimension information. The moral of an old Sufi story goes, "Wisdom is knowing the difference between the contents and the container."

The container of our future developing world is information, which will proliferate regardless of what we think or do. Information can succor suffering humanity, but it can also destroy us. Interior thinking must keep pace with the information revolution. In Europe it has somehow done so. The bulk of Europeans have found where meaning and values are born and live. They have found how third-dimensional thinking and reading can transcend information. Let me present the future European Community—and war's end.

Think of small bookstores that specialize only in third-dimensional wares. There you find nooks with tables and chairs, perhaps a pot of coffee or tea and a cat—and a new world of interactive mind. War's end means third-dimensional books expanding into their own new ferment of writers and readers, children growing up in a culture that will expand their minds before they become stuffed with undigested information.

Through literature, increasing numbers of people in the European Community and in the United States have died a thousand deaths, lived a thousand lives; in France we have been miserable with *Les Miserables* and magnified with Montaigne. We have experienced *War and Peace* in Russia and have had *Great Expectations* in Great Britain. This common inner space is so pervasive that it is like breathing—we are hardly aware of it. Nevertheless, literature cuts through ideologies and nations, and it is saving us all.

We've had Dachau; we have gulags; what is hardly noticeable amid the noise of modern politics and the polarization of ideas is the quietly growing network of ordinary people internalizing experience to a third dimension of thought. We have the mental room to create and endure common inner experiences; we have the capacity for a new compassion.

THE THIRD DIMENSION OF THOUGHT

Our purpose in following this short history of European thinking is to disentangle the thread of radical change from the general development of thinking. First, what hasn't changed? The structure of our brains has not changed radically since classical times. What of our reasoning abilities? The accumulated benefits of rational thinking have opened the universe to us, but rational thinking itself has not changed radically. Plato could have held his own with most of today's academicians.

What has changed radically is the kind of thinking associated with literature, with perspective in art, and with the scientific-industrial revolution.

But how to get a perspective on this kind of thinking. . . . Ah, perspective! "How sweet is perspective," as Uccello said in Renaissance times. When you see one of

Uccello's paintings, you see a horse, perhaps, bursting out of the foreground with men and armies gradually receding into a distant landscape. You are seeing the scene in three dimensions even though the picture itself has only two dimensions. You create the depth and the distance in your own mind, from clues the artist puts on the flat surface. This kind of picture exists *only* in your mind. Isn't the thinking process a simplified version of being "lost" in a book?

The body's feelings—emotions and intuitions—are one dimension of thought. Rational thought is the second dimension, distinguished from the body's feeling. Think of the gulf of guilt and alienation between those two worlds of thought.

Finally, we have the evolution of a third dimension of thought. Remember in school flipping through *Julius Caesar* to pick up names and places, and then creaming the test? You were using second-dimensional abilities to comply with an educational demand for information. Then recall the time when, without educational pressure, you read *Julius Caesar* for pleasure. Without your noticing it, the printed words disappeared and you entered an interior world of sights, sounds, and smells. You could feel Brutus's sword shocking through Caesar's ribs and the bright blood violating the white marble statue. It was a world of three-dimensional reality. The people and places were whole and full of life. They were not ideas or abstractions of reality. They *were* reality—more real than external reality.

There are other ways of creating this reality— painting, poetry, scientific and technological intuitions. In all of them you use rational processes in the same way you use rational language in reading: to order and stimulate your body's feelings, so that the result is a third-dimensional reality within your mind. It transcends and enfolds the first two dimensions of thinking in a new kind of reality. Rational thinking and body feelings are incompatible in the exterior material world. They can only be fused within the mind.

This third dimension of mind appears to mark the farthest evolution of the human species. If this is so, then its interior reality both supercedes and informs rational reality and body reality. The third dimension of thought cannot exist in terms of the exterior world, but only in the interior spaces of the mind.

From there, according to the Nobel laureate Roger Sperry, it exerts downward causation through other layers of reality even to the quantum mechanics of nuclear particles.

I've had to dig back to an old notebook for Roger. We were having lunch at his home in Pasadena, California, near the California Institute of Technology, where he is a professor. It's appropriate that the father of the evolutionary "mentalist revolution" in science should also be interested in physical evolution. As I do, he has rocks all over his house, and the centerpiece is an ammonite fossil four feet in diameter (like a present-day Nautilus) mounted on the living room wall. He dug the fossil up near our land in Texas.

We were discussing a speech he had made that I had edited for an anthology, *The Reach of the Mind.*

Roger noted, "Above simple pain and other elemental sensations in brain dynamics, we find, of course, the more complex but equally potent forces of perception, emotion, reason, belief, insight, judgment and cognition. In the onward flow of conscious brain states, one state calling up the next, these are the kinds of dynamic entities that call the plays.

"It is exactly these encompassing mental forces that direct and govern the inner flow patterns of impulse traffic, including their physiological, electrochemical, atomic, subatomic, and subnuclear details. It is important to remember in this connection that all of the simpler, more primitive, elemental forces remain present and operative; none has been canceled. These lower-level forces and properties, however, have been superceded in successive steps, encompassed or enveloped as it were, by those forces of increasingly complex organizational entities. For the transmission of nerve impulses, all of the usual electrical, chemical and physiological laws apply, of course, at the level of cell, fiber and synaptic junction. Proper function in the uppermost levels depends to a large extent upon normal operation at the subsidiary levels. It is a special characteristic of these larger functional patterns in the brain, however, that they have a coherence and organization that enables them to carry on orderly function in the presence of considerable disruptive damage in the lower-level components.

"Near the apex of this compound command system in the brain we find ideas. In the brain model proposed here, the causal potency of an idea, or an ideal, becomes just as real as that of a molecule, a cell or a nerve impulse. Ideas cause ideas and help evolve new ideas. They interact with each other and with other mental forces in the same brain, in neighboring brains and in distant, foreign brains. And they also interact with real consequence upon the external surroundings to produce *in toto* an explosive advance in evolution on this globe far beyond anything known before, including the emergence of the living cell."

The third dimension must therefore be the radical change in human nature that Altiero in Italy calls "the major transformation that has occurred in the political consciousness of Europeans, something which is completely new in their history." It has taken five hundred years to reach a critical mass in Europe, and now we can see large-scale results of its existence.

Garret in Dublin says that change in consciousness has emerged for the first time in world history, "but like most important revolutions in the thought of mankind, it has happened gradually enough to have escaped notice . . . yet rapidly enough to be quite astonishing in the long perspective of a world history, in which the exploitation of man by man was the norm."

Claude in Brussels, noting that war has ended in Europe for the first time in history, sees this change as the distinction between the European Community and the rest of the world.

And the ecologically minded young people of Europe maintain that the change arises from their ability to hold in their minds several different ways of thinking simultaneously. This also describes the third dimension of thought.

This radically new kind of thinking satisfies all the attributes of the European Community which distinguish it from the rest of the world and from its own past. It also explains anti-Americanism as an orientation for the third-dimensional thinking that Europeans have found difficult to put into words. I have proposed using the label *the third dimension of thought*, but any label will work. What is important is for us to understand the interior creation of reality.

Anyone can experience it anywhere in the world regardless of race, sex, creed or intelligence. It is just that in Europe it appears to have reached a critical mass in the population. Although it has appeared in similar forms in other times and in other nations, only in Europe has the balance of thought shifted.

Critical mass means that this third-dimension of thinking has been spreading through Europe at an exponential rate since the appearance of *La Celestina* in the fifteenth century. If we were able to measure the reading of novels in Europe in terms of the number of people old enough to read, the rate of increase might look something like this.

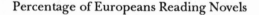

Percentage of Europeans Reading Novels

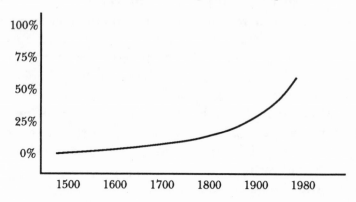

This is a new revolution in thinking that has found its way into the previously unpopulated landscape of novelistic literature. This third dimension of thinking is associated with reading, but there is no connection between literacy and the interactive creation of interior worlds in three dimensions. It cannot be learned through the pedagogy of education. Reason and memory are sufficient to do well in a multiple-choice world, but high grades or high IQs do not necessarily correlate with it. Rather, it is a mental ecological quality that grows best in free interaction. For example, time set aside for unrestricted reading during childhood is a good exercise for war's end. A truly radical change in human nature can be nurtured. It can't be taught.

Such a quality of being bypasses and transcends labels, categories, ideologies and all kinds of boundaries—boundaries between nations and boundaries between people.

The importance of third-dimensional thought for the European Community is not what it enables people to do. Rather, it is what it renders them incapable of—things like war, violence, exclusion and inhumanity.

We have begun to unravel the third dimension of thinking in the people of the European Community. I'm due in Geneva tomorrow. We'll see if we can find any evidence of it there.

ANOTHER DIMENSION

GENEVA

The old, sidewalk-crowding houses of Geneva lead to the bridge where the Rhone River spills from the lake in a silken rush. Near the shore of the lake where buildings crowd down to the water, a single jet of water shoots high in the air. Down past the old walled medieval city is a mansion in pinkish stone, which might be thought of as a palace if it weren't for its air of modesty. A doorman welcomes me and a man of great dignity receives me, takes my card, and quietly withdraws from the large hall, sumptuously but discreetly furnished. People move about peripherally in a hushed silence.

This is a unique institution, a private investment bank. The tellers are invisible, and money is never seen changing hands here.

The receptionist returns, escorts me to a gilded lift, and then pushes the button. When I emerge, a smart-looking young woman shows me to a small drawing room, the furniture from Louis XV himself. There are parchment-thin Limoges cups, an elaborate silver coffee service, and cakes set on a low table. An elderly man in a regal morning suit enters.

His face breaks from its air of contrived concern. "You old rascal."

We embrace. "Pierre, life has obviously been good to you. It's been too long."

Pierre gets us settled and pours coffee. "Ah, the good old days, they will not come again. The world is smaller, better but less exciting."

"Well listen, I have come to make it more exciting." And I tell him about my adventures in Milan with the third dimension of thought.

Pierre lays out some sheets. "So that was the reason for your request. Here is the information you asked me to gather from our computers. I've divided kinds of books into two classes: class A is fiction, historical fiction, literary history, literary philosophy, and so on, and class B includes technical, professional, sports, reference, how-to books, workbooks, textbooks, cookbooks, gardening books, and so on."

Picking up the sheets, I say, "Class A books are about third-dimensional thinking, books that use make-believe, that involve us in making up inner worlds or in thinking about ways of thinking. Class B books, on the other hand, are informational, consigning 'facts,' ideas, ideologies, systems for controlling the actions of machines and people. They're information books, about *what* we think rather than *how.*"

Pointing to the sheets, Pierre says, "Class B also includes how-to books, but here is the relevant part. The third-dimensional books tend to go to Europe. The information books go to the developing world."

"Aha! Some things begin to come together. It seems I

didn't catch on to what Federico Mayor, the director general of UNESCO, was saying to me. He kept emphasizing 'information,' the 'flow of information.' You're right; the books going to the Third World are 'information books.' The theme of the International Publishers Congress this year was The World Hunger for Books. It should have been 'The World Hunger for Information.' And—this is interesting—I discovered in Paris that the world hunger for books theme originated with UNESCO but was used by the International Publishers Association. Also, UNESCO funds many PEN centers around the world. Listen, right now UNESCO's International Board on Books for Young People has programs in Argentina, Brazil, and other countries in the Western Hemisphere, as well as in Asia and Africa. And it's the anti-American bureaucrats whom the UNESCO system protects from accountability who are choosing the books."

"I think you're letting your anger at UNESCO distract you from what is relevant," Pierre says. "My figures show that more than three times as many people read today as did sixty years ago. Actually, there are 3.5 billion more people reading today than sixty years ago, and in Europe the figure comes to hundreds of millions. To put it another way, eighty-five percent of all the readers and writers who ever lived are alive today. Is it any wonder human nature is undergoing a radical change?"

Looking at the printouts, I say, "You mean there are billions more people who can read today than there were just sixty years ago? Think of the impact of adding even a hundred million people to the numbers of Europeans who sop up most of the third-dimension books."

I hand the printouts back to Pierre. "Let me back up. I can see more clearly now what Lazlo meant. He said UNESCO really existed for Europeans, that its services in other countries were a mere rationalization for its actual function. UNESCO has been a center for developing European thought because it was created by Europeans and has been controlled by Europeans. O.K.? Well, try this on.

UNESCO export information, or B, books to developing countries primarily, and most of the billions of new people who can read are located in these countries. These people are reading but are not experiencing the revolutionary new third dimension of the mind. Most of the A books, the third-dimension books, go to Western countries, especially in Europe.

Pierre is letting excitement overcome his banker's facade. "Can you see the meaning of hundreds of millions of new people experiencing the third dimension of reading in Europe? The critical mass effect could be what is fostering the European Community. As you know, a banker tries to keep track of his customers, *how* they think, what is relevant to them, to use your phrase. What they think, whether they're capitalists or socialists or communists, isn't as important as their relations with each other and with the bank. I've been watching a long, slow change in how people think coming to fruition in Europe.

"I've kept something for you from a speech by Hans-Dietrich Genscher, currently the foreign minister of West Germany." Pierre hands me a clipping: "The progress of the European Community is one of the promising world trends. By creating a community of twelve European democracies, we won a victory over national egoism, power-political thinking and prejudice. It is the greatest and finest victory in the history of Europe. It has not cost one single human life, yet it is winning us the future."

After I finish reading the clipping, Pierre considers his coffee cup for a moment. "So how does one know if this third-dimensional grace has fallen upon one?"

"Simple. If you read a book and interact with the author to create an inner reality, you are experiencing the third dimension of thought. The book may be anything from a romance or thriller to a classic. The quality of creation may vary, but remember, the quality is in you, not in the book. Because it is individual, there is no way to predict which book would be associated with the best quality experience in your mind.

"There is no prescribed course or how-to system to confer this revolution in consciousness on you. Evolution has bequeathed it to the human race—not equally, but neither does it favor one particular sex, or race, or creed or class, or country. At the moment the European Community simply happens to be the first region to have experienced a massive shift of people toward third-dimensional thought.

"Think on this also, Pierre. The third dimension of thought is best compared with ecological consciousness. It is new in history. It is not an idea or an ideology or a belief. It is not a moral or ethical system. An enlarged interior self creates the reality within itself. In this state of being, you take care of others as naturally as you take care of yourself. Friendship, trust, love, business and professional relationships deepen to a richness never before experienced. There has never been anything like it."

Pierre stirs. "Would you say that an enlarged understanding would be an apt description?"

"You're asking me, Pierre, but I'm not an expert. Isn't that a lovely situation? No one is an expert on the third dimension of thought. There is no discipline or system to describe it. It belongs to the human race, a gift of evolution unasked for and largely unrealized. It's like being an air-breathing fish crawling up onto the land, a world no one has yet spoken for."

"Not to spoil your vision," says Pierre, "but I'm going to suggest a benign systematic approach. You have traced thinking from a first dimension of mute, unconscious body feelings, which are a whole and undifferentiated part of the natural, living earth. It is certainly to our advantage to introspectively become aware of this somatic state of being, which includes athletic prowess and health and which may include aesthetic intelligence."

"Okay, Pierre, I'll suggest a couple of ways of sneaking up on the first dimension of thought. Did you drive in today? How much of what you were doing were you aware of? Wasn't it your body's first-dimensional mind that got you here rather than your self-conscious, language-based thinking? More of our time is first-dimensional than second-dimensional. Now try this: Close your eyes and become aware of a person, a loved one, but do not make any comments about this person to yourself. Let the presence of this person rise up within you. Your body knows 'all about' this person, but this is a mute unconscious knowledge.

"Now describe the person to yourself in your own words.

"Do you notice a difference between your first 'all-about' feeling of the beloved person and your second, linguistic description? You may discover you are reducing the person to parts, to certain characteristic behaviors, colors, clothing, hair, eyes, etc. Rational thinking tends to distance itself from its object."

Pierre gives it a try. When he comes out of his trance, he says, "Yes, that's helpful. I'll work on it some more. This second dimension of language, self-consciousness and reason is easy. In our information society, reason is largely expended on the communication of information. Even a brilliant, logical conclusion that advances knowledge does not necessarily lead to understanding anything other than the logical steps that led to it. But, as you say, it gives us dominion over our world.

"The third dimension allows an inner understanding that changes us. It becomes wisdom and gives us dominion over ourselves."

"Very good, Pierre. I agree. But the availability of the third dimension of thought doesn't mean it is used. The air-breathing fish could have turned away from the land and returned to the sea. Many did. How about this: If you have it, use it or lose it."

"Let's see how this applies to business," says Pierre. "My clients, ninety percent of whom are Europeans, are just as greedy, parochial, nationalistic and violent as they ever were. But although a Frenchman may not like a German any more than he did during World War II, he has room for him now in his life and in his business. *How* he thinks about Germans has changed. He has become more tolerant of different kinds of people; they have become more relevant to him in spite of their differences.

"Well, what has happened to me personally is that I have gradually come to have a compelling conviction: There will never be another war between Europeans. I expect most knowledgeable people, if they dig into their subconscious, will agree that war within the European Community is unthinkable. But when they do voice such a thought, they pass it off with something about nuclear deterrent or the Russian threat and NATO. But we have had similar deterrents in our history and they have never stopped our warring before. No, this isn't that sort of thing. It's more like your third dimension of thought, something new and deep and pervasive. This is a mystical kind of conviction."

"Pierre, I'm sure you've made the connection between your definition of the changes in how your clients think and this conviction of yours. You've spent a lifetime successfully judging people, and I expect you've incorporated the deep-seated qualities of your clients on a subconscious level. I think you may have a prophetic conviction that is important to all of us."

"But I can't find any ideology to account for a change like this."

"That's why I'm getting interested. Your intuitive conviction is reality rather than ideology. It is about this new dimension of thinking in human beings. Listen to this: 'A major transformation has occurred in the consciousness of Europeans, something which is completely new in their history.' Altiero Spinelli said that. And he sees it as having happened within the sixty-year period of your book-reading figures. You're in the best company. Carl Jung spent years probing the collective unconscious. I think you're underestimating the weight another hundred million readers of third-dimensional books can have on Europe's collective unconscious.

"Remember George Steiner, the great professor of literature who teaches in Geneva? I talked to him in London. He said that we live in a twenty-four-hour envelope of cable television around the earth that leaves our perceptions so dispersed and overloaded with irrelevant immediacy that we are unable to focus on reading sufficiently to gain the rich inner worlds it promises. He was very pessimistic. He said the classic age of the book had lasted only a brief four hundred years and was now over. He wasn't sure literature would survive.

"Well, he's just wrong. He's got the cart before the horse. His classic age of the book is just now coming to fruition. With hundreds of millions more people reading, it seems to have shifted a balance in the collective unconsciousness of the European Community. The banker of true genius is tuned into the unconscious psyche. That accounts for the prophetic quality of your conviction."

Pierre rises. "I must tell you I expect a more thorough analysis later. But I know you have your London plane to catch."

"I'm sorry to be in a rush, Pierre. I promised I'd be in London tomorrow and then go on to Oxford for the graduation ceremonies. Your conviction is important. It makes a pattern with my recent experiences, and it's prophetic. We'll get together on it soon. My friend Francis King, the English writer, says words are more powerful than the bomb. I hear the same feeling from Francis that I do from you. Remember, THERE WILL NEVER BE ANOTHER WAR BETWEEN EUROPEANS."

THE OLD CITY OF LONDON

Flying back to London—which takes only one hour—I find myself thinking about a discussion of the third dimension of thought at the annual meeting of the Folio Society. This is a London book club which met last year in the opulent vastness of the Merchant Taylors' Hall in the Old City.

Jonathan Miller, a fine human scientist and popular film director for the BBC and the Old Vic, was present at the meeting. Miller exemplifies this change in European consciousness. He has the confidence to go beyond the boundaries of nation, science, and arts, even though they are at times mutually contradictory. Further, he is able to use them all in his life. His is the kind of thinking that we in the United States must understand in order to adapt to the changing world. "Literature conjures mental images," he said. "The images we have as a result of reading, recalling, or imagining are of a different order than the kind of impressions we have when confronted by images on the screen."

He suggested that we could all visualize Pierre Bezuhov in *War and Peace* as a real living person, even though Tolstoy doesn't tell us how many buttons he has on his waistcoat. Readers create those details as they read, with the author as their partner. There is no partnership in film because we have nothing more to create than when we see a scene out a window.

Marshall McLuhan first made this distinction when he called reading a "cool" experience and film a "hot" experience. When we read in the third dimension, we do not see the words on the page; we experience people and places. The words give us artistic clues from which we create an inner reality that is uniquely our own.

The "hot" medium of the movie, however, is similar to our perceptions of exterior experience. We do not create Dirty Harry from artistic clues; he burns himself into our senses.

Miller gave some other examples of his lively literary perceptions. Flaubert does not describe the ballroom in *Madame Bovary*, for example, only the candles on the tables. Yet his readers create for their own inner mental spaces a ballroom complete with movement, colors, and textures.

The meeting was a beautiful exposition of the third dimension of thought, which I see informing the European Community. At dinner tonight we'll discover how it's informing Oxford University.

THE OXFORD-CAMBRIDGE CLUB

My taxi is driving by Buckingham Palace down the Mall alongside St. James Park. Across the park are the Thames and Parliament. We turn off, going by St. James Palace for a short block and around the corner, and there is the Oxford-Cambridge Club fronting on Pall Mall. A familiar sensation of security and cozy belonging takes over. The columns framing the tall marble entrance are just a little shabby; the swinging double door still tries to catch me in the back as I pass through. Mounting the wide expanse of worn marble steps to the dining room on the second floor, I remember the teas that we used to have in the library. The library occupies the entire third floor and has high ceilings, panelled walls, great upholstered leather chairs, and books, books, books everywhere. The old, lean, white-haired men who seemed to live here had favorite places that everyone respected, and each seemed to be reading two or three books at a time. This was an abode of the third dimension of thought, something I didn't understand at the time. I realize now with a shock that I'm also one of those old, lean, white-haired men.

In the dining room I meet four young people—three boys and a girl—about to graduate. Could I ever have been that young? A tall, dark, severe-looking boy appears to be the leader. He introduces us to the delicate, blond girl, to a short boy, and to a blond boy whose dewy fresh skin I'm sure the girl is envying.

The leader is determined to keep things formal. "The weather is perfect, and everything is blooming in Oxford. I'm sure you will be pleased. How was your flight?"

"It was fine. It's only an hour, you know, to anywhere in Europe. It's like commuting to work every day in the United States. I spent part of my hour rereading some passages in a special book, *Unequal Partners* by Garret FitzGerald. Has anyone read it?"

Silence.

"He's been the Irish Prime Minister."

The leader, on an indrawn breath, says, "Ah, yes. I don't believe we have read any contemporary Irish politicians."

The English have a special tone of voice they reserve for the Irish and lower forms of animal life. I had forgotten.

"You should read this book. Oxford is one of the great centers of thought in the world, and the Bodleian is one of the world's great libraries. Surely it will have a copy. Dr. FitzGerald has an intriguing theory, that people have begun to manifest a way of thinking in the last sixty years that is new and unique in the history of the world."

The blond girl looks interested, but the leader quells her enthusiasm with a cold glance.

I continue, "The examples in the book are economic: Rich nations have begun to help poor nations."

"Of course everyone at Oxford has been exposed to theories on the redistribution of wealth," the leader says.

"Yes, redistribution theories are not new. Dr. Fitz-Gerald says that what is new is the *desire* of the rich Western countries to help the poor countries, an enlarged sensitivity to other people's lives."

The short boy titters. "Er, Dr. Howell, we do study history at Oxford, but I'm sure I've never read of the rich desiring to help the poor."

I've gotten myself in trouble with these young people by bringing up an Irish authority. "Then let me recommend Dr. Morris Berman, the philosopher of history. He would suggest studying history as a story of what is relevant in people's lives. Here is an example of a new condition in Europe that agrees with his theory: I have just left a French banker who has figures on the huge increase in reading during the last sixty years, which we believe correlates with the end of war in Europe. He believes the thinking of Europeans has expanded so that they can imagine others as real, living, breathing people rather than as rational abstractions. His prophetic vision is that this change is irreversible and that there will never be another war between Western Europeans."

Still no reaction. I try bringing them out of themselves with a Marshall Plan ploy. "Let me challenge you all: I claim the United States has led the way in this enlargement of sensitivity in Western culture. Prove me wrong."

Silence.

I know they are able to challenge me, they're just choosing not to get involved.

The blond boy with the peaches-and-cream complexion is trying to get into the conversation.

His eyes brighten and he says, "Dr. Howell, do you know what the sign on the W/C at the House of Lords says?"

"No, I don't."

"Peers."

It takes me a minute to get it, then I break up. Just what I needed, a good belly laugh. The English ability to get over embarrassing confrontations is one of their highest and best qualities.

Gasping, I say, "Are you sure?"

His face is pink with gratification. "I speak from personal experience."

Then the two of us go off again. Everyone else is frozen with disapproval. The blond girl is glancing at the ceiling. Hanging life-size above our table is a painting of Lord Palmerston in all his golden glory. He has been inhibiting the group all through dinner—all except the blond boy.

As we leave the dining room, we exchange a look of friendship and understanding. The young man will go far.

Stopping in the club bar for help in recovering from my ordeal, I find myself staring at a painting of Wellesley above the fireplace. This one is also life-size. Wellesley is usually depicted as a heavy, hearty man on a horse in a battlefield of rain and mud. This man is a slender dandy posing in an elegant drawing room. His clever eyes appraise me. Below his beak of a nose, his handsome, careful mouth dominates the composition. He was chancellor of Oxford.

These English and their classical approach to education—they understood education as a process of maturation, as a recapitulation of the evolution of our species. They didn't think of education as dissemination of information, as we do today.

Some of that classical sense is still present. I remember a conversation with Margaret Spencer, whose insights into English education help explain the critical mass of the third dimension of thinking in the European Community. She is a BBC commentator and consultant and a "Reader" at the University of London. In American terms a "Reader" would be a supervising Dean. I admire and respect her work immensely. She has come to embody for the British people the vital importance of reading and education.

Try her *Learning to Read*. Its approach is refreshingly accessible after the succession of high-powered doom-oriented commission reports we have been receiving in the United States.

Despite our statistics and those from UNESCO about the growth of illiteracy around the world, Margaret Spencer says studies of British young people show that their grasp of the internalization of words in reading is better than it has ever been. Just through reading, the third-dimensional thinking heretofore limited to the upper classes has been spreading throughout the population. And people are beginning to realize that this kind of internalization of thought fosters learning that is pleasurable rather than work.

Margaret is a lifelong scholar of reading in Europe. She says that *more* young people in Europe are experiencing the third dimension of thought as opposed to the rest of the world upon which UNESCO focuses. She bases her understanding on studies in orderly European schools where reliable data can be obtained. For those who would enjoy following up on this subject, *Breakthrough to Literacy* and *The Cool Web*, a book in which she participated, are included in the reading list.

These studies are of fundamental importance in understanding that the growth of the third–dimension of thought is indeed significantly associated with the emergence of a radical change of consciousness in the European Community. It will be instructive to compare the experience of third-dimensional reading in American schools. Has reading experience at any level—much less third-dimensional—increased or decreased among our American young people?

Talking with Margaret I also discovered that one of the values of third-dimensional thinking—in her terms, the inner critical social engagement—in the European Community is that a continuity of interior experience makes it much more difficult to be manipulated by government policies. This is how people are learning to bypass boundaries.

No reading lesson can teach inner thought; people learn by doing, Margaret says, and European people have learned to make the critical distinction between the power of simple thought and the dangers of simplistic thought.

She calls the personal inner growth taking place in Europe a function of the confidence to take risks. Intimate, personal interactions are risky. Crossing boundaries, national or personal, while retaining one's integrity is risky. Children take terrible risks in order to develop. Adults who wish to continue to grow also need to continue taking risks. Europe has given its people a supportive environment in which they can take the risk of imagining themselves in someone else's place and someone else in theirs.

She says that in the European Community, child and scholar are linked by a continuity of interactive third-dimensional thinking. Out of this continuity develops a largeness of mind without which tolerance for the differences in others is only a sham.

To acknowledge the existence of others is simple decency; being with others through interior thought is hard, but it is being achieved in the European Community.

OXFORD

The next morning heralds a beautiful day at Oxford. We're punting up the Thames toward the Fairy Gate that leads to the city. A splash up ahead. A group of wildly carousing students, clad in black gown and mortarboard, have just thrown one of their members into the river. The Thames flows at the bottom of the Christ Church College grounds here. These students must have just finished their final exams.

Someone pulls us in at the landing. We climb the old stone stairs of the water gate and head up past the Christ Church Quad toward Oxford's High Street. It seems as though we have left the water to emerge into a different kind of liquid—layers of thought, thick and time-laden, that have settled here over the centuries. The walls of the other colleges, shimmering as though under water, crowd the street. It is a city composed entirely of colleges with just a few pubs and stores mixed in.

We're due to meet with a group of graduating seniors shortly. Here's the Bodleian Library and nearby is All Soul's College, a college devoted to thinking rather than teaching. Between the two, perhaps, resides the most important impetus to rational thinking and scholarship in the world. But the radical change in human nature for which Europe is the model hasn't yet taken place in its great universities.

The session with the students is in a crowded room with three oak-panelled walls and one of stone, with small, leaded-glass windows overlooking the street. The students are sitting on benches set against the walls and on chairs grouped around tables, wearing black mini-gowns, formal bow ties and mortarboards. Steins of room-temperature English beer are plentiful.

I ask, "Are there any American students here?"

A perky-faced girl speaks up, "Oh! There are very few American students qualified to go to Oxford. The ones that are here are just terrible. They don't know anything about England and they don't care to. We know every-thing about the United States. They feel so superior. They know they are going out and make a lot of money. They are so positive they will get it all."

A thin-faced boy interjects, "And then all is not enough for them. Here we don't think we are better than others."

I look at him closely. "I know you. You're taking a first, graduating with honors, and you don't think you're better than others?"

He flushes. "I may be taking a first, but that doesn't mean someone else may not be better at running a business, or be more aggressive than I am. But then, I don't value material things."

A serious-looking boy who appears to be with the

perky girl says, "I've competed with Princeton and Harvard in athletics. I don't put them down. They're just ordinary people like us. Just because we're part of the intellectual class . . . I don't mean class. . . . Er, aren't we all the same then?"

I fix on the thin-faced boy who's taking a first. "You don't think you're better than others at what you do? Yet you're willing for others to be better than you at what they do. Isn't there a better way to say this? An ecological approach perhaps. It's difficult to express."

He shifts uncomfortably. "You're right, it is difficult. For one thing, it's a feeling, a feeling that we are not separated from other people. We don't want to be separated, and we feel that it is important not to be. I can know in my mind a lot of different people doing different things at the same time; when I do that, I feel in my mind that we are all equal. That's very interesting. They are only equal in my mind. There is not that kind of room . . . except in my mind."

I am beaming at him. "Welcome to the European Community."

"What?"

"My theory is that the kind of thinking you are describing is exactly what has enabled Europeans to bypass their national boundaries, and institutional and personal boundaries as well, in order to find community. I'm calling it the third dimension of thought. Tell me, did you learn this way of thinking here at Oxford?"

He's embarrassed. "No, I've always . . . at least I remember when I read the *Scottish Chiefs*, and then I did all of Scott's Waverly novels the next summer. Perhaps it was during that period. But no, not at Oxford. We want precision and logic, as well as depth, here."

As we go on, I am thinking how innocent and passionate these kids are. They are ready for a new world and they are likely to get it. We talk about the coming European Community, about how England is indeed part of Europe now, rather than the owner of a world empire. They pick up the thought that there will never be another war between Western Europeans.

The session runs down. We exchange promises of keeping up and of goodwill. At the last I say, "I have a question I want to leave with you. We've been talking about new kinds of thoughts in the world and the new ways of thinking that have made the European Community possible. But there will be some very specific choices we will all have to make in this new world. No matter how equal you are, many of you will be leaders in a future England. When it comes time to choose between the European Community and NATO—and that time will come—which will you choose? Remember, it won't be a big decision, but rather a series of small decisions relevant to everyday living."

I can tell I've reached most of them. There are troubled faces. As they leave, with eyes averted they mumble their thanks. Finally, only the perky girl and her athletic boyfriend are left.

She says, "The United States and England are friends. You know we are. But . . ." Then she squeezes my hand, and she and her boyfriend walk out into the brand new world waiting for them. I have a feeling that the United States has just been relegated to a dusty corner of future European history.

All the colleges are out now and the street is filled with students. Still in their robes, they are carrying foaming bottles of champagne, drinking some and pouring most of it on each other. Cans of shaving cream are being sprayed around liberally. They don't know what they're celebrating, but I do. They're celebrating the new world of the coming European Community. And I know my country is not included.

Yet my spirits are lifted by the thought that I'm having supper with Brian Aldiss this evening. The comforting feeling, an enveloping liquidity of thought, comes back. The outlines of the buildings are a little wavy, as though a fish might easily swim out from one of the arches.

THE OXFORD HILLS

"Dislike the United States?" muses Brian. We are sitting in the two-story living room of his Edwardian mansion, ensconced amid the lushly wooded hills outside Oxford.

He stares into the fire, his expression becoming more rocklike. "I remember things most people don't. In '45 the war was over, but I . . . we here in England would have starved to death. . . . My gut remembers that. And all of Europe would have starved to death that winter if it hadn't been for the United States. We were saved by the simple goodness of the American people. The Marshall Plan was more than statesmanship; it came from the hearts of Americans, from a new kind of people. It didn't come from the newspapers that gave them information. It didn't take us writers to create stories that would focus on solutions. It didn't need rock concerts. It came from a free people who had the self-confidence and vitality to think freely and act freely, to go all the way with everything they had. That was the feeling I had of being saved by the United States.

"Times were simpler then." He sighs and gets up to stand by the mantle. He is a big burly man, though still light on his feet. "How was so much affection and respect squandered? Vietnam first, Nicaragua now. But that's not the whole story.

"You want to know why it seems that everyone in the world dislikes or has little respect for the United States? Look back to before Vietnam," he rubs his jaw thoughtfully and continues, "and look at the storytellers like me.

Part of your answer lies in thoughts, how readers create their own inner worlds out of the stories and images we writers supply them."

"Brian, do you ever get a sense of Oxford being under water?"

He looks at me sharply for a moment. "Yes, as a matter of fact I do, but it's more a sense of water rising. Time is sedimented here, turgid. What has transpired will not flow away. You know, I've spent most of my life here. My sense is that Oxford is securely moving into a long, unchanging future."

"Strange you should say that, Brian. The graduation revelry this night has seemed to me more a celebration of a turning away from the United States. I'm feeling a bit lonely."

We stand in silence looking out at the dark outline of the hills above us.

Brian's massive hand rests on my shoulder. "Perhaps you and your country have a lonely way to go. As you say about the third dimension of thought, it's the accumulation of the history of an interior dimension of thinking. But it's not more than you can do. It may be that you will come to understand that it is what you need to do. Remember this, I believe in the United States."

THE THIRD-DIMENSIONAL
SOLUTION

FRANKFURT

Two days later I'm with Franz sitting on a bench in the plaza of Frankfurt's civic center. The plaza is on open cobbled space by the Mainz River, dotted with restored medieval buildings. The sun is warm on our faces. Franz has recently sold his publishing business for a few million dollars and retired to contemplate life. He has always been a dour man, but the big publishing conglomerates like Bertelsmann gobbling up the smaller firms has left him more lean and cynical than ever.

I am telling Franz about my meditations at the monastery near Milan. "I started this pilgrimage seeking an explanation for war's end in the European Community. I found a revolution in consciousness which no one could describe. At the monastery I began to understand that it was an evolution rather than—or as well as—a revolution. During the Renaissance the emergence of enough people in Europe able to read silently made the invention of the novel possible. The novel exploded out into the world from its center here in Europe. The explosion was a measure of the growing numbers of people with the capacity for a third dimension of thought—my label.

"And so you see, you thought you were selling a literary product. But the product didn't exist until readers were able to integrate the author's linguistic keys with their body's feelings. The product becomes a three-dimensional inner reality more vital and compelling—and in a sense more true—than exterior, perceptual reality. Martyn Goff has developed a similar understanding of reading. I enjoy him immensely, a kindred soul."

Franz tilts his face to the sun. "I'll argue terminology with you after dinner, but I'm interested in Martyn. As, you know he was asked over here to encourage reading through the same kind of book trust England has. I believe he also got something going in the United States with your Center for the Book. It never did take hold here, we're so stiff-necked. I've always liked Martyn. How is he?"

"Martyn is fine. I saw him not long ago in London when I bought this Mercedes I'm driving, a '67, from a student at Oxford. The student and his friends are still chortling over how they cheated the rich old American professor. They don't know that I've already got the Mercedes sold. It's in good shape, and Heinz wants it for his son at the University of Berlin."

"When is Heinz going to retire? You told me Paul was pestering him. He should be ready to retire after that."

"Heinz will never retire. He will die at his factory."

A light-hearted demonstration has been going on in the plaza while we've been talking, but the sound of it has changed to an uglier note. A lone American soldier seems to have been caught in the middle of it. People are shouting at him and closing in. He appears not to know what to do.

Franz is off our bench and walking toward the soldier, speaking in high German style, "Ah, Lieutenant, we have been waiting for you. So pleasant to see you. . . ." And he steers him through the crowd back to our bench.

The lieutenant, a delicately featured, thin, young man, says, "Thanks. I think I was in bad trouble back there. What you did was very smooth. Stupid of me to wear my uniform, but I was on army business close by, and I had heard there was an inn near here that is frequented by literary people. Well, I thank you."

Franz takes his profferred hand. "Not at all. I am grateful to the American army. You see, in the last days of World War II I was a teenage private in the German army headed for the Russian front. I 'got lost' and headed west, hoping I could surrender before I was shot. A U.S. army reconaissance patrol picked me up. Not only did they not shoot me, they were kind; they gave me some food even though I was their enemy. That experience opened up the possibility of a new kind of thinking that has changed my life.

"However, you were not even born then. You were born into a kinder world and can hardly know what I'm talking about. I know the inn you mean." He turns to me and says, "Let us walk this young man over the river to Saxon Town."

We are seated at a worn table, steins of beer in front of us. The young man's eyes are shining. "Wow, everyone in here seems to know you. You see, I'm in charge of publishing at the army headquarters here. There's not really anyone for me to talk to around there. My name's Jim and I'm sure glad to have met you."

The sharp, aristocratic lines of Franz's face soften. "I've been in publishing. Tell me what you do."

Young Jim blushes. "Well, I guess 'publishing' isn't the right word for what I really do. I've got a million dollars worth of the finest printing, composing and graphics equipment that money can buy, and right now I'm running party invitations for the general's wife. The general comes in, says he'd really appreciate—get that, the general appreciate?—my printing these invitations, and I put on a big show and say we have all these important jobs (which are just junk) for the field, but that I'll pull them and do his invitations for him. He's so grateful! It makes me laugh, and it makes me sick.

"You know our troops here work maybe five hours a day, five days a week—except that many weekends we'll get passes cut for Friday and Monday and have a three-day week. I would like to get the soldiers writing and publish what they are thinking. But it's hopeless. The Germans here are tired of us, so we're isolated and bored—and with that comes a drug problem so bad that no one dares talk about it. There is no KP. Local people are hired to look after us. They run the essential services. And it's inevitable that some of the locals are Russian agents. If the Russians ever wanted to attack, they could immobilize us in our bases. We're useless."

A few beers later, we're all feeling chummy and Jim is saying, "This is all a charade here. We get all these top secret strategy analyses to print. If the enemy moves here, then we'll move there—even I could figure that out. But if anything should really happen, it wouldn't be like that at all. Our great generals are just reacting. They're not able or willing to understand how people in Europe really think. They're out of it."

Franz looks mean. "What do you think the United States Army should do?"

"Get us the hell out of here before we create more ill will than we've done already. Why spend our time on strategy and maneuvers when we're losing the people? Isn't that the first principle of warfare, the support of the people? Didn't we learn anything in Vietnam?"

When Franz looks mean, it signifies he's pleased. I expect he has found a protégé in young Jim.

Jim has left for army headquarters with Franz's

promise that they will meet again next week. His expression is of someone drowning who has just been thrown a life preserver. The sun is hiding behind the rooftops of Saxon Town as Franz and I walk along by the river. We have whittled out two little boats. Franz says, "Now!" And we hurl them into the river and race for the bridge.

Franz, pounding his fists on the bridge railing, says, "I'm ahead." As his boat floats under the bridge first, he says, "I win!"

He grabs me fiercely. "It's the first time I've won. You buy the dinner this time."

Trying to catch my breath, I watch the little U.S. boat bob away into the darkness settling over the river. "Europe has won; the United States has lost."

He puts his arm around my shoulder. "Ah, so you have noticed that, old friend."

We hold onto each other, getting our breath as we descend the steps off the bridge.

"Yes, I am beginning to notice."

The lamps come on overhead. Franz is studying me, scowling. "The United States must get its soldiers out. Do you know you have 250,000 troops here? Two hundred fifty thousand troops! Do you know what that means? The population density of Canada is seven people per square mile. But in Germany right now there are *eight* U.S. soldiers for every square mile—in addition to all the Germans. Every day they remain, the United States loses more respect and sympathy here in Europe. Gratitude has gone. The feelings of European peoples are changing too rapidly. There is an excitement that is not expressed, lying underneath people's thoughts. Europe will soon be a different place, a place in which the United States has no part.

"It started with Jean Monnet. I don't think you knew him. In his last years he was not so active. Let me see, he died in 1979 at the age of ninety-one. He had been working for what he called a United States of Europe since before World War II. He was a friend of your President

Roosevelt. After the war the Marshall Plan to save Europe both inspired him and gave him a platform. It was the big-heartedness of the United States, the striking ability to make room for the concerns of others that captured our imagination. I deeply appreciate the gift of the United States spirit, which was much more important than money or goods. . . .

"But," he stabs me challengingly with his eyes, "it is our thoughts and our spirit that have carried on while the United States has faltered."

I have a flash of Vienna and feel again my shame during the Hungarian revolution. "You're right about our faltering, Franz. It started at Yalta, but I think it was activated in our national unconsciousness by our betrayal of the Hungarian freedom fighters in 1956. No one will talk about it either in Europe or in the United States. We were all guilty, but the United States unconsciously agreed to accept the focus of the guilt. And the symbolic turning point was the assassination of Kennedy in 1963. I wonder if our involvement in Vietnam wasn't the result of our burden of unconscious guilt about Hungary. Vietnam was a place where we could make a stand—but it was the wrong place at the wrong time. We didn't have an understanding of our deep interior feelings before we acted. So we merely reacted."

I grab Franz's arm. "Enough, enough, I'm going to buy you such a dinner as you have never even imagined. Let's do it all. In the morning I must start for Bonn. After that I have a date with Heinz in Stuttgart."

BONN

Making notes late at night in the little walled town that is West Germany's capital, a feeling steals over me that things could get a little scary here in Germany.

There are forces here that threaten the European Community. The principal threat comes from the Europeans who seek a supernation instead of a regional community of nations. Another threat comes from the deep, genuine grieving of the West Germans for their brethren locked away in the prison of East Germany. The West Germans are deeply involved with financing East Germany and have opened the European Community and many of its sensitive hi-tech products to East Germany.

This has uncovered an unthinkable possibility in the minds of other members of the Community, namely, a Russian-German axis. The axis between Stalin and Hitler was the primary cause of World War II. England and France could have lived with the partition of Poland. We know this because after declaring war on Germany and expending millions of lives to save Poland, at Yalta they gave it all to the ultimate horror of Stalin's bondage. They have lived with that betrayal and much more, but at the time they couldn't live with the most primordial of European fears, the Russian-German axis. Today, after living for fifty years in the European subconscious, that unthinkable axis has become a real possibility. The United States and those European nations who have never been able to speak of their complicity in the betrayal of Eastern Europe at Yalta and their betrayal of the Hungarian revolution face the possibility that they might meet around a table one day to face what finally led them to embark on World War II.

The breakup of NATO is also unthinkable, but it has become an imminent possibility. The North Atlantic Treaty Organization was established in 1950 by the American NSC-68 report, which welded together Europe and the United States in defense against Russian aggression. To question this unity has been unthinkable. But in fact, West Germany is even now beginning to pull away from NATO. The Germans are complaining that NATO has designated their country as the place where short-range nuclear missiles would fall in the event of a Russian attack. They are more frightened of being destroyed by NATO's nuclear missiles than they are of Russian tanks.

But the real reason NATO may be dissolved is the lure of the Russian-German axis. It is the only way West Germany can achieve union with East Germany. It could come about through an uneasy treaty between German power and Russian power. Or it could happen through Russian domination of Germany. Either way, the European Community would be destroyed.

If there is doubt about this as a possibility, let's take up a new word in Europe, *Genscherism*, taken from Hans-Dietrich Genscher, West Germany's foreign minister. If you recall, Pierre in Geneva mentioned a speech of his. Although he is West Germany's foreign minister, he is also an East German. During World War II he was a young Nazi in the town of Halle. Following the terms of political arrangements begun at Yalta, we Americans transferred Halle to Russia. Herr Genscher fled to the West and made his career here, but he still returns to Halle frequently. His body is in the West, but his heart remains in the East.

Listen to this pudgy man address the Bundestag, the West German Parliament: "The responsibility for the nation established by that oath [his oath of office] does not exclude my native region, the town where I was born, nor the people in the German Democratic Republic [East Germany]." Applause rippled through that normally staid institution.

This was a historic meeting of the Parliament. For the first time Herr Genscher felt confident enough to reveal the unexpressed secret of West German thinking. He is a creature we fashioned at Yalta and in Hungary, torn between East and West. He thinks of himself as a good friend of Gorbachev, and it must be clear to him that Gorbachev's peace offensive has the ultimate goal of separating Germany from the European Community and NATO from the United States.

Here is a scenario. West Germany, in its obsession to

join with East Germany, is sucked into an open border agreement that allows joint maneuvers with East German troops. Does this seem far-fetched? It is happening now! Anyone watching NATO commanders poring over maps with East German commanders on joint exercises must feel a chill running up his or her spine. For the sake of the scenario, let's imagine the nationalistic movements that threaten the stability of the Russian Empire growing more intense. In a paroxysm of repression, Russia plans the conquest of West Germany. The new party in power in West Germany is a "unification" party. When the joint maneuvers are planned across an open East German–West German border, East German troops, wearing new "unification" uniforms that resemble those of West Germany, just keep going through West Germany. Russian troops staying within East Germany immobilize the West German troops.

Within a day, East German troops occupy the critical centers of West Germany. Do the West German troops fight them? No. Not if hatred of American occupation troops has been skillfully manipulated. Do the American troops fight? No. Our bases have been sabotaged by the East German agents who are among those West Germans who maintain the bases.

Does this seem far-fetched? At this moment the U.S. government is investigating a civilian employee, Huseyin Yildirim, who worked at one of the most important U.S. posts in Germany. It appears that he has been operating an extensive East German spy ring out of our base since at least 1982. He worked as a mechanic at the base. If he had been an East German "sleeper" instead of an East German spy, he would have done nothing until the word came to sabotage the base. "Sleepers" are almost impossible to detect. There could be as many as a thousand working at our bases. In the last year alone 240,000 ethnic German refugees have been admitted to West Germany. The possibility that a significant percentage of them are on the East German payroll must be high.

We will assume in this scenario that all communications, utilities, and roads are now under the control of
the authorities of a "United Germany." Would the United
States make a nuclear response? No, it is unthinkable.
Russia could succeed where Hitler failed. There would be
no war. Rather, a high-intensity media campaign culmi-
nating in the reunification of Germany would result, and
the government would be dominated by the East Germans
and influenced by a resurgent Soviet old guard. A new
Russian-German alliance would be irresistible. The European Community would be shattered and the world in
chaos.

This scenario is not an extension of the Cold War.
The military threat of the Cold War is over. The war the
Russians are waging now is a war for the feelings of Europe with military power only one of an inventory of possible tools. The scenario is about how one thinks rather
than what one thinks. It would not be a war of ideologies.
In this scenario the Russians abandon ideology, as Gorbachev is doing, and focus on German feelings.

This scenario is not included in the United States's
strategic options because it is unthinkable. It is unthinkable because there is no *strategic* alternative. Remember
that the takeover would be accomplished in the sacred
names of nationalism, democracy and self-determination
for a United Germany. The United States would be paralyzed by our inability to bypass the boundaries of our own
ideology.

Our policymakers are not oriented to the possibility
of holding different paradigms of thought in their minds
simultaneously. Although the young member of the European Parliament could comfortably use the contradictory
paradigms of nationalistic, community-of-nations and international thinking simultaneously, U.S. leaders seem
unable to use the revolutionary new third dimension of
thought.

The rulers of UNESCO taunted us with the idea of
one-nation, one-vote, a structure we initiated. We were

paralyzed in our thinking and could not bypass that structure in order to act effectively within the organization. In this unthinkable scenario of a Russian takeover of Germany, we would be similarly paralyzed. Our leaders would have no alternative ways of thinking.

THE THIRD-DIMENSION SOLUTION

But there is an alternative. The European Community is a vital, self-confident community of peoples who share the most powerful force ever to exist on this earth—third-dimensional thinking. Russia, taking a ride on the European Community tiger, would be likely to come back inside.

If the best defense of Europe is this new spirit, it is something we must nurture. Neither money nor strategy will be useful to us. To nurture we must understand and use third-dimensional thinking in our relations with Europe. An excellent first step in this direction would be a mutually satisfactory plan to gradually remove American troops from Germany. Our troops would not, in any case, be a serious deterrent to aggression in a West Germany feeling sufficiently anti-American. Nearly fifty years after World War II our troops are still there as a conquering army, just as we still have our section of Berlin from the World War II agreements.

If there is any question in our minds about the status of our troops, we can offer to resettle them in France. The French would refuse indignantly. We must realize that our troops are an army of occupation left over from an outmoded treaty.

The biggest hole in NATO strategy—one that no one has wanted to admit—is the absence of France. France is Europe's largest nation, yet it has not been a member of NATO. However, with the development of the European Community, the stiff-necked French attitude has been changing. A French brigade is now training with the West German army, and all it would take to make France a full member of European defense would be an agreement for the gradual withdrawal of U.S. troops. France would need that excuse in order to participate.

The success of Russian aggression would depend to a large extent, first, on France being inactive and, second, on German hatred of American troops. If our bases were in the process of being deactivated, Germans would be feeling the economic losses personally. This is beginning to happen, but only symbolically; a mere four thousand U.S. troops are following their missiles out of West Germany. While this limited movement shows the possibilities for the future, a moderately staged withdrawal of U.S. troops would make the West Germans feel better about the United States. The West German troops would probably fight, and the military forces of the entire European Community could be brought to bear. U.S. troops would quickly arrive. Such an outcome could be an unacceptable risk for the Russians.

After negotiating a schedule for the withdrawal of our troops, our next step in the defense of Europe might be to begin discussions with European and Russian leaders on Gene Sharp's *The Politics of Non-violent Action*. It has already been translated into several foreign languages. Gene lays out specific plans for successful European resistance to aggression. In Afghanistan, Russians learned that aggression can become unbearable. We would also want to include Boserip and Mack's *War Without Weapons* and the British Alternative Defence Commission's *Defence Without the Bomb*. Also Liddel Hart's *Strategy: The Indirect Approach*. There is a growing sophisticated body of expertise on the very effective strategies of nonviolent resistance. The Russian leaders should be able to understand that the problems of successful aggression in Europe can be made almost insoluble if the European Community is alive and well and living on a third-dimensional mental level, able to bypass national boundaries, personal boundaries and the boundaries of paradigms of thought. The way to prevent a Russian-German axis is simple: third-dimensional thinking.

Another way to help nurture the spirit of the European Community would be to pay attention to their relations with Comecon (the Council for Mutual Economic Assistance). Its members are the USSR, the six Warsaw pact countries of Eastern Europe, Mongolia, Cuba, Laos and Vietnam. Unofficial participants include Nicaragua, Angola, Ethiopia, Afghanistan, Yugoslavia and Yemen. The European Community and Comecon signed a joint declaration of mutual recognition in 1988. Negotiations are under way to establish diplomatic relations between the European Community and the Soviet Union, Czechoslovakia, East Germany and Bulgaria. In the joint declaration, the European community held out for its right to deal individually with Comecon members, while they can only deal with the European Community as a whole, a very clever move.

STUTTGART

I pull into the grounds of Heinz's house hidden off a country lane. His house is still old-fashioned and spacious. Nothing has been moved since his wife died. His son, Erich, thin, dark, and intense, is home on vacation from the university in Berlin, and his daughter Marta is living at home with Heinz while attending the university in Stuttgart. Marta takes after her father, small and a little plump.

Paul, satisfied with his machinery, has gone back to London and his cross-channel tunnel negotiations. So Heinz is relaxed and pleased to see me. But his kids seem a little withdrawn, almost hostile; at other times they would hang around me with interest and affection.

Heinz has maintained his traditional German family life, and after a polite dinner the kids give us a delightful Bach concert, Marta at the piano and Erich playing the violin. They're good; they've been doing this ever since I've known the family.

We accomplish the transfer of my car to Erich as we end the evening in the library. It is a comfortable old room with three walls of solid books and easy chairs scattered about. Marta asks me to go with her to a meeting at the university the next morning. She has a glint in her eyes, and I suspect treachery, especially when Erich perks up and says he wants to come, too.

I notice that Erich has been reading a copy of *Pravda* printed in German. *Pravda* is translated from the Russian and reprinted in Vienna, an expensive undertaking, but I understand the demand is enormous.

"How do you like *Pravda*, Erich?"

Erich replies a little stiffly, "I like it very much. We get it the next day. We also get *The Moscow News* in German. It's republished here in Bonn."

"Pravda means truth. *Pravda* says they are telling us the truth under glasnost this year; so they must have been lying to us last year. I guess 'pravda' is a more appropriate name this year than it was last year."

A look of intense suffering crosses Erich's face. I try to make amends. "It's wonderful that Russian leadership has decided openness of thought is to their ultimate advantage. . . . I guess my generation just doesn't understand, hmmm?"

"Yes sir," says Erich fervently.

DOUBLE STANDARDS

Next morning at the university, we're shown into a large, bare, white-painted room decorated with life-size posters of Sitting Bull. The professor sponsoring the activity shows us around. "We are collecting medicines and volunteers to go to the United States to help these oppressed peoples achieve self-determination," he says.

It's irritating to watch Erich and Marta assume their smug and self-righteous demeanor. They should have been around on the Texas frontier. The Comanches were the deadliest light calvary ever to sweep across the face of this earth. They determined themselves without any help. I remember the cut bank of the creek on our place where my family hid from the last Comanche raid. Their great war chief was Quanah Parker. His mother was Cynthia Parker, a white woman taken captive on one of their raids. The Indian always took the name of his mother's family. Our county in Texas is called Parker County. Quanah used to go to Washington in all his beads and finery to astonish and impress government dignitaries. They didn't realize he was actually making fun of them.

American Indians surely have a right to self-determination. But if West Germans want to talk about helping poor, oppressed people to achieve self-determination, what about the rights of the East Germans, the Polish, the Czechoslovakian and the Hungarian people? The Bulgarian and the Romanian people? The Latvians, Estonians, and Lithuanians? I doubt if there is a German organization at the university dedicated to going into any of those countries and working to help those oppressed people.

As we leave, I say, "Erich do you believe that even with all the glasnost and perestroika one can conceive, Russia will allow the countries of Eastern Europe to leave its empire? Gorby has warned that pluralistic parties do not mean that these countries can leave Russia's "socialist" system. What about your countrymen in East Germany? Are they not—in the midst of glasnost—still dying on the electrified wire at your border as they try to escape to freedom?"

Erich shouts, "That is our affair. You stay out of it. Stay out of our affairs!"

He is too mad at me to drive us home, so Marta and I
take a taxi. She huddles in one corner looking upset. I
used to make a grotesque face at her that would send her
off. I try that.

She giggles. "You are terrible." Then she looks
puzzled. "Why did he shout like that?"

"Maybe he didn't want to have to face the double
standards that were being applied: one for the Russian
Empire and a different one for the United States."

Marta nods slowly. "Yes, I see. A double standard
erects walls to outside thought. Why, that would be a kind
of self-imposed censorship, not letting ourselves realize
that we accept the bad things the Russians do but get all
excited about some bad things the United States does."

"Yes, it would be replaying the honest, honorable,
comfortable Germans who didn't want to hear the
breaking of glass on Kristallnacht."

"We young people will never be like that. We are
different. Erich is just going through a stage."

"I hope so, Marta, because you're the ones who are
going to have to bring Europe into being as a free, open
society of self-determined people who are capable of an
enlarged sensitivity to thought from wherever it comes,
even from old, worn-out, used-up Americans."

Heinz is taking me on one of Germany's fast trains
this morning. His firm had a small role in producing
some of the machinery involved.

Erich drives us to the train in the old Mercedes I had
bought him. He's going to drive it on to Berlin.

As he lets us out I give him a hand-drawn map.
"Erich, here is the route to take to Berlin. If you take this
little road here, you can actually see the East German
border. But if you take the main roads and are careful
where you look, you will never even notice the double-
spaced fences of electrified wire or the mine fields or the
killer dogs and killer soldiers that patrol the border.
Most West Germans take care never to see the border, just

as good Germans of another time managed to be unaware of what was happening to the Jews."

Erich grits his teeth and grinds the gears as he speeds away.

FAST TRAINS

The train is speeding through the green German countryside at two hundred miles per hour, but we seem to be just floating along. The water in the glass isn't even vibrating. This is one of the cars rented to business as a commuting office between the cities of Europe. It has a complete electronic center with fax and phones and television. The car has work areas, couches and easy chairs.

Heinz says, "There are twelve members of the Community now, and soon there will be eighteen. They will represent more than 400 million people with a gross national product far in excess of the United States's." It will be the most powerful influence in the world.

"Does it remind you of the time when the original thirteen states of your country were evolving from the Articles of Confederation to your present constitution? The world was never the same after that, although here in Europe we didn't realize it for a long time. The United States wasn't powerful, but it changed the thought of the world; it changed the way the world thought about self-determination, freedom, equality.

"The change we are instituting here in Europe is the transcendence of nationalism. There will still be individual hatreds of different kinds, but there won't be mass patriotic hatreds. We're leaving behind primitive nationalistic emotions.

"Here we are all able to talk to each other on a common ground. It was the businesspeople, not the politicians, who first learned to have this room in their thoughts.

From one of the comfortable couches I reply, "It's the fact that your businesspeople have a common literature that makes possible the growth of deep interior thought."

I read Heinz an excerpt from West German Chancellor Helmut Kohl's speech in Brussels: "It is also about giving the Community a social dimension, a common monetary base, and achieving understanding in the largest possible number of fields, in foreign policy and also in security policy."

"Have you heard Peter Koestenbaum speak, Heinz?"

"Yes, I was one of the German businesspeople chosen to attend one of his international sessions. I have also read several of his books."

"Well, over the years he has mentioned various conversations with European businesspeople that have astonished me. I remember his telling about one time in England when an executive was arguing for a particular marketing strategy; to make his point he quoted a passage from Shakespeare—from memory. Someone else noted that Milton's metaphysics threw quite a different light on the proposal—and the executive proceeded to quote Milton from memory."

"What's so astonishing about that?" says Heinz, "German businesspeople frequently speak in such a manner. After all, we are civilized."

"Come on Heinz, you're just rubbing it in. You know American businesspeople don't go around making literary allusions to each other. Peter also told me about an argument in Italy between two executives who quoted Montaigne and Descartes to stake out their positions.

"The atmosphere in your house is of decades of living with books. There is a sense of the continuity of rich inner lives, what I'm calling third-dimensional thinking. But tell me truthfully, what's your feeling about other European businesspeople?"

Heinz looks out the window for a moment at the German countryside. "It's tradition. The middle classes since World War I have been expanding, pushing both the aristocracy and the peasantry out of our cultures. Yes, the people I know—executives, middle management, and senior workers alike—live in an atmosphere of reading and thought, as you call it, a "third dimension." It is not their level of education but rather a tradition passed on from one generation to the next to be careful, to take thought, to test consequences inwardly before actually trying them out. There are times when just holding a familiar book in my hands induces a kind of creative, reflective contemplation that I find useful in my work."

"That explains something to me, Heinz, about the policy of your unions toward the European Community. You know, their leaders look so prosperous and proper. In Brussels, Mathias Hinterscheidt, the secretary general of the European Trade Union Confederation, said that the German unions have the most to lose when the national trade barriers are abolished in 1992. And I think he was also expressing the feeling of unions in France and the Benelux countries. Labor is cheaper and less demanding in southern Europe. He said the average German worker gets about eighteen dollars an hour—the highest in Europe—while a Portuguese worker gets about two dollars and fifty cents an hour for similar work. In 1992, there are bound to be shifts in production and labor between countries.

"However, what struck me most about the German unions is that they are not opposing the dismantling of national barriers, and they say they have no plans to do so. They seem to feel a mutual responsibility to serve society, as well as to be served by society. They're not just thinking about their own interests."

Heinz's eyes sparkle. "Yes, we Germans are the best. You know that union members sit on my board of directors. It is true now all over Germany. It is called Mitbestimmung, co-determination or something like that in English. We have a thirty-eight-hour workweek and a

month's vacation yearly, yet we are the most productive
nation in the European Community. It's all based on the
quality of the individual. Our workers are highly educated
and motivated. And yes, their quality comes from
deliberate reflective thinking and care.

"But the European media are another matter. My
feeling is that these people read little, have no culture of
reflective thought and have few inner resources to understand the consequences of their actions. This lack is even
more true in the emerging information culture of computers—and it is beginning to extend to intellectuals.
Their lives are not as grounded in traditions of personal
libraries as they were in the past."

"But what about the Greens and Greenpeace, Heinz?
I'm becoming interested in the potential of these young
people."

"I can't say that I am sympathetic to their style of life.
It is not oriented to a culture of inner reflection. On the
other hand, they seem to be developing the kind of
thought you describe as the third dimension, and in some
cases they are even going beyond it."

Sometimes Erich startles me with his grasp of
interacting processes on a scale that is beyond me.

"They are creating an interior reality of ecological
relations and consequences that may be greater than I can
even imagine. We are about to be replaced, my friend. But
perhaps we are in view of a pleasant future."

We are pulling into the station and Heinz is
practicing his sales pitch. "When the tunnel under the
channel is finished, we could go all the way by train at
two hundred miles per hour. You know our new superconducting trains will soon be operating commercially."

"You mean we Americans have developed the new
lower-temperature superconducting materials and you
Europeans have stolen a march on us, putting them to use
before we have done anything with them? We Ameri-

cans are running as fast as we can to catch up with Europe, but the train is pulling away and we're going to miss it?"

"I'm afraid so." He smiles. "But remember, there is always another train."

PART Four

The Meaning of the
European Community

THE RUSSIAN HAMMER

STOCKHOLM

The northern nations of Sweden, Norway, Finland and Iceland, along with Austria and Switzerland, do not belong to the European Community. They have been paralyzed with fear under the Russian hammer and, as neutrals, have formed their own trading group called the European Free Trade Association. Now that Russia has recognized the European Community, however, the original pressure has diminished. The date 1992 will also mark the establishment of the European Economic Space, a comprehensive agreement between the European Community and the European Free Trade Association. It is assumed that 1992 will also mark the beginning of a gradual merging of the nations of the European Free Trade Association into the European Community. Norway and

Austria are already making preliminary moves in that direction.

The European Community will inevitably loosen its commitment to NATO and to the United States in order to bring the neutral European Free Trade Association nations into their fold. We had better be prepared, because it will happen. NATO was based on a two-super-power nationalism that is no longer viable as the Russian military threat is perceived as diminishing. This is another reason that the purpose of NATO diminishes.

I remember the clear waterways and green pines that make Stockholm the Venice of the midnight sun. In Stockholm the presence of bookstores everywhere and the nature of even casual conversations reflect the prevalence of third-dimensional thinking.

My thoughts turn to the émigré Russian poet Joseph Brodsky, who received the Nobel Prize for Literature in 1986, and I pull out my notes on his acceptance speech.

> "The Nobelstiftelsen, its wood paneling reflecting soft swirling light, is the ancient hall where Brodsky is to receive his Nobel prize. The Swedish king enters and the ceremonies begin. "Your Majesties, Your Royal Highnesses, Ladies and Gentlemen. . . .
>
> "For someone far from his motherland," Brodsky says, his round puckish face still young looking, "it is better to be a total failure in a democracy than a martyr or crème de la crème in tyranny. Regardless of whether one is a writer or a reader, his task consists first of all in mastering a life that is his own, not one imposed or prescribed from without, no matter how noble its appearance may be.
>
> "Literature is not a byproduct of our species's development, but just the reverse. The point is

not so much that virtue does not constitute a guarantee for producing a masterpiece, but that evil, especially political evil, is always a bad stylist. There is no doubt in my mind that should we have been choosing our leaders on the basis of their reading experience and not their political programs, there would be much less grief on earth.

"Literature is much more dependable than a system of beliefs or a philosophical doctrine,' he says. 'I have no wish to darken this evening with thoughts of the tens of millions of human lives destroyed in Russia in the first half of the twentieth century in the name of the triumph of a political doctrine. The number of people who perished in Stalin's camps surpasses by far the number of German prison camp victims.

"And I am speaking precisely about literature, not literacy. Lenin was literate, Stalin was literate, so was Hitler, Mao Tse-tung.

"I who write these lines will cease to be, as will you who read them, but the language will remain, not merely because language is more lasting than man, but because it is more capable of mutation."

God bless you, Brodsky. You have revealed the secret of the kinds of thoughts that are nurturing the European Community. Those who read and internalize literature are less prone to human destruction and more capable of human community.

Brodsky represents the new third-dimensional people who do not wish to be martyrs to "someone else's logical idea." To writers like Brodsky, who have escaped life on the edge of the abyss, the Russian Empire is "a utopia smelling of corpses," to use his words.

It is the small forces, like "less destruction" and "more community," in the people who are patiently developing the ability to internalize thought that will move the world. Policies, ideologies, treaties, and alliances will all fail unless they are built upon the third dimension of thinking.

When the northern countries join the European Community, the border with the Russian Empire will have moved northwards to the limits of land, from Greece in the Mediterranean to the Arctic Sea.

As the train arrives at the West German border, the fear exuded from East Germany becomes palpable. This is the most dramatic physical interface between the anvil of anti-Americanism and the Russian hammer. East Germany is the best example in the last fifty years of the differences between the accumulation of third-dimensional thought in the European Community and the repression of thinking in the Russian Empire. Like anti-Americanism, life under the Russian hammer is a good way to understand the European Community by experiencing what it is not. Leipzig is a good example of East German living. Juergen Gunther, a man I admire, lives there.

LEIPZIG

Leipzig is an interesting East German city because it has few Western visitors, yet it is East Germany's second largest city. The first reference to Leipzig appears about A.D. 1000 as a town at the foot of a castle.

Leipzig has a rich ancient tradition. Movable type was invented in the mid-1400s by Gutenberg in Mainz, Germany, but Leipzig became the publishing center. By 1500 Leipzig had twelve publishing houses. Goethe went to school here; in fact, one of the most famous scenes in his *Faust* drama takes place in Leipzig's Auerbachs Keller Tavern, which opened in 1615. The Hans Zum Koffeebaum has been in business since 1500, its entrance ornate with Turkish carvings.

But things are a little bleak these days. The square, now called Karl Marx Plaza, has that communist look of being reserved for ordered mass demonstrations. Individuals crossing it look conspicuous and vulnerable.

Nevertheless, Leipzig is still a major publishing and university center. It's an appropriate point from which to gain perspective on the influence of the Russian empire on the European Community.

Juergen Gunther is head of Boersenverein communist literary publishing in Leipzig. I have always been a sucker for communist academics and literary people. They tend to be charming, punctilious, cultivated and sincere, and Juergen's a model of the type. He is an elegant dresser, a serious thinker and a sincere devotee of literature.

The list of the books he publishes is a treasury of the world's classics. People living in this, the most repressive of Russia's East Europe, still have access to perhaps eighty percent of the literature of the past, even though they have no access to the free literature of the present.

I wonder what it would be like to live here in the prison of the human spirit that is East Germany. The material bleakness wouldn't bother me. I don't pay much attention to that sort of thing in my daily life. No one starves. People here are healthy. Those Olympic gold medal winners come mostly from Leipzig universities. I don't think my inner life of study and research would be much different. If it were my native country, I think I could live here fruitfully; Juergen seems to, except for a wound I have glimpsed opening its red mouth behind Juergen's eyes, a wound I had first seen as we sat in the countryside behind a small restored castle, sipping tea and conversing pleasantly, lost in the world of books and literature. The wound remains. I have been making sense of its meaning recently, here on the edge of the Russian empire.

Recently, the most adventurous East German writers, encouraged by glasnost, began to write tentatively beyond the line allowed for academic study, about the subject of human freedom. They and their publications were ruthlessly rooted out by the secret police, beginning with a raid on the library of the East Berlin Zionsgemeinde, until now they have either escaped to West Germany or they have been silenced. The East German censors have even banned the Russian publication *Sputnik* for its glasnost and five Russian films for being "too open."

THE EMPIRE

Even with glasnost, the only way to survive in the empire—that is, outside the westernized cosmopolitan intelligentsia of Moscow and Leningrad—is not to think. It is fine to be concerned with academic thoughts past and far away, but to survive, don't think about the present.

Nizametdin Akhmetov, a young poet from a nationalist minority in Russia, had been sentenced to the Gulag. When he persisted in thinking even in the Gulag, he was put in a so-called mental hospital. He says, "The medicines they feed and prick me with would be bought with pleasure by Satan for his hell. They seek to deprive you not only of physical liberty but also of mental liberty, to deprive you in fact of the capacity to think."

In some ways, however, Russian literature has been enriched by its readers and writers having lived so close to the abyss of nonthought. I can feel it when I am in East Germany—the need for thought, the need to touch my deepest feelings as if they are all I have left.

Living on the edge of the abyss, East Germans commonly refer to Americans as "soulless." Alexander Yakovlev, Gorbachev's right-hand man on foreign policy and the United States, feeds this kind of double-think. Ironically, in 1985 he wrote a book entitled *On the Edge of an Abyss*, the abyss being American power. To quote from it: "We must deal with a country where freedom is suppressed, where violence flourishes . . ."

This is an example of the real abyss, the two-dimensional kind of thinking in East Germany where freedom of thought is repressed with the violence of ultimate savagery.

Literature sees "the vomit on the floor," as in Albee's *A Delicate Balance.* Russian dissident writers in exile have benefited from the prevalence of Russian vomit on the floor. They are close to the distinction between the new age of third-dimensional thinking and the old age of second-dimensional rational thought. They can smell the difference.

Solzhenitsyn, author of *The Gulag Archipelago*, edited an early collection of essays entitled *From Under the Rubble.* He and other contributors have insisted on "the primacy of spiritual life over the outward forms instilled by education." Only individual thought matters. "We are history," says Solzhenitsyn, agreeing with Maury Berman that neither political policies, strategies, or ideologies can make human history, It is the deep thoughts of the psyches of enough people that make history. Solzhenitsyn and his Russian contemporaries have understood the necessary distinction.

Milan Kundera, a writer in exile from Czechoslovakia who is a Nobel laureate, also makes the critical distinction between third-dimensional and second-dimensional thinking, between "the novel that examines the historical dimension of human thought and the novel that is the illustration of a historical situation." The latter is nothing more than information put in story form. It represents the second dimension of rational informative thinking.

In his novel and movie *The Unbearable Lightness of Being*, Kundera describes the Russian invasion of Czechoslovakia twenty years ago. One night at dinner Lady Eccles had verbalized for us the horrors of that flight. She described how Soviet tanks rumbled into Prague in the night, and the country found itself occupied by half a million foreign troops. The ultimate horror, she said, was not the torture and executions, but the extinction of third-dimensional thinking. Interestingly, Lady Eccles is the wife of another Nobel laureate, the neurologist Sir John Eccles. That night Sir John confirmed her point, for he could scientifically prove that mind supercedes body, and thus that the destruction of mind is the destruction of the essential reality of the material world.

After the brutal repression of the Hungarian revolution, the Czech government of Alexander Dubcek still did nothing to resist the Russian rulers, but they did allow a faint glimmer of humanity that came to be known as the Prague Spring. They had been "good" communists. But the essence of Russian rule through fear was that people were always "guilty" and that they never knew when retribution would descend on them. So it was with Czechoslovakia.

Dubcek obsequiously and abjectly begged forgiveness, and Brezhnev, Russia's leader, stated the famous Russian doctrine, "Communist rule is irreversible." Dubcek became a nonperson, and his country was subjected to the brutal repression that Kundera described so well.

Twenty years later, Dubcek became a person again. He was even permitted to make a speech in Italy, during the time I was at the monastery in Milan. The Czechoslovakian government, however, had meanwhile embarked on a new program of thought repression to rival that of East Germany. The new Helsinki Agreement, guaranteeing human rights and the "effective exercise of those rights," had been signed at that time in Vienna by countries from all over the world, including Czechoslovakia. A few hours after the signing, the Czechoslovakian police attacked a peaceful rally in Prague, thus signaling the beginning of a massive terrorist campaign against citizens that lasted for six days. Fourteen hundred people were arrested, among them Vaclav Havel, the internationally known playwright. He was sentenced to nine months in jail. The Czechoslovakian jails are among the worst in the world, with little heating, scraps of garbage for food, and primitive cells packed to bursting with prisoners. Hunger strikes and suicides are daily occurrences. And, as in Kundera's novel, even after one is released, the persecution does not stop.

These are serious charges, but they are not disputed by the government. Gorbachev had said he would pull out some of the eighty thousand Russian soldiers stationed in Czechoslovakia, which may have set off this new repression. In the Russian empire there can be openness by decree one day and repression by decree the next.

The cultures of these East European possessions of the empire disclose the reality of the Russian empire. It is an empire in the classical sense.

As citizens of the United States, we find it hard to understand this reality. We are more than a union of states. Ours is a broad land that nurtures individuals of all races, nations or creeds. They can go where they want and with whom they want. The Russian empire, by contrast, is composed of many different nations. The dominant ruling elite is of Western stock and lives around Moscow and Leningrad in the Russian Soviet Federated Socialist Republic, the RSFSR. This elite rules an empire of fifteen republics—the Ukraine and Byelorussia, which are represented in the United Nations; Armenia; Azerbaijan; and the Slav and Siberian republics—plus Estonia, Latvia, Lithuania, East Germany, Poland, Czechoslovakia, Hungary, Bulgaria, and Romania. From the beginning of its history, the Russian empire has continued to grow through ruthless conquest and repression and by instilling overwhelming fear in its possessions. This imperialistic imperative *is* Russia.

Mykola Rudenko, a Russian World War II hero, writer and now expatriot says, "The Soviet Union is an empire encompassing entire indigenous nations, some large, some small and some of which are thousands of years old."

Akhmetov, the minority poet who survived the torture of Russian mental hospitals and fled, is now returning to Russia. He fears, however, that he will return to repression. He says that glasnost "is unlikely to extend to the national minorities in the Soviet Union."

His fear was demonstrated dramatically after the Armenian earthquake on December 7, 1988. On December 10th, even as people from all over the world were racing to help with rescue efforts, the Russian secret police were raiding the Armenian writers union headquarters. The secret police were using the disaster as an excuse to throw into the Gulag people who had been tagged previously as having dared to think. Members of the legislature were also included.

Rafael Popoyan, an Armenian literary critic, summarizes the situation. Bulky in his clothes, his breath blowing a cloud in the still cold air, he is standing in the square by the opera house in Yerevan, Armenia's capital. The square used to be filled with people listening to impromptu speakers on politics and the arts. Now it is empty, surrounded by Russian tanks. "Don't try to take pictures," he says. "You'll be arrested. They've seized this moment of tragedy to destroy the Armenian national movement for good. These troops could be helping earthquake victims. You see what Russian imperial priorities are."

Given the "bred-in-the-bone" Russian historical imperative, the empire will never let any of its possessions go. West Germany will never win union with East Germany except by allowing itself to become dominated by Russia. Jailers—and Russia is one—anywhere become brutalized over time, and East German troops and police, traitors to their countrymen, have become even more brutalized than their Russian masters.

Milovan Djilas, the writer and dissident from Yugoslavian communism, points out the dangers of the West German drive for union with an East Germany after nearly fifty years of Stalinist repression of free thinking. "The indiscriminate projection of Western values onto other cultures," he says, "is a sign of Western conceit and parochialism and is politically dangerous."

The United States participated in creating these dangers. The horrors of repression I have been experiencing vicariously in Eastern Europe exist because the United States betrayed these people at Yalta after World War II and in Hungary in 1956. It is the heritage of our betrayal from which they suffer. Eastern Europe has been a wound in the side of the European Community for fifty years, and it will always be a drain on its spirit. The European nations connived with us when we turned these peoples over to Stalin's butchers, but at that time the Europeans were weak and we were strong. The responsibility is ours. The reason for harping on this betrayal is that it has been repressed. We must somehow transform it from information into inner experience in order to understand the European Community.

At this point I find I have just received a letter from Lazlo.

Dear Dr. Howell,

Our mutual friend Paul asks me to convey to you his best wishes. As I said to you in Paris, I very quickly discerned that Paul is almost as cunning and devious as I am. Events have borne this out.

Paul interests me as a specimen of the type of person who has learned to internalize thought through reading, not novels, but plans, specifications and business prospectuses. Apparently, he internalizes these forms of communication into interior realities of the motives, thoughts and plans of the people involved in the business project.

He asks me to tell you that his involvement in the cross-channel tunnel is proceeding satis-factorily—thanks to me, I might add, if you would not think me immodest. The success of this project is important as a physical symbol of England's attachment to the continent.

If you are still where I think you are, I must applaud your choice. The winds of change blow most strongly against the ramparts erected against them. I'm afraid my friend Honecker does not sit comfortably on his East German throne these days. But we are not concerned with such as he. This note is merely to let you know that in spite of your disinclination to meet with me, you will soon have that pleasure.

Well, I have been pretty obvious since returning from the monastery, so tracing me here wouldn't have been difficult. However, I have no intention of meeting him. I can get along without that pleasure.

RUSSIA

We in the United States have bequeathed to the European Community the kinds of thoughts embodied in the New Deal and the Marshall Plan and, conversely, we have connived in the betrayal of thought in Eastern Europe. I have connived at a smaller betrayal. It is the story of a Russian friend of mine.

Andre, as I will call him, is a retired Russian professor of early European literature from Leningrad who had come to Harvard to do some work at the Wi-dener Library. He was blond with a thin face and fanciful eyes. He had been a decorated lieutenant in the Russian army during World War II and was smart enough to parlay himself into a university position that could not possibly get him caught in the middle of power plays within the party. His sponsor at Harvard was my friend George, a professor of Spanish literature. I was in international affairs. We three were young and romantic. We hit it off well.

George was just back from Spain, where he had found the proverbial old trunk in the attic full of undiscovered letters. Part of his find related to a character from a play written in the 1400s, the intriguing Spanish lady you will recall as La Celestina. We got in the habit of including La Celestina in our conversations. We began taking her out to dinner with us, demanding a chair for her, ordering for her. I remember one night we took her dancing at the Copley-Plaza. We would cut in on each other and finally got into a drunken altercation in three languages over her favors. Then we got thrown out.

We became fast friends. I started calling Andre *Tovarich*, or comrade. Andre returned to Leningrad. Due to his command of English and knowledge of America, he was asked to host groups of visiting scholars from the United States and England. Over the years we managed to keep up our friendship.

In those days, the Gulag system of prison work camps proliferated in Russian society, even in the cities. It is not so obvious now, but in past years you could see and smell it everywhere. The Gulag was not so much a prison system as a means of working starving prisoners until they died. You would see groups of barefooted women working on city streets guarded by lounging armed guards. Women especially were often condemned to the Gulag for merely talking to foreigners. Small Gulag forced labor camps were also built as part of forced labor factories with barbed wire and machine gun towers at the corners of the compound.

Now the Gulag has retreated to isolated locations away from the lives of Russian citizens, but it still exists. Despite what Gorbachev may say or try to do, the Gulag will always be there. In isolation the entrenched Gulag bureaucracy becomes even more immovable, less subject to directives from the Moscow intellectual elite.

Anyone over twenty in Russia knows this about the Gulag, and Andre in particular knows it. He knows it every hour of the day and every hour of the night.

To continue the story, Andre is still playing host to visiting groups of English-speaking scholars from the United States and England. Glasnost is upon us. Everyone is being open.

The rest of the story belongs to Francis King. Francis is a well-known British author and international president of PEN. He was responsible for a group of writers Andre was guiding through Russia. He is a little frail and this kind of travel is tiring. "It had been a good trip, much less suspicion than the last time. People actually were coming up to talk to us. We had just reached the Ukraine and settled into a standard issue hotel. I was aware of some local dissatisfaction with attempts to impose the Russian language on the Ukranians as the only language to be taught in school."

The Ukranians are not Russian. They read and write with Roman letters instead of Cyrillic. They are Uniate Catholics rather than Russian Orthodox. Their language and poetry predate their conquest by the Russians, and they still speak their own language. They are the largest of the Soviet republics next to the Russian Republic, the RSFSR.

"I was being pressured to come on a special side trip just decided on for the next day. I said I was just too tired, but it seemed that if I didn't come, the others wouldn't come. On the basis of our friendship I finally said I would go.

"It was a dreadful side trip, and I came back to the hotel exhausted. I opened my bag and went cold all over. My things had been searched! It had been well done. I would never have noticed if I weren't such an obsessively precise packer. In the old days one would have expected it immediately upon arrival. But in this case my good Russian friend, our host, had betrayed me. And through me he had betrayed the whole group. Through them, he might have betrayed some wretched Ukranian who had handed one of us some nationalistic protest literature. You could read the protests in the paper. People had freely voiced their concerns to us. To try to trap someone was pointless. It was insane.

"I couldn't speak about it the next day. Fortunately, the trip was almost over. We never spoke of it. I was deeply shaken. I will never go back."

Memories of Andre and his small betrayal have been coming back to me. Francis didn't speak. I must speak for him.

Andre, I know you as the best of the old Russian academic elite. I also know you personally as my friend from long ago. The story about you that I'm including in my book *War's End* is known to your government, and I think it is important that we feel comfortable putting it into words. There is betrayal in this story, and I'm including myself in the betrayal.

I had never really faced up to my knowledge that you had been around the Gulag archipelago all your life. You'd seen the gray workers with the hollow faces and dull eyes trudging past, just as the "decent" Germans had seen the gray Jews trudging past their cattle cars.

Why hadn't I ever questioned how you really lived? Because I wanted you to be good as I wanted to be good. I wanted a society in which material things were scorned and everyone worked for everyone else. I wanted that to work. It was a high-minded aspiration of selflessness, sacrifice and morality, a reaching beyond our grasp.

I had always gotten along so well with scholars from communist countries. We all lived in the high reaches of scholarly discourse. I had found myself beginning to live and survive just as you had, by never making the distinction between logic and mind, between information and dreams.

Why didn't I have this out with you when I could still look you in the eye, when you could still look me in the eye? Too late. Your commonplace behavior has put me in the position of being in the Gulag looking out.

Remember, we used to talk about the withering away of the national state as the ultimate goal of communism. Your little betrayal of Francis King, in a time of glasnost and perestroika, is important because it marked the gulf between the Russian system and the communist goal. But Andre, tovarich, there is a third-dimensional solution to heal this gulf.

It is happening in the European Community now. Nationalism is being transcended while national differences are being cherished and preserved. It is happening through the accumulation of a critical mass of third-dimensional thinking among the people of free Europe. It is the *only* way glasnost and perestroika can work in the Russian empire. It depends on a revolution in consciousness in the peoples of the empire.

I can see beginnings. We may not live to see it come to flower, but I have hope that our children will. We will not meet again, but perhaps we can share the hope.

Goodby, Tovarich.

IT WOULDN'T BE
MAKE-BELIEVE

LONDON: BLOOMSBURY

The flight from Berlin to London takes one hour and fifty-five minutes—I'll be in time to attend a luncheon at Francis King's. As you will recall, Francis was the leader of the writers Andre guided through Russia. He has a lovely old Victorian home with a small, classically designed garden in the heart of London, not far from Bloomsbury.

Francis has lived here forever, and the house is full of him and his art. The walls are solid with paintings, and behind each is a story of cunning acquisition in some part of the world. Tables are covered with eclectic treasures, books are piled everywhere; it is a cozy house filled to bursting with the past and with the physical manifestations of a long, full, literary life. To be intimate and personal with Francis, get to know his house first. Francis has recently been given a party to celebrate the publication of his twenty-third book. A visit to any London bookstore will find at least two or three of his titles.

Francis has prepared lunch himself. As he sits down at the table he is clearly a comfortable man, comfortable in his full face and slender figure, comfortable in his role as host. "We'll be going to Korea soon for the international PEN congress. Don't you think if political conversations between nations were more literary, they would be more meaningful? Otherwise, how do you know what you're saying, or want to say, without art? In Korea we will try to begin literary conversations that will transcend nations, because that is what art can do.

"I suppose literary America grew from literary London. We tend to hold the same social theories and liberal politics. Of course, I realize that literary America is diverse and uncomfortable with itself. Here, literary thought is cozy. We're comfortable with ourselves."

Francis broods over his dessert for a moment. "Let me say this very seriously. Literature changes you. The important distinction to make is that it isn't change in literature that changes you. It is literary thought itself, regardless of its nature. Literary thought is living thought; to live you must change. I think that's where we diverge from the United States. The underlying thought of our culture has continued to change. In the United States literary styles have changed, rather frantically at times, but the underlying thought of American culture has not changed. That's sad.

"In English—no, European—culture, as I've said, the word has become more powerful than the bomb. I'm afraid that hasn't yet happened in the United States."

I am thinking to myself that Francis is merely being polite, and what he really means is that he feels sad that Europe is outgrowing its old friends across the sea.

As I'm leaving, Francis says, "By the way, I'm going to be reviewing *Driving Miss Daisy* tomorrow. It's a play

imported from America. Would you like to come?"
Francis is also a major theatre critic. The only thing
modern in his house is the word processor connected
directly to the *London Daily Telegraph.*

At the theatre bar during intermission, Francis says,
"How astonishing that Wendy Hiller can become on
stage an authentic southern Jewish lady."

A friend comes up to us. "Francis, how are you? Have
you seen the flyer for this new play, *American Hero*?
There's a picture of a soldier in uniform coming out a
door with his duffle bag. The blurb says, 'When they
begin to make you a hero, look out. They're getting ready
to start another war.'"

It is worthwhile to listen to how others, especially
our friends, think and feel about us. They might be right.
We have made many mistakes: Vietnam, Grenada, Nicaragua. We've been nailed for our mistakes by our friends
and our enemies, and we have to live with them now.

But the feelings people have about us are more
important than our mistakes. Unconscious feelings generate words. The wordsmiths of Europe have scary feelings
about us. They seem to feel that we're unpredictable, and
meddlesome.

However, let's not forget there are other kinds of
smiths. For a dramatic contrast let's walk from Francis's
place through Mayfair past the Dorchester Hotel, the
entrance swarming with top-hatted attendants in livery.
Spending one night there would cost from four or five
hundred dollars up to thousands. Henry Kissinger would
entertain royalty and foreign ministers in a suite at the
Dorchester.

We walk on a short distance, duck through an arch
and find ourselves suddenly in the other England of
Shepherd's Bush. Shepherd Street is a narrow lane; just
down the street there used to be a market for common
folk. Here is a little luggage shop.

Meet Mr. Chase. He and his family before him have
been here for many, many years. "What do I think about

America? Please, I don't think about it. What is there to think about? Do you know what good leather is, how it gets that way and stays that way? This is a thing to talk about. . . . Although we do enjoy 'Dallas' on the telly. It's on mornings and evenings now."

Leathersmiths don't squeeze their feelings like wordsmiths do; their primary concerns are shoe leather and family, not the United States. But I suspect that the other London of Mr. Chase has the same deep fear that literary London has, of a United States where people don't know their place in society, where there are no unconscious social norms to ensure that everybody knows what others will do next. In England there is an underlying sense of belonging to a cozy continuity of living that does not exist in the United States.

In the 1870s at the height of Victorian England, parts of west Texas, for example, were blank spaces on the maps of the world. The land had never been inhabited; even the very few Indians were nomads. There are practically no human bodies buried in the soil there. Even our New England traditions are only hundreds of years old.

In the old world of Europe one walks on soil made of thousands of years of human bodies. And the residue of the human mind is just as deep—ancient human images of self-restraint and reconciliation.

But from across the sea, from the alien soil of America, comes a music wild and strange, always changing. . . . It is about living farthest out, about full hearts, innocent and naive. That music stirs a deep atavistic fear in European minds, a fear of unrestrained, uncensored human action.

Leaving Shepherd Street we walk down the Mall and across St. James Park to Birdcage Walk. On the way we pass statues of George Washington and Abraham Lincoln. The people who erected and care for those statues are our long-standing friends.

HYDE PARK

We're arriving at an Embassy dinner. Rolls-Royces are pulling up before the marble entrance. We mount the steps; a tall man in gleaming livery steps forward and takes my card. He thumps his staff on the floor and announces me.

Our friend John the editor, dropping cigarette ash on his vest, says, "I say, I don't think I want to go to New York again. I was reading how fiercely one is ostracized there for smoking. America swings to such extremes! By the way, I meant to mention the last time we met that the United States was copying an older England when Kennedy wrested the leadership of the world away from us without a shot being fired. His 'one brief shining hour' was real. Since we talked, my memory of those times has become clearer. I did believe in your Camelot. It was real for me here in England. Don't think that because you made it up out of your own thoughts that it wasn't real."

"Let me mention that some good things happened right after Camelot, John: civil rights, women's liberation, flower children."

"Of course, you were still following England's lead," John says, "phases we had already passed through, except for the dope, of course. We don't do that."

It seems that the people of Europe are more threatened by American chaos than by our big political mistakes. We are so young, so unpredictable! We make up values as we go along, while the continuity of literary Europe depends on restraint of action, on self-censorship derived from an understood norm.

After World War II, Europe had simple feelings of respect and affection for the United States. During the sixties these were symbolized by the Camelot archetype of America. The United States seemed to be a magic place of hope for the Western world. With the assassination of

Kennedy the magic of Camelot vanished, and Europe rejected the American archetype of hope for social images of a cozy despair.

Now Europe is changing again. There are more individual initiatives and there is less despair, but the underlying fear of what the United States may do next becomes discomfort on an intimate level. And discomfort is transformed into a pervasive dislike.

Turning toward the bar, I find Lazlo in front of me. He is decked out regally in all the finery he could put into a tux, with a couple of additional decorations to finish it off.

I push him into an alcove. "You've been messing in my life. There have been too many coincidences. . . ."

Lazlo smoothes his lapels with his fingertips as though I had mussed them up. "My dear friend, or enemy, it is up to you. My understanding of loyalty and trust is that they must come from the heart, not from outward circumstances, n'est-ce pas?"

"Well, yes, dammit. But what gives you the right to play God, Lazlo?"

Lazlo allows the intimation of a smirk. "I have occasionally indulged myself in that surmise."

I burst out laughing. "You're too much for me. Let's go get a drink."

With an elegant gesture Lazlo motions me to precede him. "I believe you were referring to your friend Paul. Let me assure you that he was quite discreet. I even wonder if he managed to get the better of me in our negotiations. He is deceptively clever. . . ."

"Sorry I blew my top, Lazlo. I've gotten in over my head. I started out to observe the European Community for a straightforward book. I've been running all over Europe like a hunting dog quartering a field for a scent. I've got a feeling for how ongoing events are fitting together in Europe, but I've got to work on pinning them down by myself. In the midst of all my friends, I find I'm alone in the European Community, just as my country is alone."

"No, you're not."

"What?"

"You're not alone. I'm going to help you."

"You don't understand. I have to go it alone. The feelings I'm following are interior, and I have to go back to the United States to be with my true self."

"I do understand, and I agree with you. But I can help you now. Tomorrow I'm driving to Southampton. I have reserved the best suite on a luxurious ocean liner for the last leg of its transatlantic voyage, which is to Le Havre. You can get a plane from Paris. I feel sure that on the way I can arrange an environment that will be useful to you in accomplishing your immediate task."

"I believe we're talking to each other now, Lazlo. No games."

"That is correct. No games this time."

"Well, let's drink to it. . . ."

"Then I will come by your house at eight o'clock in the morning."

"I guess there's no point in giving you my address. I'll be ready."

"As a matter of fact, I do have your address."

While we are standing around with drinks waiting for dinner, Lazlo and I are joined by John. Lazlo is saying to me, "Writers are image makers in a land of make-believe."

John, turning to him, says, "What do you mean, make-believe?"

Lazlo says, "Writers make us believe things."

John says, "No they don't. It's simple. A fact is a fact. You believe it because you see it."

"You are talking about images," Lazlo says. "You see someone being attacked by a dog. You receive an image through your eyes and you believe it. But the images of literature are equally factual. For instance, you read words about being attacked by a dog. If you are caught up in the literature, you're not even aware of the words; you see the dog and the dog exists in your thoughts. You 'make up'

the image in your mind, and you can make yourself believe the mental image even more readily than the
image you saw with your own eyes."

John says, "Well, let me point out that the quality of
one's belief depends on the writer of the words, the
storyteller. You wouldn't believe you saw a dog attacking
someone unless the images made a story, a continuity of
experience. Our knowing is narrative knowing."

"Ah, yes," Lazlo says, "truth, whether fact or fiction,
involves a story. How familiar. A good author strings
images together in a story to reach the inner spaces of
your mind. Check yourself the next time you are talking
about someone. Aren't you, in some sense, using the
information in the story as an excuse or to justify an
emotional feeling you have? And if you can become aware
of the emotion, don't you also become aware of the
images . . . ?"

Leaving John and Lazlo, each having met his match,
I come upon Brian Aldiss. "Give me the professional
writers who work for a living," he says, "not the American superstars who write one book and make a fortune.
However, I will say that the American professionals are
about to outdo us. . . ."

Nearby, Margaret Drabble, creator of the literature of
the Great Social Dream, is standing straight and indomitable. She has just spent the afternoon counseling a group
of foreign writers and will soon be off for more good
works this night. "These young ones," she says, "are in-
fected by the American Gimme Generation. They think
only of 'what's in it for me,' and they think only in
terms of money. It's a little sad."

As I turn away I can see through the two-story
windows the lights of the big village that is London
stretching out into the night.

I feel a surge of affection for all the kind, dedicated
people who have shared themselves throughout Europe. I
want to thank them and let them feel that it's all right to
dislike the United States sometimes. We Americans are

unique. There is no place on this earth that hasn't contributed its seed to the United States. With so many different kinds of people, it's hard to know who we are or even if we are. That's why we Americans need so much to have others believe in us. Wouldn't it be all right for our friends in literary London to dislike us if they believed in us? After all, they're mostly using their anti-Americanism to orient their own thinking. But we Americans are afraid that people who dislike us won't believe in us.

We can also sense that it is hard for anyone to believe in us: we have no roots, no common traditions, no soil that is comfortable with us being on it. We have only the contentious ideas of freedom and equality. We have made the United States up out of our own thoughts!

We have to make ourselves up all over again every day.

Europe is safe, cozy, warm and intimate, but how about a breath of fresh American air? It feels good—living all the way, not constantly concerned about fitting in and being comfortable.

As I leave, John and Lazlo almost tumble down the stairs after me. Lazlo is holding the editor upright. We link arms, and I say, "I'm going to teach you all a homely song. It's about my America."

Lazlo says, "I don't sing," and tries to pretend he doesn't know us, even though he is holding John up on one side.

And we walk down the street toward Hyde Park, singing "It was only a paper moon . . . Um, Um, what's the next bit? Umm, Umm . . . BUT IT WOULDN'T BE MAKE-BELIEVE IF YOU BELIEVED IN ME . . ."

Going to bed finally, with that tune still running through my mind, I'm thinking that my time here is drawing to a close and . . . what? It's true that we Americans are much too influenced in our actions and thoughts by the fear that other countries won't believe in us. We're vulnerable. That's the way we are and that's okay.

GOING ALL THE WAY

WINCHESTER CATHEDRAL

The next morning at eight my doorbell rings. At the door is a man in a chauffeur's uniform. Beyond him looms a gleaming black Rolls-Royce limousine. He takes my bag and opens the door. Lazlo is ensconced in the vast interior with a basket of fruit and snacks arranged on the bar.

"I thought we would drive on through," he says, "so I had Georges acquire for us a Fortnum and Mason basket. Orange juice?"

He settles back into the plush leather seat. "You and your editor friend were rather vulgar last night, tramping about an elegant section of London singing that ditty. What was it?'

"It was nice of you to help sober him up. I could tell you were suffering from the vulgarity of it all. I thought the so-called ditty was profound: 'It wouldn't be make-believe if you believed in me.'"

During the car ride, I tell Lazlo about my recent experiences and my theory of how an understanding of the third dimension of thought could pull all the disparate aspects of the European Community together. He is a suave and courteous listener.

We motor through King Arthur country, Stone-henge, Aylesbury, Old Sarum. As we near Winchester, Lazlo is looking thoughtful. He activates the intercom. "Georges, take us to Winchester Cathedral."

As we get out, he says, "This may suit our purpose. Pardon me for a time. I'll meet you in the library."

I wander up to the library, a series of low, barrel-vaulted rooms containing books from the 1400s. There is something magical about a collection of really old books, no matter what the books are. In a nook some women are seated at a table. They are taking books down from the shelves, carefully wiping each page and then returning them.

"Are you volunteers from the town?"

Nod, nod, "Yes," and back to work.

I ask the nearest one, "How does it feel?"

"What? Feel? Actually, I suppose it feels rather good. Quite good in fact. Of course, we do it because it preserves the books. Women from the town have been doing this for as long as anyone remembers."

"May I do one while you watch me?"

"Well . . . if you're very careful."

It does feel good, caring for these books. There is a concentration of quiet thought here, quietly persevering through the ages of the cathedral.

Lazlo comes in. "Ah, my friend, come, the cathedral awaits. I beg your pardon, ladies, for my intrusion."

As we leave, I'm afraid the women will start dropping curtsies. I wonder if Lazlo maintains his regal presence when he's in the bathroom.

"Have you bought Winchester Cathedral, Lazlo?"

"At the moment I have only rented it. They were about to close, and I was able to arrange for our privacy for an hour. No one will be in the Cathedral but you and I. Come along through here."

The Cathedral is an awesome place. The vast ceilings disappear into a dark glory, and from the stained windows a fading, many-colored light plays on the floor. The presence of a once and future king seems to occupy the shadows.

Lazlo guides me along one wall. "Here we are, the round table of King Arthur. I am unable to recreate Camelot, but I believe the atmosphere here is as close as one can come."

We climb up a short flight of stairs to the altar. The only light in the Cathedral is above the choirmaster's stall behind the altar where there is room for us to converse.

Lazlo sits but I remain standing by the altar. "You know, Lazlo, in this place one can only tell the truth. I thank you for arranging this situation, but if you want to go with me, you will have to go all the way."

His eyes shift for a second, then he straightens and looks at me sincerely. "I think, my dear man, I will only speak the truth to you in this place, and I have already discerned that you are incapable of less." But there is a palpable tension in the air, and I have obviously touched a nerve. Lazlo has more riding on our meeting than I had realized.

"I have had your briefcase brought in as you requested," he says.

I move over to sit by Lazlo. "Listen, why did you decide to stop here?"

"I chose this place because the literature of King Arthur has been part of the living thought of Europe since the 1400s, and together with the potent myth of Camelot it is therefore a sanctuary charged with the energy to enable us to continue our discussion of the third dimension of thought."

"You're using my word, Lazlo. Please tell me your feeling about it after our discussion this afternoon. I think I laid out my findings pretty thoroughly."

"I would be happy to. I agree with your theory, and it seems to me that this kind of thought exists in a tenuous but glorious reality that is more real than the exterior world.

"Briefly, as I understand it, many different people internalize and share the same deep thoughts. These thoughts become interactive when each person adds something new to them. The thoughts become progressively enriched and, by their collective forces, eventually become an entirely new way of thinking. As it develops, one might say that it becomes an added dimension of thought.

"Such a point of view does not appear too outré when one considers that in the last fifty thousand years, our brains and bodies have not evolved at all. Yet in that same period of time certain ways of thinking have evolved exponentially.

"Indeed, some say that what is in one's mind is the reality, that thought looks into the material world as though looking into a mirror where it sees itself. This is how thought evolves, just as one changes by first seeing oneself. The novel has become the center and the symbol of this evolutionary development of thought."

"My word, Lazlo, that is brilliant and succinct. Listen, I want to respond to that by introducing you to the character I mentioned this afternoon, La Celestina. She has become a true third-dimensional person living in my mind over all these years. Are you game?"

"Indeed I am."

"Well, in my mind she stalks into this circle of light wearing a tight Spanish dress. She gives you a hot glance, and she says to you, 'So you think to dismiss the novel as a thing when it is *me*? I have had many books written about me. How many books have been written about you? I am a woman who, when you get me in your blood, you cannot get me out; you are in thrall.

"'Me, I am eternal. As long as there are men, I will live. And I become more, not less. I will tell you how this happens. You think in words, and they are logical. You know them. Now, they sink down into the bed of your feelings, your deep desires, which you do not know and which do not have words. The you that speaks can never know them except through love. Only in the bed of love— and trust me, I know everything about it—unbeknownst to you, a new life is born. A new kind of being. It lives only inside you, and you are possessed. You will never be free again. You are forever changed.'

"So, what do you say, Lazlo?"

Lazlo seems amused. "I would reply to her, 'Madam. I can hardly argue with one of your considerable experience.'

"Let me assure you," he goes on, "that thoughts have consequences. Thoughts can kill and they can heal the physical body. When I use the word *thought* in this context, I do not mean theories, ideas, logic or reason. Neither do I mean opinions and other surface kinds of information. These can neither kill nor heal nor evolve. I mean, rather, the deep feelings we manage to integrate with rational language and share with one another. These are the springs of the third dimension of thought.

"I can only say that third-dimensional thinking is evolutionary. It never supplants but always builds on what is there. For instance, in the European Community, people informed by this thought do not deny their nations. They keep what is useful and learn to work around the problems, such as rigid national boundaries, in order to arrive at community. We can say it is ecological because it is whole and enfolds all life."

I'm getting the creepy feeling that Lazlo is trying to draw me out in order to win me over and use me, somehow, and I think the third-dimensional material was what he was waiting for. I wonder what his purposes are, if this is all a sham.

I pick up my briefcase. "Well, I'd like to show you some small artifacts of the new European Community that you may have missed."

I take out and unfurl a flag with a circle of twelve yellow stars upon a blue background. "The flag of Europe. A year ago it was seldom seen. Today this flag is seen flying everywhere throughout the European Community. It is all the rage."

Then I remove a watch from my case. "Here is an item found in all the stores; it has become very popular. This Eurowatch marks the hours with a tiny flag for each member of the Community."

"Here is something else you may not have seen. This maroon passport will replace all twelve passports now being issued. This represents common citizenship in the European Community.

I take a small binder from my case. "This is a decision of the European Court of Justice in Luxembourg. It may well be the most important action the Community has taken so far.

"Listen, Lazlo, this is a decision involving civil small-claims cases, and I am familiar with its provenance. In such cases, one of the parties is often poor and unable to afford professional legal representation, putting him at a disadvantage compared to the party who can.

"To remedy the potential for inequality before the law, the Court has directed national governments to simplify and clarify their small-claims laws and courts so that any citizen can understand them and represent himself.

"You might say that it would be simpler to assign a public lawyer to represent parties unable to hire one—that is a solution in the United States—but the European Community has chosen to confront a unique, fundamental question. To what does equality refer? What is its object?

Is it I, myself, who am equal before the law, or is it my interests? Is it my thoughts, my values, my soul that are accorded equality before the law, or am I to be merely an abstract entity, an interchangable part in a state-created adversarial game played by professional lawyers? In such a game, I am powerless, and my lawyer's only purpose is to serve the self-interest of an abstract person.

"But the European Court of Justice is to be applauded for finding that your self-interest is a paltry thing compared to yourself. The Court decreed that the state must not confront you as an abstraction but as a person. For the first time in history, the function of the state has been transcended and altered in order to accommodate the consciousness of people. The Community recognizes that if I am able to interact as myself, I will grow and become an ever more valuable member of my community. My maximum value to the Community is my participation as my full self.

"It's not like me to make speeches this way, but I am simply overwhelmed in this case by the wisdom of the Court. It heralds a new kind of human relationship and affirms the fundamental role of the Community as the nurturance of the radical change in the consciousness of Europeans. In such ways is the European Community made possible."

Lazlo seems genuinely moved. His eyes shining, he says, "I must say that it is a monumental decision, and your description and experience are something I have been waiting for.

"I am fascinated by your small exhibits, which I have, in fact, overlooked. Please go on."

I hold up a sheaf of bills. "Here is the new European money, European Credit Units, a single monetary standard to which all members of the European Community may refer.

"And here is a document I'm sure you haven't seen, a single customs document for shipping goods to replace the thirty a truck driver now needs for going from, say, Copenhagen to Athens."

"This is more important than you might think," Lazlo says. "Without specific government rules and regulations, businesspeople have formed most of the character of the European Community cooperatively. I have been serving on an informal citizens' commission monitoring their efforts, and I can say that only a year ago less than thirty percent of European business executives were aware of, or even interested in, the developments toward relaxed trade regulations. Today, however, so far as I can determine, nearly all European businesspeople are aware of them, and seminars and advertising campaigns about the new Europe are proliferating. There is a kind of fever of new ways of thinking about Europe and above all a new confidence in each other's abilities."

Leaning toward me, he says, "But I fear this fever. If Europe goes too far, all is lost. A majority of all Europeans now want to elect a president, which I believe would be disastrous. We must at all costs avoid a supernationalism. The problem of nationalism is not that it differentiates between people; rather, nationalism becomes a disease that takes on a life of its own. The nation becomes its own excuse for existence and begins to sacrifice its people in order to protect itself and ensure its existence. The nation-state has only one imperative, to continue to exist forever.

"Men of goodwill like Ian Clark worship the sanctity of the nation-state. By sanctity they mean the inviolability of a nation from being warred on by another, but it is precisely in order to protect its sanctity that a nation energizes itself for war. Warmongering is inevitably part of the fundamental nature of nationalism.

"The only solution Clark and his friends find for this dilemma is a world government with the power to enforce sanctity among all the nation-states. If they could turn the United Nations into such a powerful world government, they would merely have created another nation-state, a supernation, whose imperative would then become its own continuance.

"The only viable alternative to this dilemma is the model of the European Community that keeps the valuable aspects of nations, their human differences, but transcends the inhuman imperative of continued existence and power no matter what the human cost.

"The European Community stands as a revolutionary model for the transcendence of nationalism, not for an intensification of nationalism. The nature of the European Community has grown from our ability to embrace intimacy in diversity. We do not want or need uniformity. The European Community exists now as a web of agreements between people without a stifling central bureaucracy, and this is the source of its irreversible energy and popularity."

His voice rises in intensity. "For example, we have transcended the need for uniform laws. A lawyer qualified in one member country can practice anywhere in Europe. And each nation has its own unique problems in this unity in diversity. Germany and France find themselves opening to a kind of competition in thought, business, and art which they find distasteful—for example, the Italians are unable to think of contracts as binding, while to the Germans they are sacrosanct. For the small Benelux-type countries it means adjusting to bigness. For the Spanish, Portuguese, and especially for the Greeks, the problem is in developing a kind of thought and literature that will enable them to care for and cooperate with others in mutual trust."

I break in, "Lazlo, you have it! This is what it is all about. It's not about better ethics or better rules. The European Community is about the room in your head to accommodate differences and to trust, based on successful experience, that others also have room in their thoughts for you. That is what my experience shows, that the balance has shifted and only in this last year. Europe has finally accumulated enough people with interior thought and inner space that it has become worthwhile to trust one another. All of us have been feeling the balance shifting without knowing what it was."

"Our time is limited," Lazlo explains. "I suggest I condense our discussion to a few simple propositions.

"First, the European Community was not planned, it was born. We are not sure of the parentage, but we are delighted with the offspring. It is a miracle. War has ended in the European Community, and this is an indisputable fact. Indeed, the quotes you have just shown me—from such diverse and prophetic figures as Parliament member Altiero Spinelli, Prime Minister Garret FitzGerald, and Nobel laureate Joseph Brodsky—all testify to the existence of a consciousness that is new in the history of the world.

"Second, the European Community is not being caused or created by a single planning or governing body or by a constitutional convention. Nor is it following the lead of one strong leader. European politicians seem to be only concerned with trying to stay out in front of and rationalize the results of a new third-dimensional way of thinking and relating between people.

"Third, I think we must also lay to rest any possible economic causes. The European Community is not being forged by economic forces. There are predictions of future economic growth of seven percent or more. And European businesses are announcing plans to purchase goods and services from each other more frequently. The loosening of national restrictions on trade and business is, of course, conducive to economic growth and vitality. But I have to say that such loosening is made possible by the growth of mutual trust, not by economic theory."

"Let me add something here, Lazlo. I'm thinking of Margaret Drabble and her book *The Radiant Way*. I'm quite taken by her and her books. She seems to assume that these changes are being driven by socialistic theory, but I think she also goes beyond that in her idea of the 'Great Social Dream.'

"I can imagine her, sitting as she does with a straight spine, and talking about it. It was, as I understand it, the development of a kind of thought that could include the concerns and needs of others. But the 'Great Social Dream' was also a burden. Some were to look after the others. In spite of theories, fortunately, that is not what has happened in the European Community. Now all are looking after each other, and I think that is a better dream.

"In other words, when one who is capable of caring for others wakes in the morning, she can be confident that in the course of the day she will encounter at least one other person who is capable of mutually caring for her."

"Some were to look after the others. Now, we are to look after each other. One must pause in reverence," Lazlo says.

"We have a new revolution of thought, which we have called the European Community. But the revolution is invisible to us because we are as yet only beginning to develop the language to describe it.

"I think we are now ready to judge my fourth proposition, which is conflict. The conflict between the United States and Russia no longer monopolizes the international stage. The Cold War is over. However, a new conflict is underway, and it is invisible because it is about the power over people's minds.

"The conflict, simply put, is between those seeking to impose a planned supernation and those who understand that the European Community has grown organically from the people. Those who are wise will be faithful to its roots and leave it to fulfill itself. Make no mistake. If the European Community fulfills its potential, other powerful regions of nations will follow. The earth will eventually become an ecologically fruitful and peaceful place."

I remember the sad, liquid eyes of Juergen Gunther from Leipzig. "Pardon me for interrupting, but I think I should mention a few thoughts about the Russian Empire.

A process of rapid change is sweeping people's thinking in the Warsaw Pact countries, and that will result either in the effective destruction of the East Europeans in a spasm of nationalistic repression or in the formation of the Russian Community. It is not possible to revert back to the chaos of nation-states. This revolutionary change is frightening, especially for those who have been in control, whether they be business executives, commissars, or politicians. Nevertheless, any nation-state not ameliorated by community inevitably controls more and more of its citizens' lives, whether its ideology be democratic or communist or whatever, and control leads to stasis. People must change in order to live. The European Community retains the useful qualities of nationalism while allowing change, and the energy released by such a change could save Russia and leave its empire as a community. Russia's only hope is that the European Community succeeds; its people have the potential for a rapid development of the third dimension of thought.

"And while I'm at it, Lazlo, I'll make a few additional points: One, the nature of the European Community will be its ability to accommodate differences in others while working to reach common goals.

"Two, not a governing bureaucracy, but the people will decide the nature of the European Community.

"Three, the evolution of a third dimension of thought that has never before existed in the history of the human race is making the European Community possible.

"Four, the European Community will be the harbinger of a new form of human relationship in the world, the promises of which are beyond our present conceptions.

"Five, President Franklin Roosevelt's New Deal was the forerunner of Prime Minister FitzGerald's discoveries of enlarged sensitivities in the European Community. The Prime Minister places the beginning of the change about sixty years ago, which means it occurred during Roosevelt's term of office. The Marshall Plan was the first international expression of the new thought. And it was necessary, not as material aid but as thought, for the eventual development of the European Community.

"The new third dimension of thought made its first appearance in a social sense in the United States. On behalf of the United States I say to this new child of the world, 'God bless you! May good fortune favor you.'"

Lazlo bows to me. "I will undertake to respond to your kind good wishes on behalf of the European Community. I've been hearing from you about how Europeans dislike the United States. That dislike served a temporary purpose to help orient Europe to the expression of the third dimension of thought, but dislike will turn to indifference in the future, I am afraid. Europe is where the action is now. The United States is an old friend whom Europe has outgrown. The European Community will be glad to have U.S. trade or support, but only on our terms. I say this in the friendliest way, and I wish the United States good luck as it, hopefully, develops its third dimension of thought."

"Thank you, Lazlo, but I must say you remind me of Harold Pinter, who seems to be so full of rage at the United States. He, like the modern painter, moved from three-dimensional to two-dimensional representation in order to demonstrate the vital necessity of conceptual purity in our lives. We are often confused by the rich and misleading diversity of our modern consciousness.

"In his writing he plays the purity and sparseness of the characters' dialogue against the inner confusion of their lives. In the same sense, he plays the action against their contradictory speech. That is how he achieves literary purity. I wonder if he is merely playing anti-American statements against an American archetype in order to create a pure description of the European Community."

Lazlo is fastening the catches on my briefcase and rising to his feet. "We have overstayed our time. We will have to hurry to catch our ship."

He peers about. "I do not discern the shade of King Arthur here. Perhaps he got bored."

"Cut that out, Laz. You're making fun of my ancestor."

"Did I understand you to address me as Laz!"

"Did I? I guess I did."

Lazlo looks intrigued.

THE ENGLISH CHANNEL

We have arrived just in time to catch our ship. As we are being shown to Lazlo's luxurious supersuite, the liner maneuvers into the sound. Lazlo's suite is located behind the flying bridge and next to the captain's quarters. The hills of the Isle of Wight slide by and soon we are in the channel. The North Sea is like a mirror. I have never seen it so smooth. Somewhere below us is the hell of noise and high pressure which is the construction of the cross-channel tunnel. Paul will be involved.

"You know, Lazlo, we have all been oppressed for the last fifty years by the concern—symbolized by the nuclear bomb—that our continuing mastery of the material processes of our planet would destroy us before we learned how to live together. But if the people of the European Community can fulfill their promises, their example can mean the end of war for all of us. What was it I said about Margaret Drabble?"

A lassitude has come over Lazlo, as though he has time now that he didn't have before. Looking peacefully out to sea, he murmurs, "In the Great Social Dream, some were to look after the others; now we are to look after each other."

"That's it. Hundreds of millions of new thinkers capable of internalizing reading and thought have finally achieved a critical mass and made mutual caring possible. Dear Margaret, I like her a lot. I wonder what she would say about that. I'll have to ask her the next chance I get."

Wandering on in Lazlo's unusual silence, I say, "The phrase *third dimension of thought* is a label. Before a label can become a name, people have to understand the process and find it relevant to their daily lives.

"Well Laz, your observation on how these changes could not have been caused by politics or economics, but only from new ways of thinking, was very well said."

"Yes, I thought so too."

"But you didn't relate these things to the United States, which was the point."

"Your point, not mine."

"Well, *I* began this investigation—and Laz, I have been dumbfounded by your seriousness today—and I thought for one moment we both had the exact same goal. I began in Texas with my family, asking myself if their future could be seriously affected by the changes taking place in the rest of the world. Is saving the world important to their future? And, of course, there is no question about it. No concern in their lives is as important as the continued development of the interior thought processes that are forming the European Community and making peace in the world.

"I also asked myself what kind of thought in the world was important to my family's future, what peoples were important and where were they located? The peoples important are obviously the peoples of the European Community, and also because they are right next door to the Russian empire.

"The thoughts behind the New Deal and the Marshall Plan planted the seeds for the European Community's breakthrough, but now they're moving ahead of us. We in the United States have to move, too. I think of Rilke's saying, 'There is no place at all that is not looking at you. You have to change your life.'

"The United States started it all, Laz, but where do we fit in now?"

A breeze is picking up from the French coast and Laz's murmur, like a benediction, is carried on it. "Europe will need someone to talk to."

PARIS

Lazlo's breakfast room opens onto a walled rose garden. I find him there with a cup of coffee reading a paper.

"I've finally figured out your ambiguous utterance, Laz. You said that the European Community would need the United States to talk to in order to keep its balance. In isolation the European Community might risk becoming a superstate, on the one hand, or it could disintegrate over West Germany's attempts at unity with East Germany. There are forces at work here that you're not disclosing."

Lazlo looks up from his coffee and shudders delicately. "Good morning. One hopes for a more pleasant topic to greet the day."

The two days spent with Lazlo before returning to the United States have been a paradise of Parisian elegance and Middle Eastern splendor. He thinks a volume following *War's End* that would also apply psychology to an understanding of war and regional community in the rest of the world would be valuable. He has offered to use his resources to make it possible. I have agreed.

Lazlo wants me to go with him to Egypt where he's apparently planning some intrigue involving a UNESCO-supported rebuilding of the Alexandrian Library, once one of the seven wonders of the world. Madame Mubarak, wife of Egypt's president, is in charge of the project. Lazlo seems to think Madame Mubarak would look upon me kindly.

Filling my plate with breakfast goodies at the sideboard, I say, "I am acquainted with Madame Mubarak, Laz. I had lunch with her and her four bodyguards once, and we appeared on the same lecture platform. I admire and respect her immensely. Her efforts to develop third-dimensional thinking in Islamic culture may be the only hope for peace in the Middle East now. The way she is co-ordinating writers' centers with reading centers is marvelous. In any case, you go to a lot of trouble to leave the impression you know every important world figure intimately. Why would you need me?"

Lazlo shrugs. "Please, cynicism does not become you. It is your American naiveté and innocence that make you valuable. The most valuable quality you Americans have is that at heart you really don't want any power in the world. But we're straying from the point. Accompanying me to Cairo will also be useful for our book following *War's End.*"

I settle myself at the table. "Laz, I have committed myself to being with you in Cairo, but first you're coming to San Francisco to help me finish *War's End,* right?"

He has insisted on San Francisco and extracted an additional commitment to take him to the redwood grove commemorating the establishment of the United Nations. While there, he says, he will reveal to me the circumstances that "have made a certain delicacy desirable." He has assured me that when I know all, I will approve of what he is doing.

I doubt it. But I expect he has a better grasp of what's going on in the world than anyone else.

In the meantime, he has booked me on the Concorde for the United States of America tomorrow.

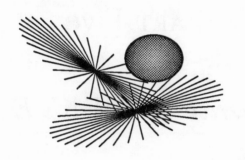

PART Five

America and War's End

THE NORTH AMERICAN COMMUNITY

THE UNITED STATES OF AMERICA

It's good to be home. The United States was the inspiration for the development of the European Community, but we have lost Europe's trust, and they have shut us out. War has ended in Europe, and Europeans don't trust the United States to understand how that has become possible.

The European Community is also increasingly confident of their ability to remain at peace with the Russian Empire. They don't need anything from us any more, and we don't seem to know how to relate to people who don't need us in material or strategic ways. We only know how to buy people with money or manipulate them with strategic policies.

Lazlo said that Europe would need someone to talk to, and it is logical that the United States should be the one. The only tragedy is that in the last twenty-five years we have believed our value to the world was our material, rather than spiritual, wealth. Washington and Jefferson knew, Lincoln knew, Franklin Roosevelt knew, and Kennedy embodied it all. But since Kennedy our leaders have forgotten.

The most valuable thing we have to share is our thoughts, our ways of thinking. There is an old Christian passage: "Lay not up your treasure on earth where moth and dust doth corrupt and thieves break through and steal. Rather lay up your treasure in heaven. . . ." Could we substitute the word "spirit" for "heaven"? Or "ways of thinking"? What Americans have of value to offer is our spirit, our ability to make ourselves up out of our own minds.

In 1783, upon winning our revolution, George Washington declared that we "seemed to be peculiarly designated by Providence for the display of human greatness and felicity. Heaven has crowned its other blessings by giving the fairest opportunity for political happiness than any other nation has ever been favored with, and the result must be a nation which would have a meliorating influence on all mankind."

In spite of the goodwill we have lost in the world since President Kennedy, the United States still has a "meliorating influence on all mankind." Let us take stock of ourselves.

We are still the leader of the world. We have the one and only essential quality for world leadership—that we, the people of the United States of America, traditionally do not seek material gain from leadership. We seek, rather, to help others. We have shown the world what it means to help weaker nations instead of dominating them, and our spirit was the first sign of a radical change in human nature. No matter how much we are disliked, people throughout the world look to the United States as a world leader.

We are largely a compassionate, big-hearted people who root for the underdog and who try to be fair.

We would rather live in the United States than anywhere else.

We can be depended on.

We govern ourselves, and we have had to be self-reliant.

We are free and work hard.

We all have opportunities to better ourselves.

Women and men succeed in working and living together, and in fact have the best chance for equality than in any other country in the world.

More than any other defining factor, we are the only truly pluralistic nation in the the world. We have people here from every part of the world.

At this crucial point in world history, we can no longer afford to take our resources for granted. If you need examples, just look around at some of the many European expatriates who have chosen to live in the United States in order to take advantage of our dynamic culture.

Hachette-Filipacchi is a French publishing company that may be the second largest in the world. Daniel Filipacchi, one of the partners and head of its magazine group, has been living in the United States part-time for the past seventeen years. Still young-looking and handsome, Daniel is European sophistication, elegance—and ruthlessness—personified. Yet his enthusiasm for America is like that of a child at F.A.O. Schwartz. He talks about the jazz, the glass towers, the cinema, about everything being so fresh and young. He speaks of the United States as a place where creativity is fostered.

Francis Ford Coppola talks about the tremendous freedom in the United States and about America's talent. He believes our energy comes from so many different kinds of contentious people living together, and he sees the United States as having more creative potential than any other country in the world.

We are seeing the exhaustion of ideologies—of

Marxism, but also of capitalism and democracy. Something new is in the air. It has the freshness and smell of the youth, energy and innocence that Filipacchi and Coppola have the artistic instinct to find here. We must be aware that our spirit is our country's most precious asset.

THE ONLY GAME IN TOWN

The quintessential move toward peace would be the formation of a community, including the United States, similar to the European Community. When we can discern a shift in the balance of thinking here, when more and more people begin to bypass the boundaries of special interest groups and institutions to serve each other mutually, when the reality of others outweighs our own self-concerns, then we will be ready to move toward a North American Community based on the European Community model. In the European Community ordinary people have managed to preserve and cherish existing institutions and national differences, while going beyond those institutions to achieve greater goals that serve them all. Can we in North America do any less?

How would a North American Community start? In fact, it has already begun in the form of our trade agreement with Canada. The acrimony that developed in negotiating that fairly simple agreement indicates how much inner growth must take place in both countries before we can make further progress.

The simple question the peoples of Canada and the United States must ask themselves is, Are we personally ready to transcend and go beyond our nationalism in order to achieve a greater good? Answering this question puts into perspective the radical change in human nature that the European Community has actually undergone.

But the trade agreement has already moved us closer together than we may realize. People traveling on routine business used to be hassled at the Canadian border, both coming and going. Now they just show up with proof of citizenship and go right through—for a stay of up to a year. Architects in Canada and the United States are also working on common credentials that would certify them to work in either country.

The European countries, with more acrimony between them than Canada and the United States could dream of, started out with a trade agreement after World War II. It has taken them forty years to work out the European Community. Canada and the United States don't have that much time, but we won't need much. The European Community has shown the way.

Our free trade agreement with Canada means that all barriers—tariffs, quotas, trade regulations—will be removed by 1999. It does not envision a community such as the European Community where nationalism is transcended by harmonizing taxes, antitrust policy, labor law, monetary policy.

We in the United States have to realize that we are a nation born from revolution. Our goals were freedom and equal opportunity. Canada, on the other hand, developed slowly from a colony into a nation. Having inherited its character from England, Canada has as its goals peace and the common good through the power of enlightened government.

Many Canadians feel that the new trade agreement threatens their culture. John Turner and Ed Broadbent, Canadian political leaders who opposed the agreement, recognize that in the European Community the French do not feel their culture is threatened by the Italians, even though the French dislike the Italians; nor do the Spanish feel threatened by the Germans, even though the Spaniards can't stand the German tourists. Canadian leaders know the Canadian culture is not actually at risk, and their arguments against the agreement are spurious. Even though Canadians, especially the intelligentsia, hate Americans, they can still find room for us in their third-dimensional inner spaces in order to form a community with us.

The campus of McGill University sits on the rising ground of the fortresslike hill dominating downtown Montreal. Students there have the same complaint about the United States as do their counterparts at Oxford and Dublin and Bonn. A blond, strapping girl, obviously of Scots extraction, says, "People in the United States know nothing about us, but we know everything about them. They don't even know we exist, nor do they care. But we have a culture and standards of art and scholarship that far exceed those in the United States. We have values, and one of them is to remain independent of the United States."

Paul Johnson, the author of *Modern Times*, the book Margaret Drabble mentioned in London, says that the most prevalent form of "racism" is anti-Americanism. It is certainly prevalent in Canada, more so even than in the European Community.

But in fact the United States is aware that Canada exists, and the Canadian resistance to community could change quickly. Mexico would be the catalyst. In 1988, a bill was introduced in Congress to create a North American Free Trade Area that includes Mexico. No one took the bill seriously because the economic benefits were not immediately obvious. The problem has been to recognize that a "Free Trade Area" is not about economics but about transcending and bypassing nationalism. It is exactly the same kind of small move that began the formation of the European Community. After World War II, Eisenhower's administration pushed for political union in Europe, for a United States of Europe. Our planners were looking for an ideological solution to war. Fortunately for the future of humankind, however, circumstances forced us to remedy specific problems relevant to people's lives rather than to impose a supernation. The first step to the European Community was the Iron and Coal Agreement. In North America we need to find solutions to our daily problems in exactly the same way.

Also, a North American Community would shift the present Canadian focus on the United States to the prospect of intimacy with Latin cultures very different from their own. The Canadian intelligentsia would find that appealing.

We need to take the North American Free Trade Area bill seriously as a first step toward a North American Community. That would shake up the Canadian intelligentsia to face what is truly at stake here: the possibility of a new world of peace and prosperity—war's end.

A North American Community could include the Caribbean, the six Central American countries of Costa Rica, Guatemala, Honduras, Nicaragua, El Salvador and Panama, as well as Mexico, the United States and Canada. As in Europe, some countries—Cuba and Nicaragua, for example—would not join at first, but over time the benefits would become apparent to all.

Canada is the world's second largest country, rich in mineral and natural resources. It is poor in population, however, with only seven people per square mile—one of the world's lowest population densities. Mexico has an abundance of people, whose number is increasing exponentially every day. Mexico also has an abundance of oil. The diversity of culture, technology, human and natural resources in the North American Community would make it practically self-sufficient, in contrast to the European Community and the Russian Empire.

Page 244 is a map of the North American Community; page 245 contains a table showing the gross national product and population of each of the three communities.

THE NORTH AMERICAN COMMUNITY

THREE COMMUNITIES

	Gross National Product (in U.S. dollars)	Population
European Community	2.5 trillion	325 million
Russian Empire	2.5 trillion	471 million
North American Community	5.0 trillion	361 million

Every member of a North American Community would benefit, and the diversity of countries would balance the fear of U.S. dominance. The rest would be up to the spirit of community in the United States. We would have to go out of our way to demonstrate a lack of interest in using power only for our own strategic interest. We would have to grasp the opportunity for an interdependence of all people serving each other.

U.S. citizens fear being swamped by hordes of hungry people from south of the border. We seem to think of this as a one-way street, as ourselves serving others. Think of it instead from a community point of view. In a North American Community, Americans could also travel freely south of the border. Rich investment possibilities await us in the south, along with a supply of cheap labor. This is already happening in the maquiladora factories along the Mexican side of the border, with nearly half a million Mexicans employed in various kinds of joint ventures with the United States. Before long, as we created more jobs in Mexico, the pressure of people wanting to come to the United States for jobs would diminish.

The difference is between general policies based on national self-interest and day-by-day solutions based on community interest.

There are no real barriers to a North American Community. The overwhelming gift from the European

Community is showing us that community can be realized, that nationalism can be bypassed, that war can end.

The world wants and needs our leadership. After all,
we started all this. We can provide the spirit to create
opportunities, or we can shrink within ourselves and
continue to attract the hatred of the world as a symbol that
failed them. There are no rules. A transnational community cannot be bought or imposed. It is something you
discover. It is not a system or ideology to be learned.
Enough of us have to be the right kind of people.

THE BUSINESS OF THE UNITED STATES

A North American Community would mean a lot
more business for the United States—in this hemisphere,
in the world and particularly in the European Community. Current business growth in the United States is
only about two or three percent, as compared with the
European Community, which projects a seven percent
growth rate in 1992. The reason ascribed to the increase
in Europe is the ability of businesses to bypass national
boundaries and trade freely with companies that work
most advantageously with them.

Traditionally, American businesspeople have been
renowned for their ability to get around boundaries of all
kinds—government regulations, internal revenue rules,
trade restrictions, competition. Whatever the problem, we
could still get the job done. This robust approach to
business has unfortunately succumbed to the overwhelming power of the network of bureaucratic government and
professional and special-interest boundaries that circum-
scribe our lives.

One way to confront this problem is to revive our
unique kind of equality. We Americans have had an
attractive sense of equality that foreigners perceived as an
inner self-reliance—"I'm as good as anybody"—rather

than equality as an exterior measurement—putting equal signs between people. For decades Europeans have been both impressed and appalled by the can-do attitude of American business. They have been appalled when American businesspeople muscled their way into foreign markets that were supposed to be safe from competition and impressed when we came up with products that everyone knew couldn't be built.

The practice of third-dimensional thinking in a prospective North American Community can be the businessperson's best friend. We can learn from the young people of Oxford who are obviously superior to others in those qualities most highly valued by their society. Yet they yearned for and found equality with others by creating them as real people in the inner spaces of their minds.

This requires the third-dimensional ability of having room in our own interior reality for hundreds of thousands of other people. Then we can be equal with others because the others have become part of our selves. Even though this equality with others exists only as a third-dimensional inner reality, it suffuses everything we do.

If we Americans can integrate our traditional sense of equality with an inner equality with others in the third dimension of thought, we will have much greater business success. We will be able to avoid breaking boundaries even though we are getting around them.

In the European Community we must confront a pervasive and often unconscious dislike of Americans. They don't trust us to cherish and protect differences in others while going around them to do business.

Europeans unconsciously and intuitively recognize the existence of third-dimensional thought in others. Americans who can combine the old "I'm as good as anybody" thinking with third-dimensional thinking will find good friends and partners and associates in the European Community.

Don Petersen, chairman of the board of Ford Motor Company, in a speech in Italy quoted Peter Koestenbaum's approach: "'People,' Dr. Koestenbaum says, 'need to feel worthy, a need that is reflected in four important desires: the desire to be self-starters, or entrepreneurs; the desire to exhibit courage, or take responsibility; the desire for love or belonging, or being part of the team; and the desire to stand for something, to have values, principles, integrity.'"

Peter says that the courage to act comes from the deep structures of the psyche. There is no system of specific rules to follow. In the third dimension of thought, others become part of you, and the courage to act responsibly for them becomes natural and inevitable.

Love, to share the self with others, requires the sense of belonging to the future, of working together toward future goals.

To stand for something—values, ethics—is also intimately linked to our progress toward a North American Community. When the United States reaches a critical mass of third-dimensional thinking, all of these qualities will be instantly recognized by the European Community because they are concentrated there. For the United States they represent the door to a profitable business future with the European Community and, eventually, with other regions of the world that learn to transcend nationalism in community.

If we each ask, Am I personally ready for a North American Community? the answer will probably be, No. How do we get ready? The next chapter will lay out basic conditions and give some examples of how the European Community model might work within the United States. There is no other viable alternative for us. We must move toward a North American Community. It is the only game in town.

NURTURING THE NORTH
AMERICAN COMMUNITY

How can we contribute to the growth of a North American Community? Our first step would be to look at our institutions and special-interest groups, because they are just like nations, each with its own boundaries. How can we transcend our own internal boundaries? To begin with, only as individuals can we accomplish a breakthrough of thinking. Governments don't think, laws don't think, societies don't think. We, privately and individually, must discover for ourselves how to bypass boundaries. Let's take the boundaries of our educational establishment as a first example.

EDUCATION

Remember Nobel laureate Joseph Brodsky in Stockholm? His words are simple: "Literature, not literacy."

Literacy is a measurable skill that fits neatly into a professional structure. But becoming literate does not in itself lead children to literature, to creativity and the development of inner lives. Let us cherish our educational institutions but go beyond their institutional boundaries to help our children learn to love literature. If they do, they will no longer view reading as a technique isolated from their lives. The words will disappear from the page and children will live what they are reading. Remember what Francis King said: "Literature is what changes you. The word is more powerful than the bomb."

Marva Collins, a teacher on the west side of Chicago, decided to try to bypass professional educational boundaries. The west side is like New York's South Bronx, only tougher. Marva turned a couple of rooms in her home into classrooms and started a school, the Westside Preparatory. Now it has more than two hundred fifty students and a waiting list of several hundred. She takes "unteachable" students, and every student who graduates is now completing high school or enrolled in college.

In Marva's third grade, the students are already reading Shakespeare. One way to tell if children have done their homework is to give a test asking for specific information that they could know only if they had read the assignment. But that would be a literacy test, confirming only that the children are able to read.

Marva *knows* they have read the Shakespeare assignment because she sees how they have changed. They even look different. They have experienced the miracle of being "swept away to a secret world," of being unable to put the book down. The teacher's understanding bypasses the system and gives the children the freedom to practice this new dimension of their minds.

Parents can also bypass educational boundaries. If you are a parent, you may remember having found your child with her nose in a novel. "Mary, you're not doing anything. Why don't you clean your room?"

Be careful. Mary may believe you, and a door opening in her mind may close forever. She was practicing opening the third dimension of her mind, creating inner realities of people and places. No process in the education of a child is more important than plugging into this revolution in consciousness. Nurturing this quality is the most important gift parents can give to their children.

This going beyond the boundaries of the educational establishment is more important to Marva Collins than fame and fortune. She has turned down the position of U.S. Secretary of Education. She has turned down the job of Superintendent of the Los Angeles County School System, one of the largest school systems in the country. Marva believes that a community in which we all serve each other is a more important goal.

SCIENCE

Another example of how we can approach a North American Community concerns the special-interest group of professional scientists. This example came to me recently when Don Polkinghorne and I were working on a recent issue of *Methods: A Journal of Human Science.* Dr. Polkinghorne is acknowledged to be one of the world's leading experts on methodology in the human sciences, which include the disciplines of psychology, sociology, anthropology, and others. His latest book is *Narrative Knowing.*

Don points out that "truth" is achieved through an agreement by consensus among professionals in a given scientific discipline. This body of truth changes slowly as certain truths are eventually found untrue and new truths are written into the discipline. In other words, scientific truth is what scientists say it is. But science has become too important to leave to scientists only.

Tradition in the scientific discipline holds that professionals—those who profess the discipline—are all equal as they form a consensus about what is "true." We can extend this vision to all curious, intelligent people who are dedicated to truth. If we thus go beyond the boundaries of the scientific profession itself, to include in the consensual process anyone who is seriously willing to commit to reading and understanding the necessary evidence, there would be millions of intelligent people serving the common goal of truth.

By finding room within the scientific community for interaction with nonprofessionals, we could create a new interdependent kind of community. Such a community would honor and respect the professionals of the discipline, and the professionals would value the help of nonprofessionals capable of an extra dimension of thinking.

Truth is an inner reality. If this third-dimensional thinking reached a critical mass in the United States, this would be of enormous benefit to science. There are encouraging signs. Just a few years ago most serious scientific conferences in the European Community and in the United States were limited to academic participants. Today these proceedings are attended by various intelligent, and curious participants, both professional and nonprofessional alike.

The same sort of approach can be taken in other professions—law, medicine, government. Professional "truths" become merely information when their transmittal to nonprofessionals is a one-way street; professional disciplines must offer a two-way street of mutual interaction. Truth can be created as reality in an extra dimension of thinking beyond professional boundaries. Professionals of all kinds need nonprofessionals to test truth against their own experience and to argue about results. *War's End* is written with precisely this kind of environment in mind. Please argue with me; I need to hear from you.

JOURNALISM

Since the early days of journalism, "the news" seems to have deteriorated and sunk into a corporate morass called "the media." It is more credible, better done, but it has become less relevant to our lives. Once we all participated in the exciting common goal of finding out the truth about what was going on. The youthful energy of a partnership between reporter and reader that existed then provided a key to the same kind of inner three-dimensional experience of life provided by literature.

The change came after World War II. I remember sitting behind a grundgy desk with my tie pulled down, clothes rumpled and socks sagging. I was thinking about how to stretch my penurious pay to cover a night on the town when in walked a former colleague. His blond hair was slicked back; he smelled of the barber shop and his manicured nails glistened. He was wearing a perfectly tailored blue silk suit.

"What do you think you're doing, McCall?"

"I've taken a job as a public relations representative."

"A what?"

"You know, public relations. I know you've been covering these War Labor Board hearings and my client . . . Well, I've written a story for you that gives a balanced view . . ."

He was sliding some neatly typed papers on the desk. "I thought we could go out on the town tonight—I have an expense account—and talk about it."

I began meticulously tearing his copy into strips and dropping them into my wastebasket. "You Benedict Arnold, I was feeling sleazy when you walked in, but now I feel slimy. Get out!"

He started backing out the door. "Really, you don't know how helpful I can be. You'll see . . ."

McCall was the future. The world is more complex now, and the media have become highly organized. The news is more credible. Still, think of George Orwell's *1984*, which predicted that a lot of terrible things would happen. Nineteen-eighty-four arrived and they hadn't happened, or had they? The book is most terrifying when the hero, fighting against tyranny, is finally broken. He spends his days reading the government news about wars and events in the world outside. Information never stops flowing. Bytes and bits of facts from anonymous sources are fed to him until he knows everything about . . . what? He ceases to live in an interior dimension.

We must cherish and protect our media. And we must improve them by going beyond their professional boundaries. The important news is the news we make ourselves, the news we ourselves witness and the news we report. I'm surprised at how much of the news I receive is from people I know—a young man working for a computer company, for example, tells me about a hard disc coming out soon, a woman at the bank tells me about the government examiners being pulled from the job before they can finish an audit properly. These are idle conversations, but they stick with me after the morning paper has become a blur.

A mortgage banker I know who handles hundreds of millions of dollars in investments points out that his customers are the real insiders in the stock market. A man working for a washing-machine company will get a feel for a coming breakthrough long before the experts do. What he knows is relevant; it's news. The annual report may not be.

We're fortunate to have media professionals serve us the news, and we can also serve them. In the North American Community we can all learn to serve each other in a community that is both intimate and free.

In special-interest groups, people's thinking is apt to become as small as their own self-interest. To serve each other mutually, we must acquire in our interior thoughts a new dimension of room for others, carrying the spirit of our great liberal traditions beyond laws and government control to mutual service.

BUSINESS

Just as I was getting ready to meet Lazlo in San Francisco, Paul and his wife Jocelyn flew in from Europe; he had just finished negotiating his construction contracts for the tunnel linking England to the continent. Paul read part of a rough draft of *War's End.*

"It's what I would have expected," says Paul, slamming the manuscript on the table. "You give everyone credit except the people who make things, the ones who keep your world running for you."

Jocelyn stretches her lithe body and rolls her eyes as Paul forges ahead. "Who do you suppose is doing this third-dimensional thinking in Europe? The intellectuals? The only kind of thinking they know is intellectual, logical. Do you suppose they know how the water gets to their kitchen tap when they turn it on? They don't understand the world they live in."

I remember Heinz saying that Paul was a "poet of machinery," that he could look at a set of plans and imagine the whole machine in operation with all of its parts moving. And Lazlo had mentioned that Paul had a feeling for the intricacies of how a group of people were thinking during negotiations.

"You're messing up my theory, Paul."

"No I'm not, I'm making it workable. Do you remember the man who is in charge of my equipment? He keeps the whole operation running."

"Well, I'm not sure, Paul. . . ."

"I'm going to tell you how I found him. I had walked through dozens of factories looking for the right person when I spotted a master electrical control panel holding maybe twenty-five switch boxes. Out of each box a pipe carrying wires rose to the ceiling, where the pipes then connected to the different machines on the production floor. Every pipe was exactly parallel to every other pipe. They were all bent to the same degree. When they changed directions, the change was always ninety degrees.

"I found the electrician and asked him why he wasted so much pipe and wire being precise when he could have cut across to the machine he was hooking up. He asked me what I thought was more important, his thoughts or those pipes. He said that everything that moved in that plant was moving in his head. Anything that went wrong, he knew exactly where and what it was. He said that those pipes represented what was going on in his head and that that was the real plant—in his head. I hired him on the spot." Paul settles his bulk back in the chair in triumph.

"But you're talking about businesspeople, Paul. Everyone knows that they think only of their own self-interest and that their only motivation is greed."

"You think you're so damned funny. You know a good executive thinks about how the whole economy is affected by what he does. Honor, honesty and concern for others are what keep him successful. In a good business situation—the kind I create—we help each other. And if it's not possible, I just back off."

"How many situations like that do you find, Paul? Are they increasing or decreasing in the United States?"

Paul considers this carefully. "They're rare. Maybe they're increasing in Europe."

"Are these paragons of business virtue open to the thoughts of us intellectuals?"

"I didn't say they were perfect."

"But don't you think they could profit from reading my book, if I get it all together?"

"Sure, I'll pass out copies for you, but not to management in the big corporations. They're not real businesspeople. They don't make anything. They're bureaucrats who don't read or think in your third dimension.

"You remember the book by Peter Koestenbaum on philosophy in business that you gave me? I sent a copy to the president of a multinational corporation headquartered here in the States. I'm on the board. At the next board meeting the president gave an exposition on the book, focusing on how philosophy and ethics should be paramount in corporate leadership. He then put everyone down by asking if anyone had read the book. No one had except me, and I kept quiet.

"After the meeting, on a hunch, I looked up the executive vice-president's secretary and asked her whom she had sent the book to. I hit it on the first try. What had happened was the president had called the vice in, given him the book, and told him to give him a one-page résumé in advance of the board meeting. The vice then sent it down to a lower-echelon junior executive and told her to give him the one-page résumé. She apparently read the book and sent back a good synopsis. None of the top people had read the book; they had only used it to stab each other in the back. As the board members returned to their own companies, I'll bet that scenario was played again and again."

Paul never talks this much. If nothing else, the manuscript has opened him up.

"Do you think the United States has a chance, Paul?"

"Sure it does. Listen, I think there are possibilities for your North American Community. It could work. There is still a greater reservoir of potential in the ordinary people of the United States than in all the rest of the world."

Paul gives me a look. "After all it was this country that made me possible."

COMMUNITY

I had sent the first part of the manuscript of *War's End* to Larry Dossey, president of the Isthmus Institute and author of many highly regarded books in human science, including *Space, Time and Medicine.* He calls and we have a valuable visit about the book, including how he views the third dimension of thought and its significance in U.S. foreign policy.

Larry is tall and slender, with a quiet intensity. He is saying, "The relaxation of the boundaries and restrictions between the *nations* of Europe is an event that depends, perhaps, on a deeper and more general fact: that boundaries between *minds* are not fundamental. As you were describing your experience in European countries, my thoughts turned to look for the deepest, most comprehensive explanation for how the third dimension of thought, mediated through literature, actually leads to a community of nations.

"We *do* make ourselves up as we go along! You point out that the mind is accepted as a factor in some interpretations of modern physics. There is also evidence that it changes reality at the *macroscopic* level—and not just through communication between people, but directly in the world-at-large: the way societies actually function, how people behave, what they eat for breakfast, what they dream at night, etcetera. I could go on. . . ."

"I like that, Larry. You're getting at just how the third dimension of thought emerges in the culture of a society."

"Right, it's a positive force. Jung pointed out that there is a deep drive in the unconscious self toward wholeness and integration—a tendency toward the Divine, as he put it. Maybe this is why 'it feels good' to most people when they experience the third dimension of thinking as wholeness. They are being true to their inner nature. If political community, manifesting itself on a societal level, is a corollary to the drive toward the wholeness that exists in this revolution in consciousness, perhaps it also 'feels good.' If so, we might expect these political developments to gather force with time.

"We've been talking about the North American Community. Ultimately, community at that political level will never work until one *feels* the validity of community at the psychological or spiritual level. I think you pointed this out in our failed policy in Central America: we didn't develop a base of thought before intervening."

I jump up. "That's it! We in the United States must *feel* community to arrive at a critical mass of third-dimensional thinking."

Larry replies, "I agree. If it is true that the third dimension of thought is intrinsically unbounded, the primacy of the individual ego would be transcended and replaced by a different form of awareness. This is why, of course, some people don't like the idea of community: it means giving up boundaries. I have often thought these people have a disease that might be called *spiritual agoraphobia*. Like their counterparts who suffer the *psychological* form of agoraphobia—fearing vast spaces, crowds, and so on—*spiritual* agoraphobics fear the infinity in time and space that is implied by the vast interior room for others in third-dimensional thinking. They prefer boundaries, things closed in, restricted, personal, local.

"There is also *political agoraphobia*. Political agoraphobics incessantly warn against the loss of national identity, being taken over. They do not know how to think in complementary ways, which, as you have pointed out, means the ability to hold different *ways* of thinking—paradigms—about the world in one's mind at the same time. Unable to think in a complementary fashion, they do not see that the fullness of the individual—or of nationhood—can only be realized by transcending it. They are unaware that a hypertrophied nationalism, like an inflated ego, is deadly."

While writing down my conversation with Larry, I am reminded of the mental adventure at the monastery near Milan—St. Augustine's discovery that a few people could read silently, could internalize written words. It took a thousand years for that evolutionary development in thinking to emerge in the Renaissance as the third dimension of thought, finding expression as perspective in painting, as internalization of mechanics in science, and as internalization of language in the novel. The novel as literature was the practice of third-dimensional thinking. It took another five hundred years of practice for it to emerge in Western culture as care for others, as in the New Deal and the Marshall Plan, and finally to result in a community in Europe.

This practice has reached a critical mass in Europe, enabling people to bypass national boundaries in the European Community. This bypassing of boundaries can lead to a critical mass of third-dimensional thinking here in America. Bypassing the boundaries of education, science, the professions and the media in our society will show us the immediate benefits and open us up to a mental third dimension that can make community possible.

Do you remember Morris Berman, the historian and author who pointed out that relevant experiences are interior experiences? He goes further, using Hegel and Sheldrake to postulate a rippling effect in the transmission of thought, how thought can float through a culture. This explains how a critical mass of third-dimensional thought can explode within a community that is caring and intimate but still nourishes differences. It can happen here.

The only way of passing on the possibilities for peace and prosperity inherent in a community of North American nations is to bypass boundaries in our own nation. We will then find people in other nations who will respond to third-dimensional thinking. They are there. They are using that kind of thinking in their interior lives, but someone has to be the first to demonstrate that it works in community.

THE LAST BEST HOPE

FOREIGN POLICY

A consensus of world opinion would show that since World War II the United States has had two overwhelming successes in foreign policy. The first was the Marshall Plan, which was the inspiration for the European Community. The success of the Marshall Plan lay in the perception of Americans as a warm, big-hearted people.

Our second success was President John F. Kennedy, who during his presidency was the most revered and most loved political figure in Europe. Let us not forget that our successes were built on an indomitable spirit; while we may have lost some ground in the last twenty-five years, we can recapture it in the opportunities ahead.

Our future success in foreign policy will depend on our internal strength and on our ability to nurture the growth of a North American Community. If we can do that, our influence could extend to other parts of the world. Even Russia might benefit.

Consider, for example, the influence of the American Bar Association in Russia. Solzhenitsyn and other dissident writers have been calling for law as a way of thinking for the past ten years. Russian law has always been a procedure for rationalizing the government's absolute and arbitrary control of the thoughts and actions of its citizens. Now, however, there are signs that the American Bar Association's alliance with Russia is paying off. Soviet specialists are beginning to use the American judicial system as a model for a Russian system of independent judges, jury trials and the right of counsel.

Our Association for Humanistic Psychology has been involved in Russia for several years now. Forward-looking Russian psychiatrists have recently accepted Freud's thinking, a milestone as important as the acceptance of law in Russia. My publishing friend Juergen in Leipzig is responsible for pioneering the publication of Freud's works. The Soviet psychiatrist Dr. Ivan Belkin writes, "It has become clear that the sphere of the subconscious is an immense source of reserves of the human psyche." Thus Russian professionals are beginning to recognize the subconscious as a reality worth studying.

As our businesspeople and professionals and tourists invade the Soviet culture, American words are also creeping into Russian. How about "biznessayet" (doing business), "kidnepping," "Breikdensing," "parking," "sadden def overtaim," as well as "sponsori," "no-khow" and "finansirovat dzhoint venchur" for a melding of cultures?

American music has also invaded Russia. I am thinking of a dinner with Dave Brubeck and his wife, Iola, at the conclusion of their recent Russian tour.

"We have never had such passionate responses," Iola said, "and you know, we have played in practically every country in the world."

Dave, still with the lanky cowboy figure he had as a young man and still shy, said, "The important thing is the inner communication of music, and that comes across with particular power in Russia. Everyone in the group can feel it."

"Music, as is so often the case in revolutions, paved the way for glasnost and perestroika," I remember saying. "Rock concerts, using American costumes and showmanship, have been put on by young Russians for other young Russians for many years. It was the one kind of expression the government never seemed able to suppress."

I told Dave and Iola about having been with Yevtushenko not long before. He was then appearing at the Village Gate in New York. Yevtushenko shares Dave's approach to art, and his poetry recitals in Moscow get the same kind of reception from the young.

"He's the one dissenting Russian writer the government has never felt it could repress. After the Village Gate he appeared at the Kremlin Palace of Congresses in Moscow. He is truly a citizen of both the United States and Russia and he is loved in both places. With the royal treatment the Russian government is giving you, Dave, you may soon be in the same position."

Dave replied very softly, as he does, "Talking with music comes first, only then comes talking with words."

Dave is a genius, and I wondered why I hadn't understood that before. It helps explain how jazz helped the United States win the thoughts of Europe in the twenties, thirties and forties, and it explains the recent change in Russia. Dave and artists like him and all kinds of American visitors are the United States's most effective ambassadors in winning the thoughts of the world.

As I later watched Dave and Iola cross the expanse of

the empty square to their hotel, I thought they looked a little lonely in the night. The life of a vanguard on the cutting edge of society is often lonely, but like Dave we must as a country have the necessary strength and vision to take a risk for our greater good.

Julian Semyonov's Russian bestseller *Tass Is Authorized to Announce . . .* is very revealing of current Russian attitudes toward the United States. With his close-cropped hair and beard, Semyonov resembles Ernest Hemingway, to whom he is often compared as a writer. Semyonov is an "authorized" writer; his books are "authorized." Notice in the title, Tass is "Authorized." It is not part of Russian thought to release something unless it is authorized. Semyonov's Russian heros represent average Russian thinking. His book sounds quite similar to American thrillers.

The book begins with two of the Russian heros having coffee. Their waitress is telling them about her holiday last year on a beach in Romania.

One of the heros is a KGB agent. He notes that the holiday sounds peaceful and that it would have been impossible thirty years ago for a waitress to take a holiday abroad. He further comments that it would have been impossible for secret police to be acting—as they are in the story—as agents of peaceful foreign relations.

Later, discussing a minor female character, the KGB agent asks what her complaints are.

The author says that she complains about the same things we all do: slipshod habits, security-mania, laziness, overstaffing, bureaucracy.

The American CIA villains are the slimy tools of big business. There is, however, an American hero. He is a journalist—morose, crumpled, his hand shaking as he lifts his drinks—who says, "As far as I'm concerned all you Russians are Ivans. It's great to use one name for a whole nation."

"Why do you say that?"

"Because we Americans are so divided, each for himself, and we have no common purpose. But Russia is a monolith. Whatever they tell you to do, you do it."

One of the Russians says that he should reread Tolstoy or Dostoyevsky, that he's just wrong about Russians as a flock of sheep, and he should read Russian literature.

The American journalist finally blows the CIA's plan to replace a communist regime in an African country with a capitalist regime. He goes on television and announces, "I do not agree with the ideology of Russian communism. Once we were allies, but even in our present state of opposition, certain rules of the game must be observed unless we want to break our heads on the sides of tanks."

In the book, there is no single Russian hero, but a group of heros, in this case peaceful KGB agents, who act as a collective and who experience no individual character development. The American hero is a tortured, doomed individual who does, however, grow as a person. He chooses to betray the CIA to get an innocent KGB agent out of jail.

The book is available in the United States in English. More Americans ought to read contemporary, as well as classic, Russian literature to get a sense of the thoughts of the average Russian reader. As with the Europeans, the Russians are certainly well informed about our culture, and we need to prepare ourselves for life in the coming new world by understanding how they think. Instead of fearing the Russians, we could learn to talk to them and be friends. After all, we have much in common. We are both diverse, passionate people living on a large continent.

In order to effect real change, however, U.S. leaders have to catch on to what is happening. In Paris Lazlo hit me with the concept of a war for the thoughts of the world. Since then I have been rolling it around in my thoughts, trying it out in different scenarios, getting the taste of it. It is clear that the Russian leaders have accepted Gorbachev's discovery of how the revolution in consciousness is changing the European Community. They are seriously and carefully considering the possibilities that this new third dimension of thought holds for the world and for themselves.

The danger for us is that when Gorbachev tells the United Nations that ideology is no longer an issue in international affairs, U.S. policymakers don't hear him. They think it is just propaganda. But we had better believe Gorbachev. He is out to win the thoughts of the world, and he is even sacrificing the ideology of communism in order to advance the Russian Empire.

And in the European Community the number of people who think of themselves as communists is diminishing; in fact, they can no longer agree on what communism is. An Italian communist is hardly distinguishable from a Swedish social democrat. There are practically no communists left who believe that a true Marxist regime will ever be possible, and fewer still believe that Stalinism or the past aggressions made in its name are defensible. In Moscow the "new thinkers" backing Gorbachev don't even call themselves communists. Gorbachev says his policies are an expression of Leninism rather than of capitalist democracy, yet fewer and fewer Russians are willing to defend Marxist-Leninist doctrines.

Gorbachev has succeeded in breaking the NATO alliance. It isn't apparent yet, but with his "peace initiative," he has already won the first major contest—for influence over Germany. "Peace initiative" in Russian means another way of carrying out its imperative to empire. U.S. foreign policymakers don't even know where the real war is. They do not seem to realize the enormity of the threat to our nation, and that it is a revolution in consciousness that is causing world change.

Power politics and diplomatic strategies will not put NATO back together again. NATO was based on old and trusted ideologies, but a strong, successful European Community is more important than NATO. The least—and the most—we can do is to understand the new way of thinking in the European Community, and support it. The only way to support it is to learn to live together peacefully in community as they are learning to do. Between us, we and Europe can give Russia the opportunity to evolve from empire to community.

A Russian Community would be modeled on the European Community. Gorbachev's sacrifice of ideology may open Russia to the development of third-dimensional thinking. It might develop along with our North American Community. We could help each other. Whatever it takes to encourage the development of a Russian Community from the Russian Empire should be a global priority for the United States.

The beginnings of a Russian Community are already under way. In Poland the Russians are allowing—encouraging, even—a multiparty system. A lower house, the Sejm, will open one-third of its membership to non-Communist candidates and will be dominated by Solidarity. The upper house, the Senate, will be open to democratic elections but will have a limited role in government. Similar multiparty reforms are taking place in Hungary. There is now an open border between Hungary and the European Community. These reforms are driven by the Russian war for the thoughts of the world. The Communist party will still be in control, but Russia is already bypassing boundaries, taking steps toward a Russian Community rather than a Russian Empire.

Page 268 shows a new world order of communities.

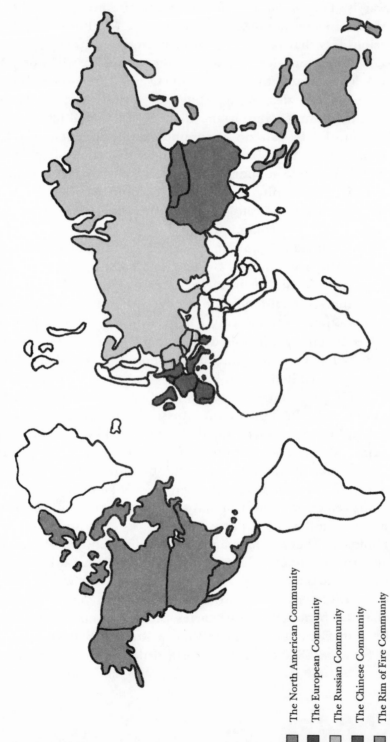

WORLD ORDER OF COMMUNITIES

The North American Community

The European Community

The Russian Community

The Chinese Community

The Rim of Fire Community

A NEW WORLD ORDER

The conditions for developing a community based on an enlarged sensitivity to others are the same in Russia as in the United States. What we American citizens can do individually for our inner growth and development will have more influence on a possible Russian Community than all the policies, strategies, monetary inducements and sanctions our leaders may devise.

The development of other transnational communities in the world would be an inducement for Russia to follow suit. Five possible communities are shown below.

FIVE POSSIBLE COMMUNITIES

	Gross National Product (in U.S. dollars)	Population
European Community	2.5 trillion	325 million
Russian Community	2.5 trillion	471 million
North American Community	5.0 trillion	361 million
Rim of Fire Community	3.0 trillion	350 million
Chinese Community	0.3 trillion	1 billion
Totals	13.3 trillion	2.5 billion

The table leaves out South America, whose nations would qualify for inclusion in one of the other transnational communities. They could eventually join a North American Community or even the European Community. Or they might form a South American Community, the beginnings of which already exist in the Andean Group and the Organization of American States.

The Rim of Fire Community would be composed of those nations bordering the volcanic rim of the Pacific Ocean: Japan, Korea, Taiwan, Singapore, the Philippines, Indonesia and perhaps Australia and New Zealand.

Except for the Chinese Community, the communities would have similar populations and gross national products. However, China is catching up, and it is limiting its population growth. The Chinese people are good guys. They're always looking for a way to make a buck, as are we. The government's repression of students may set China's progress back for a year or two, but no more. The armed forces will see to that; they need technological advance for their own power. The people of Japan and China are highly intelligent and industrious. The history of the novel in Japan is older than in Europe, and China's tradition of novel-like literature is even older than Japan's. Third-dimensional thinking is growing among these peoples. Like Russia, China has ethnically diverse peoples who speak their own languages. It also has the tradition of empire, which could turn into community.

Neither China nor Russia are U.S.-type democracies, nor will they ever be. There are many ways for people to live in freedom and equality, not just our way. Our kind of democracy is perhaps the most effective, but we must not make it as rigid an ideology as communism.

There is a very real possibility for the development of these communities of nations. The beginnings of community are to be found in all of them. India is an enigma. It will surely be able to make a valuable contribution to peace, but what its contribution will be is not clear at the moment.

The chaos of a future world without such communities would be dangerous indeed. Communities of nations that find peace and prosperity *within* themselves may well find peace *amongst* themselves. War could end for half of the world. The five communities make up almost half the total world population and an overwhelming percentage of its total gross national product.

Such communities need not and, indeed, should not seek to impose a universal ideology on the rest of the world. It is sufficient to remedy problems relevant to the lives of their own people, one at a time, bypassing as many rigid controls and boundaries as possible.

THE CHASM IN THE WORLD

Half of the world's population is left out of the five transnational communities, but community by its nature grows outward. It is in touch with the organic rhythms of our living planet. Given time, community will be an opportunity for all people. The third dimension of thought is an opportunity now for anyone anywhere. However, there is a chasm in the world that separates people from each other. This chasm runs through all nations. The most recent and most dramatic example is Salman Rushdie's book *The Satanic Verses*. Anyone who publishes, sells, buys, reads or goes into a bookstore carrying the book risks assassination. Bomb threats are involved.

Naguib Mahfonz, the Egyptian Nobel laureate, charged the late Ayatollah Khomeini with committing "intellectual terrorism." Many Moslems around the world agree with Mahfonz. This is not a religious issue, regardless of Khomeini's rhetoric. It is a chasm that divides those of the third dimension of thought—who have room in their minds for different ways of thinking, room for the reality of the existence of others—from those who do not, those who believe in the old curse, "If you're not a member of my group, you're not human." It divides terrorists from those who oppose terrorism. It is directly related to the development of literature, art and science. It has something to do with the critical mass of third-dimensional thinking in Western culture. But in the end it is all of these things and none of them. We recognize tolerance when we see it. Whether it's across our back fence or across the world, we know the edges of this chasm. We are on the other side of the chasm of thought from those who can only see a stranger as nonhuman.

The Rushdie terrorism dramatized the existence of peoples who have not advanced beyond Cato, the Roman politician. Cato was as rational as we are today, but he was incapable of third-dimensional thinking. He was capable of Carthagenian genocide. He sowed the fields of Carthage with salt and killed or enslaved all of the men, women and children. When terrorists like Khomeini make wild threats of exterminating us, we should believe them. They mean it.

UNESCO met and merely noted Khomeini's death threat. Director General Mayor made a major statement, but his condemnation of violence was couched in UNESCO double-think: "It is every person's duty to respect other people's religions," but "It is also every person's duty to respect other people's freedom of expression." Remember the policy directive from UNESCO in Paris. "Whilst respecting the freedom of writers, states will nevertheless ensure that they do not flout the prevailing philosophies of their states." This is how those on the other side of the chasm control UNESCO.

In a like fashion the president of the United Nations, Perez de Cuellar, denounced Khomeini's actions, but the Assembly of the United Nations did nothing. The balance of power in the United Nations lies with those on the other side of the chasm. We should preserve and cherish the United Nations as a meeting place, but not as the leader into a new world order. A supergovernment ruling us all is unattainable and is unacceptable to free people. We must go beyond the United Nations to the organic, slow and sure development of communities of nations. This is attainable and it will bring peace and prosperity to the world.

If any good has come from the Rushdie terrorism, it is that it may have broken the triangle of power that has existed between UNESCO, PEN and the International Publishers Association. PEN Centers in the European Community and in the United States have valiantly opposed the terrorist threats, as have the publishers of the United States and England. International PEN is clearly divided between those who support and those who oppose this terrorism. The International Publishers Association has experienced a dramatic split. Only time will determine if the IPA can find the courage to resolutely oppose this death threat to the third dimension of thought. UNESCO appears to be irrevocably under the control of nations on the other side of the chasm in the world, but PEN and the IPA could be among the most valuable international organizations to nurture war's end among transnational communities.

SAN FRANCISCO

The sun is rising over San Francisco Bay. A friend and I are sailing with the tide on a thirty-five-knot wind out of the Golden Gate into the Pacific Ocean and north a few miles up the coast. We're going to Muir Woods. Since this is a spiritual pilgrimage, I want to go this way to avoid the crowds of visitors who throng the park each day. A large share of the visitors to this national park are international. We anchor in a little cove. There is a small sandy beach between two headlands. The sun tips each small wave with a point of light. It's a perfect day. I leave my friend to putter around on his boat while I row to the beach in the dinghy. My friend leans over to look me in the eye. "Remember, I only go through the Gate on the tide. If you're not back here before it turns, I go without you and you're left behind. Got it?"

Muir Woods is in a valley, and the stream running through the valley empties into the ocean at this cove. I'm hiking up over a ridge, which is faster than following the stream—just a few miles. The ocean side of the ridge is open heath, but as I crest the ridge, I enter the stillness of forest. The path is so soft with pine and fir needles that even breathing seems to be noisy. The only breath here should be the slow, year-long breathing of the trees. I pause while a deer moves silently below, browsing along the ravine. It seems the slow cycles of birth, death and regeneration have been proceeding uninterrupted since the forest began to grow here. Now I'm getting into the redwoods. I notice one tree that must be more than a thousand years old, about the time it took for St. Augustine's silent reading to develop into a novel.

This tree has been growing the entire time the human species has been developing third-dimensional thinking, rising straight up to the sky and the universe beyond. I come to a glade on the valley floor which is the home for a little brass plaque on the side of a short log.

HERE IN THIS GROVE OF ENDURING REDWOODS,
PRESERVED FOR POSTERITY, MEMBERS OF THE UNITED NATIONS
CONFERENCE ON INTERNATIONAL ORGANIZATION
MET ON MAY 19, 1945
TO HONOR THE MEMORY OF FRANKLIN DELANO ROOSEVELT,
THIRTY-FIRST PRESIDENT OF THE UNITED STATES,
CHIEF ARCHITECT OF THE UNITED NATIONS
AND APOSTLE OF LASTING PEACE FOR ALL MANKIND.

I sit down on the pine-needle carpet. That's it, mission completed. I have fulfilled the promise I made to Lazlo in Paris. It seems a lifetime ago. The stillness is broken by a murmur of voices in the distance, getting closer. I take out a much-creased piece of heavy vellum paper and open it to read once more. The letterhead is that of a firm of lawyers in Paris.

Dear Dr. Howell,

I regret to inform you that Lazlo Kanosz died from a massive heart attack last week. It was not unexpected. A year ago his doctors had warned him that he was living on borrowed time and suggested a sedentary life. He rejected their advice, saying he had too much to do.

Shortly before his death Mr. Kanosz directed that an item, which he described as being valuable to you only, be turned over to you if he should die before meeting with you. It is a chest and is in the hands of a law firm in Cairo, whose separate letter is enclosed. Upon presentation of yourself and proof of identity at their offices the chest will be delivered to you. I was not apprised of its contents.

Please feel free to contact me for any purpose. Mr. Kanosz was a valued client of our firm and a personal friend of mine.

Respectfully,

Charles Poincare

I carefully fold the paper and put it away. Looking off through the great trees, I say, "I promise, at least, to go to Cairo."

The voices are coming closer. Unable to face people right now, I slip away into the healing trees.

I am beginning to understand Lazlo's secret.

I can imagine a young Lazlo in the Congo facing Dag Hammarskjold's death. He would have vowed to be the guardian of Dag's poetic vision of world peace and unity, which ranged far beyond the petty politics and strategic interests of his position as secretary general of the United Nations. Dag saw a strange and mystical fusion of spirit in the future of humankind.

In all Lazlo's years at the United Nations, would not a shell of clever cynicism have been necessary to protect his vow? When he could no longer find any hope for the future in the United Nations—and he would have been more knowledgable than anyone else about the U.N.—he drifted into an ambiguous relationship with UNESCO.

By the time he ran into me, he must have realized that UNESCO was no longer useful for his purposes. He needed a new tool, and I was handy, sniffing around trying to understand the European Community. Perhaps he decided I could be of use.

I expect that, in order to carry out his promise to Dag, he envisioned a North American Community as the next step after the European Community, perhaps as a backup in case the European Community should fail. He must have seen the human species evolving within a world of transnational communities. We didn't discuss it, but a North American Community as the inevitable conclusion of my investigation was probably obvious to him, if not to me.

I can only surmise the reasons for other aspects of his byzantine maneuvers. Why did Lazlo try to involve and then protect me? No strategy or policy could impose a system of transnational communities on the world. These communities can only develop from within.

The tragedy of Lazlo's life was that he knew his strategies could not create community. His dream rested within the minds of ordinary people. Yet his life of bureaucratic diplomacy and strategy made it impossible for him to trust us. Like Moses, he was made in an outmoded world and could not cross the river Jordan.

I like to think he was content when he died. Thinking back to our last time in Paris, I sense there was a hint of satisfaction in his outlook. Perhaps he had taken his dream as far as he could, perhaps it was a dream for others, not for himself.

It was Lazlo I had in mind when at the last moment I sought permission to open this book with lines from Frederick Turner's epic poem *Genesis*. It seems appropriate to repeat a few of them here in the book's ending.

> How those men and women worth a story
> Burn and consume the powers they're kindled by;
> And how their acts, mortal and cast away,
> Are crystalled in the melt of history.

The diamonds to be found in the melt of history are not of great leaders but of people like Lazlo and the others with whom we've become familiar in this pilgrimage. Also people like you who have been impelled to read this far. The third dimension of thought is an inner reality that—one person at a time—is changing the world. Look! Our story is a mine glittering with the diamonds of all kinds of diverse people. It is only about people.

I know of no organized support for a North American Community. But I can imagine the existence of powerful—perhaps clandestine—groups who would oppose a world order composed of such communities. Such a world order would strip these groups of their power and control because neither the communities, the nations nor the individuals who live in them could be manipulated any longer.

Any forces opposed to a North American Community would have to confront the growing numbers of third-dimensional people, and such a confrontation would only create and increase support for a North American Community.

Successful opposition will be oblique. There will be the bland assertions of experts that "it is an interesting idea, but it will not happen. It's just not reasonable— human nature you know." And surely there will be lists of reasons that it would be politically and economically impractical. Except, except . . .

Except that the European Community is happening. It is ambiguous, it is faltering, but it is happening. The countries of Europe are learning to cherish and preserve

278   AMERICA AND WAR'S END

their individual nations, cultures and ethnic differences, while cooperating to bypass the rigidity of national boundaries. War between nations ends when the balance starts to shift to the third dimension of thinking.

The European Community looms as the inescapable answer to doubts about the practicality of a North American Community. If they can do it, we can do it— and better.

Forty years ago Einstein said that the ability to split the atom had changed everything except the way we think. And in those forty years even the way we think has changed—for the first time in history.

We have to do two things. First, we must become aware that the future of the world is too important for us to be overly concerned with general problems of ideology or strategic interest. We need to take care of the problems that are relevant to people's lives and take care of them one day at a time.

Second, we must become aware that we are in danger of winding up on the wrong side of history. We have mislaid our spirit. We led people to expect more from our early, liberal breakthroughs than we could then deliver. We can redeem ourselves by focusing our concern on the many opportunities ahead of us, opportunities to go beyond boundaries, to go beyond liberalism, to mutually serve each other. There is no one who is not capable of some service to others. Our way of living together must make room for that.

I'm tired, and I must climb this last ridge to get back to the boat. The tide is about to turn.

The United States was the first to express the revolution in consciousness which has made a new kind of community possible. We can lead the way to a new world order of regional communities of nations.

As we approach our task, let us remember Abraham Lincoln's message: "The United States is the last best hope for the peoples of this earth."

READING LIST

Abler, W. L. (1978). "Asymmetry and evolution." *Behavioral and Brain Sciences, 2.*

Abshire, David M. (1988). *Preventing World War III.* New York: Harper & Row, Publishers.

Aldiss, Brian. (1987). *Ruins.* London: Butler & Tanner Ltd.

Allen, James J. (1961). *European Common Market and the Gatt.* Riverton, VA: The University Press of Washington, DC.

Annett, M. (1972). "The distribution of manual asymmetry." *British Journal of Psychology, 63.*

Annett, M. (1980). "Sex differences in laterality-meaningfulness versus reliability." *Behavioral and Brain Sciences, 3.*

Annusire des Communatues Euro. (1984). Government publication.

Arkin, A., Antrobus, J., & Ellman, S. (Eds.). (1978). *The mind in sleep.* New York: John Wiley & Sons.

Avanesov, G. A. (1982). *Principles of criminology.* Moscow: Progress Publishing.

Bacon, F. (1878). *The works of Francis Bacon* (Vol. 1). Cambridge: Hurd and Houghton.

Bainton, Roland H. (1960). *Christian attitude toward war and peace.* New York: Abington Press.

Baradat, Leon P. (1986). *Soviet political society.* Englewood Cliffs, NJ: Prentice-Hall.

Barchardt, Klaus. (1986). *European unification: The origin and growth of the European Community.* Luxembourg: Office for Official Publications of the European Community.

Barton, Griselda, Meek, Margaret, & Warlow, Aidan (Eds.). *The cool web.* London: The Bodley Head Ltd.

Barzini, Luigi. (1983). *The Europeans.* New York: Simon & Schuster.

Bateson, Gregory. (1979). *Mind and nature.* New York: E. P. Dutton.

Berman, H. J. (1963). *Justice in the U.S.S.R.* Cambridge, MA: Harvard University Press.

Berman, Morris. (1986). *The reenchantment of the world.* New York: Simon & Schuster.

Berman, Morris. (1989). *Coming to our senses.* New York: Simon & Schuster.

Broca, P. (1888). *Memoirs sur le creveau de l'homme.* Paris: C. Reinwald.

Brown, G. S. (1972). *Laws of form.* New York: Julian Press.

Bruner, J. (1962). *On knowing: Essays for the left hand.* Cambridge, MA: Belknap.

Bugental, J. F. T. (1967). *Challenges of humanistic psychology.* New York: McGraw-Hill Book Company.

Butler, W. E. (1983). *Soviet law.* Sevenoaks: Butterworth (Publishers) Ltd.

Capra, F. (1977). *The Tao of physics.* New York: Bantam Books.

Carter, Ashton B., Steinbruner, John D., & Zraket, Charles A. (Eds.). (1987). *Managing nuclear operations.* Washington, DC: Brookings Institution.

The challenges of Eurofutures. (1984). Commission of the European Community.

Cimbala, Stephen J. (1987). *Extended deterrance.* Lexington, MA: Lexington Books.

Colman, A. D., & Bexton, W. H. (Eds.). (1975). *Group relations reader.* Sausalito, CA: Grex.

The community today: Commission of the European communities. Luxembourg: Office for Official Publications of the European Community.

Conquest, Robert (Ed.). (1968). *The Soviet police system.* London: The Bodley Head Ltd.

Cousins, Norman. (1986). *The human adventure: A camera chronicle.* Dallas: Saybrook Publishers.

Cunliffe, Barry. (1979). *The Celtic world.* New York: McGraw-Hill Book Company.

Davis, Howard (Ed.). (1987). *Ethics and defense.* New York: Basil Blackwell.

Defence without the bomb. British Government Publications.

De Quiroz, J. B., deCoriat, L. F., & Bensayag, L. (1961). *Fonoaudiologica, VII*(1).

de Tocqueville, Alexis. (1969). *Democracy in America.* George Lawrence (Trans.). J. P. Mayer (Ed.). New York: Doubleday, Anchor Books.

Dossey, Larry. (1982). *Space, time and medicine.* Boston: Shambhala Publications.

Douglas, George H. (1986). *Women of the twenties.* Dallas: Saybrook Publishers.

Downie, N. M., & Heath, R. W. (1974). *Basic statistical methods* (4th ed.). New York: Harper & Row, Publishers.

Drabble, Margaret. (1985). *Oxford companion to English literature.* New York: Oxford University Press.

Drabble, Margaret. (1987). *The radiant way.* New York: Alfred A. Knopf.

Eccles, Sir John, Sperry, Roger, Prigogine, Ilya, & Josephson, Brian. (1989). *The reach of the mind: Nobel prize conversations.* Dallas: Saybrook Publishers.

E. C. index. (1985). Europe Data.

Endicott, John E., et al. (Eds.). (1977). *American defense policy* (4th ed.). Baltimore: Johns Hopkins University Press.

The European Community: Institutions and policies. (1983). Francis Pinter.

Facts sheets on the European Parliament. (1983). Strasbourg: European Parliament.

Feld, Werner. *The harmonization of the European Community's external policy.*

Feld, Werner, Jordan, Robert, & Hurwitz, Leon. (1983). *International organizations: A comparative approach.* New York: Praeger Publishers.

FitzGerald, Garret. (1979, January). *Unequal partners.* Switzerland: Tad/Inf/Pub/78.6 GE 78–71738 (8640).

Flynn, Gregory, & Rattinger, Hans (Eds.). (1985). *The public and Atlantic defense*. Totowa, NJ: Roman and Allanheld, Atlantic Institute for International Affairs.

Foshay, A. W., & Morrissett, I. (Eds.). (1978). *Beyond the scientific: A comprehensive view of consciousness*. Boulder, CO: Consortium.

Freud, S. (1961). *The interpretation of dreams*. New York: Science Editions. (Originally published in 1899.)

Gatlin, D., & Ornstein, R. E. *Psychophysiology, 9*.

Geldard, F. (1953). *The human senses*. New York: John Wiley & Sons.

George, Stephen. (1985). *Politics and policy in the European Community*. New York: Clarendon Press–Oxford University Press.

Geschwind, N. (1978). *Anatomical evolution of the human brain*. Towson, MD: Orton Society.

Gevartar, W. (1978). *NASA, code RES*. Washington, D. C.

Giannini, J. (1977). *Journal of General Psychiatry, 99*.

Gibson, J. J. (1966). *The senses considered as perceptual systems*. Boston: Houghton Mifflin Co..

Gilman, Stephen. (1981). *Galdo's and the art of the European novel: 1867–1887*. Princeton, NJ: Princeton University Press.

Gray, Colin. (1977). *The geopolitics of the nuclear era: Heartland, rimlands and the technological revolution*. New York: Crane, Russak & Co.

Greening, Tom (Ed.). (1984). *American politics and humanistic psychology*. Dallas: Saybrook Publishers.

Gregorios, Paulos Mar. (1987). *The human presence*. Warwick, NY: Amity House.

Gregorios, Paulos Mar. (1989). *Enlightenment East and West.* New Delhi: B. R. Publishing Corporation.

Gruhn, Isebill. (1985). *Europe, Africa, and Lome III.* Lanham, MD: University Press of America.

Hamilton, Edward K. (Ed.). (1989). *America's global interests.* New York: W. W. Norton & Co.

Haugeland, J. *Behavioral and Brain Sciences, 2.*

Hilgard, E. R. (1986). *The divided consciousness: Multiple controls in human thought and action* (2nd ed.). New York: John Wiley & Sons.

Hoffman, Stanley. (1968). *Gulliver's troubles.* New York: McGraw-Hill Book Company.

Holloway R. (1981). *Angelus, 8.*

Holroyd, Michael. (1988). *George Bernard Shaw: In search of love.* London: Chatto-Windus.

Holsti, K. J. (1972). *International politics.* Englewood Cliffs, NJ: Prentice-Hall.

Hopkins, Michael. (1985). *European Community information: Its use and user.* Mansell.

Houser, Rita. (1960). *A guide to doing business in the European Common Market.* Dobbs Ferry, NY: Oceana.

Howell, Pat (Ed.). (1988). *The second Gutenberg revolution.* Dallas: The Mentor Society.

Hubbard, David G. (1986). *Winning back the sky.* Dallas: Saybrook Publishers.

Hughes, H. S. (1958). *Consciousness and society: The reorientation of European thought, 1890–1930.* New York: Vantage Books.

Hurwitz, Leon (Ed.). (1983). *The harmonization of European public policy: Regional responses to transnational challenges.* Westport, CT: Greenwood.

Jeffares, Norman A., & Kamm, Antony (Eds.). (1987). *An Irish childhood*. Glasgow: William Collins & Co. Ltd.

Jefferies, John. (1981). *Guide to official publications to European Community* (2nd ed.).

Johnson, Paul. (1983). *Modern times*. New York: Harper-Colophon Books.

Jones, R. M. (1968). *Fantasy and feeling in education*. New York: New York University Press.

Kaldor, Mary, & Anderson, Paul. (Eds.). (1986). *Mad dogs: The U.S. raid against Libya*. London: Pluto Press.

Keating, Michael J., & Jones, J. Barry. (1985). *Regions in the European Community*. New York: Oxford University Press.

Kirchner, Walter. (1984). *History of Russia* (6th ed.). New York: Harper & Row, Publishers.

Kissinger, Henry A. (1979). *The White House*. Boston: Little, Brown & Co.

Koestenbaum, Peter. (1987). *The heart of business: Ethics, power and philosophy*. Dallas: Saybrook Publishers.

Koestenbaum, Peter. (1989). *Socrate et le business*. Paris: InterEditions.

Korobeinkov, B. V. (1985). "Crime prevention in the U.S.S.R." *Crime and Social Justice, 23*.

Lafore, Laurence. (1970). *The end of glory*. New York: J. B. Lippincott Co./Harper & Row, Publishers.

Lane, David. (1985). *State police in the U.S.S.R.* New York: New York University Press.

Laqueur, Walter. (1980). *The terrible secret*. London: Weidenfeld and Nicholson.

Laurens, Roy. (1985). *Fully alive*. Dallas: Saybrook Publishers.

Lefever, Ernest W., & Hunt, E. Stephen (Eds.) (1982). *The apocalyptic premise.* Washington, DC: Ethics and Public Policy Center.

Leibniz, G. W. (1898). *Leibniz—The monadology and other philosophical writings.* London: Oxford University Press.
LeMay, M. (1978). *Behavioral and Brain Sciences, 2.*

Lesgold, A. M., Pellagrino, J. W., Fokkema, S., & Glaser, R. (Eds.). (1978). *Cognitive psychology and instruction.* New York: Plenum Press.

Liddell, H. B. (1954). *Strategy.* New York: Frederick A. Praeger Publishers.

Liska, George. (1967). *Imperical America: The international politics of primacy.* Baltimore: Johns Hopkins University Press.

Lodge, Juliet (Ed.). (1986). *European union: The European Community in search of a future.* New York: St. Martin's Press.

Lunt, W. E. (1957). *History of England.* New York: Harper and Brothers.

Mackay, David. *Breakthrough to literacy.* Chicago: Longman.

Mahler, M. S., Pine, F., & Bergman, A. (1975). *The psychological birth of the human infant.* New York: Simon & Schuster.

Mally, Gerhard. *The European Community in perspective.* Lexington, MA: Lexington Books.

Mark, Hans. (1988). *In search of the fulcrum.* Berkeley, CA: University of California Press.

Marquand, David. (1979). *Parliament for Europe.* J. Cape.

Martin, Lawrence. (1985). *NATO and the defense of the West.* New York: Holt, Rinehart and Winston.

May, Rollo. (1985). *My quest for beauty*. Dallas: Saybrook Publishers.

May, Rollo. (1988). *Paulus: Tillich as spiritual teacher*. Dallas: Saybrook Publishers.

May, Rollo, Rogers, Carl R., & Maslow, Abraham. (1986). *Politics and innocence: A humanistic debate*. Dallas: Saybrook Publishers.

McLeod, R. B., & Pick, H. L., Jr. (Eds.). (1974). *Perception: Essays in honor of J. J. Gibson*. Ithaca, NY: Cornell University Press.

Medish, Vadim. (1987). *The Soviet Union* (3rd ed.). Englewood Cliffs, NJ: Prentice-Hall.

Meek, Margaret. (1982). *Learning to read*. London: The Bodley Head Ltd.

Meissner, G. (1859). "Untersuchungen uber den tastsinn." *Nationelle Medicin*, 7.

Milligan, W. J. (1984). *Challenges facing new nomads*. World Council of Churches.

Morris, Brian, Crane, Peggy, & Boehm, Klaus. (1981). *The European Community: A guide for business and government*. Bloomington: Indiana University Press.

Mueller, John. (1989). *Retreat from doomsday: The obsolescence of major war*. New York: Harper & Row, Publishers/Basic Books.

Myers, Kenneth A. (Ed.). (1980). *NATO: The next thirty years*. Boulder, CO: Westview Press.

Nogee, Joseph L., & Donaldson, Robert H. (1985). *Soviet foreign policy since World War II* (2nd ed.). New York: Pergamon Press.

The North Atlantic Treaty Organization: Facts and figures. (1984). Brussels: NATO Information Service.

O'Brien, William V., & Langan, John, S. J. (Eds.). (1986). *The nuclear dilemma and the just war tradition.* Lexington, MA: Lexington Books.

Offner, Arnold A. (1975). *The origins of the second world war: American foreign policy and world politics, 1917–1941.* New York: Praeger Publishers.

Opening of historical archives of European Community to the public. (1983). Commission of European Community.

Operation of the trade agreements program. U.S. International Trade Commission.

Ornstein, R. (1972). *The psychology of consciousness.* New York: Harcourt Brace Jovanovich.

Overton, David. (1983). *Common market digest.* New York: Facts on File.

Overturk, Stephen Frank. (1986). *The economic principles of European integration.* New York: Praeger Publishers.

Pavlov, I. P. (1932). *Psychopathology and psychiatry: Selected works.* Moscow: Foreign Language Publication House.

Peirce, C. S., Hartshorne, C., & Weiss, P. (Eds.). (1931–1935). *Collected papers of Charles Sanders Peirce* (Vol. 6). Cambridge, MA: Harvard University Press.

Penfield, W. (1975). *The mystery of the mind.* Princeton, NJ: Princeton University Press.

Pfaff, William. (1986, June 23). "Europe: A slumbering, politically withdrawn giant." *International Herald Tribune.*

Polkinghorne, Donald E. (1987). *Narrative knowing.* Albany: State University of New York Press.

Polkinghorne, Donald E. (Ed.). (1986). *Methods* (Vols. 1, 2, 3). Dallas: Saybrook Publishers.

Puchala, Donald. (1983). *Policy making in the European communities*. New York: John Wiley & Sons.

Puchala, Donald. (1984). *Fiscal harmonization in the European communities: National politics and international cooperation*. Francis Pinter.

Rallo, Joseph (Air Force Academy). (1987, September). "The E. C. and multinational enterprise." *Europe*.

Riasanovsky, Nicholas. (1984). *A history of Russia* (4th ed.). New York: Oxford University Press.

Ricoeur, P. (1970). *Freud and philosophy: An essay on interpretation*. New Haven, CT: Yale University Press.

Rosenberg, R. A. (1973). *The anatomy of God*. New York: KTAV.

Rosenthal, Glenda G. (1982). *The Mediterranean basin: Its political economy and changing international relations*. Woburn, MA: Butterworth Publishers.

Rosenthal, Glenda G. (1983). *The European Community: Bibliographic excursions*. Francis Pinter.

Schell, Jonathan. (1982). *The fate of the earth*. New York: Alfred A. Knopf.

Schmookler, Andrew Bard. (1988). *Out of weakness*. New York: Bantam Books.

Seabury, Paul, & Codevilla, Angelo. (1989). *War, ends and means*. New York: Basic Books.

Semyonov, Julian. (1987). *Tass is authorized to announce . . . .* New York: Riverrun Press.

Severin, F. T. (Ed.). (1965). *Humanistic viewpoints in psychology*. New York: McGraw-Hill Book Company.

Sharpe, Gene. (1974). *Politics of non-violent action*. Boston: Porter Sargent.

Shevchenko, Arkady N. (1985). *Breaking with Moscow.* New York: Ballantine Books.

Singer, J. L., & Pope, K. S. (Eds.). (1978). *The stream of consciousness.* New York: Plenum Press.

Snow, Donald M. (1987). *National security.* New York: St. Martin's Press.

Solomon, Peter H. (1978). *Soviet criminologists and criminal policy: Specialists in policy-making.* London: Macmillan.

Solzhenitsyn, Aleksandr I. (1978). *The Gulag Archipelago* (Vols. 1–3). New York: Harper & Row, Publishers.

Sondermann, Fred (Ed.). (1979). *The theory and practice of international relations.* Englewood Cliffs, NJ: Prentice-Hall.

Spencer, Margaret. *Breakthrough to literacy.* The Bodley Head Ltd.

Sperry, R. W. (1968). "Hemisphere deconnection and unity in conscious awareness." *American Psychologist, 23.*

Talbott, Strobe. (1984). *Deadly gambits.* New York: Alfred A. Knopf.

Terrill, Richard J. (1984). *World criminal justice systems: A survey.* Cincinnati, OH: Anderson Publishing Company.

Tugendhat, Christopher. (1986). *Making sense of Europe.* New York: Viking Penguin.

Turner, Frederick. (1988). *Genesis.* Dallas: Saybrook Publishers.

Ulam, Adam B. (1973). *Stalin: The man and his era.* New York: Viking Press.

Walzer, Michael. (1977). *Just and unjust wars.* New York: Basic Books.

Watkins, M. (1977). *Waking dreams.* New York: Harper-Colophon Books.

Watson, Hugh Seton. (1956). *From Lenin to Malenkov.* New York: Praeger Publishers.

Watson, J. B. (1924). *Behaviorism.* New York: W. W. Norton & Co.

Wood, David. (1987, September). "Future technocrats? Recruits to the higher civil service of the E.C." *Europe.*

Wundt, W. (1902). *Principles of phsyiological psychology: Vol I.* New York: Macmillan.

INDEX

A Delicate Balance 122, 199
Abraham Lincoln 278
African National Congress
115
Akhmetov 202
Alexander Yakovlev 198
all about 156
Altiero Spinelli 83, 98,
127, 227
Amadou M'Bow 71
American Bar Association
262
American Hero 211
Anna Liffy 117
Antonia Fraser 33
Articles of Confederation
187
Association for Humanistic
Psychology 262

Averell Harriman 38
Birdcage Walk 212
Bonn 176
Breakthrough to Literacy 164
Brian Aldiss 168, 216
Brussels 85
Bundestag 178
The California Institute of
Technology 147
Camelot 50
Canada 240
Cato 272
the chasm in the world
271
Chinese Community 269
Claude 119
Claude Deplessy 88
The Coffee Run 110
Comecon 183

Coming to Our Senses 119
Congo 275
Contras 34, 111
The Cool Web 164
Cosimo de Medici 139
The Court of Justice 92
Critical mass 149
Crocodile Club 97
Cross Timbers 26
customs document 224
Czechoslovakia 201
Dag Hammarskjold 75, 275
The Dail 113
Daniel Filipacchi 239
Darwin 133
Dave Brubeck 262
Defence Without the Bomb 182
Dick and Jane 122, 135
Don Petersen 248
Don Polkinghorne 251
Don Quixote 140
Dr. Federico Mayor 65, 70, 104, 152, 272
Driving Miss Daisy 210
Dublin 108
Easter Sunday 118
Einstein 278
Eleanor Roosevelt 77
Ed Broadbent 113
equality 246
Eric 184
Ernesto Cardenal 112
Ethiopia 103
European Commission of Human Rights 93

European Community 22, 84, 93, 119, 154, 164, 167, 171, 177, 183, 189, 193, 204, 223, 232, 237, 247, 261, 276, 278
European Community Commission 88
European Court of Human Rights 93
European Court of Justice 223
European Credit Units 224
European Economic Space 193
European Free Trade Association 193
European Parliament 83
Eurowatch 223
Faust 196
first dimension of thinking 133
flag of Europe 223
"For Better or For Worse" 120
Francis Ford Coppola 239
Francis King 206, 209, 250
Franz 171
Frederick Turner 42, 276
From Under the Rubble 199
Garret FitzGerald 107, 113, 161, 227
Geneva 151
Genscherism 178
George Marshall 88
George Steiner 157
George Washington 238

German Democratic
  Republic 178
Gorbachev 266
Great Expectations 145
Greenpeace 101, 190
Greens 190
Gulag 205
The Gulag Archipelago 199
Gunther Ball 28
Hans-Dietrich Genscher
  154, 178
Harold Pinter 33, 112, 230
*The Heart of Business: Ethics,
  Power and Philosophy* 85
Heinz 172, 183
Helsinki Agreement 200
Hitler 180
Hungarian revolution 41,
  177
Hungary 203, 267
Huseyin Yildirim 179
Ian Clark 73, 78, 225
Index on Censorship 34
informative 143
International Publishers
  Association 65, 272
Ivan Belkin 262
J. A. Koutchoumow 64
Jacques Delors 89
Janet McCally 114
Janos 35
John Andrews 56, 64, 213
John Turner 241
Jonathan Miller 159
Joseph Brodsky 227, 249
Juergen Gunther 196, 228

Julian Huxley 71
Julian Semyonov 264
Julius Caesar 146
Jungian archetype 47
Khomeini 272
King Arthur 220
La Celestina 139, 221
Lady Eccles 200
Larry Dossey 258
Lazlo 76, 106, 108, 118, 127,
  203, 214, 218, 233, 237,
  274
Learning to Read 163
Leipzig 196
Les Miserables 145
London 31
London Daily Telegraph 211
Luxembourg 102
Madame Bovary 159
Madame Mubarak 233
Margaret Drabble 53, 216,
  227, 231
Margaret Spencer 163
Marshall McLuhan 60, 159
Marshall Plan 25, 88, 169,
  232, 261
Marta 184
Martyn Goff 57, 172
Marva Collins 250
Mathias Hinterscheidt 189
Maury Berman 199
Methods:A Journal of
  Human Science. 251
Michael Holroyd 53
Milan Kundera 199
Milovan Djilas 203

Mitbestimmung 189
Modern Times. 55
monastery 129
Morris Berman 119, 260
The Moscow News 184
Mozambique 103
Muir Woods 273
Mykola Rudenko 201
Naguib Mahfonz 271
Narrative Knowing 251
NATO 177, 266
Nelson Mandela 115
Nicaragua 111, 169
Nietzsche 142
1985 Single European Act 98
1992 24, 27
Nizametdin Akhmetov 198
North American Free Trade Area 242
North American Community 240, 251, 276, 277
novel 143
O'Connell Street 117
Odyssey 135
Oedipus Rex 133
the old city of London 158
On the Edge of an Abyss 199
Oxford 247
The Oxford-Cambridge Club 160
Paul 77, 108, 119, 203, 242
PEN 153, 272
Perez de Cuellar 272
perspective 139, 145
Peter Koestenbaum 85, 188, 248

Pierre 152
Poland 177, 267
political agoraphobia 259
The Politics of Non-violent Action 182
Pravda 184
President Eisenhower 88
President John F. Kennedy 88, 261
Proinsias deRossa 116
Queen Berenice 141
The Radiant Way. 227
The Reach of the Mind 147
The Reenchantment of the World 119
Renaissance 139
Richard Hoggart 71
Rim of Fire Community 269
Roger Sperry 147
Rule of St. Benedict 137
Russian Community 267
Russian Empire 179
Russian Soviet Federated Socialist Republic 201
Russian-German axis 177
Saint Thomas Aquinas 138
Salman Rushdie 271
Sandinistas 112
The Satanic Verses 271
second dimension of thinking 133
Shepherd's Bush 211
Socrate et le Business 85
Solzhenitsyn 199
Sophocles 133
South American Community 269

Space, Time and Medicine 258
spiritual agoraphobia. 259
Sputnik 198
St. James Park 212
Strasbourg 83
Strategy: The Indirect
 Approach 182
Stuttgart 183
supernationalism. 225
*Tass Is Authorized to
 Announce* . . . 264
third-dimensional
 thinking 139, 145, 149,
 154, 222, 229, 247, 252,
 270
Treaty of Rome 98
Trieste 129
Trinity University 109
Uganda. 103
*The Unbearable Lightness of
 Being* 199

Uncle Tom's Cabin 142
Unequal Partners 106, 161
UNESCO 69, 102, 152, 272,
 276
United Nations 75, 272,
 275
United States Army 174
Vaclav Havel 201
Vietnam 169
War and Peace 145, 159
War Without Weapons
 182
Wellesley 163
West Germany 178
Winchester Cathedral 219
World Hunger for Books
 153
Yalta 177, 203
Yevtushenko 263
Zionsgemeinde 198